FRUIT

FRUIT

AN A-Z REFERENCE AND COOK'S KITCHEN BIBLE WITH OVER 100 RECIPES

KATE WHITEMAN AND MAGGIE MAYHEW

southwater

This edition is published by Southwater

Southwater is an imprint of Anness Publishing Ltd, Hermes House, 88–89 Blackfriars Road, London SE1 8HA
tel. 020 7401 2077; fax 020 7633 9499, www.southwaterbooks.com; info@anness.com

© Anness Publishing Ltd 1998, 2005

UK agent: The Manning Partnership Ltd, 6 The Old Dairy, Melcombe Road, Bath BA2 3LR;
tel. 01225 478444; fax 01225 478440; sales@manning-partnership.co.uk

UK distributor: Grantham Book Services Ltd, Isaac Newton Way, Alma Park Industrial Estate, Grantham, Lincs NG31 9SD;
tel. 01476 541080; fax 01476 541061; orders@gbs.tbs-ltd.co.uk

North American agent/distributor: National Book Network, 4501 Forbes Boulevard, Suite 200, Lanham, MD 20706;
tel. 301 459 3366; fax 301 429 5746; www.nbnbooks.com

Australian agent/distributor: Pan Macmillan Australia, Level 18, St Martins Tower, 31 Market St, Sydney, NSW 2000;
tel. 1300 135 113; fax 1300 135 103; customer.service@macmillan.com.au

New Zealand agent/distributor: David Bateman Ltd, 30 Tarndale Grove, Off Bush Road, Albany, Auckland;
tel. (09) 415 7664; fax (09) 415 8892

A CIP catalogue record for this book is available from the British Library.

Publisher: Joanna Lorenz
Senior Editor: Linda Fraser
Copy Editor: Jenni Fleetwood
Indexer: Hilary Bird
Designer: Nigel Partridge
Photography: William Lingwood (recipes) and Don Last (fruits)
Food for Photography: Bridget Sargeson (recipes) and Christine France (fruits)

Previously published as *World Encyclopedia of Fruit*

1 3 5 7 9 10 8 6 4 2

NOTES

For all recipes, quantities are given in both metric and imperial measures and, where
appropriate, measures are also given in standard cups and spoons. Follow one set, but
not a mixture because they are not interchangeable.

Standard spoon and cup measures are level.
1 tsp = 5ml, 1 tbsp = 15ml, 1 cup = 250ml/8fl oz

Australian standard teaspoons are 20ml. Australian readers should use 3 tsp in place
of 1 tbsp for measuring small quantities of gelatine, cornflour, salt etc.

Medium eggs are used unless otherwise stated

CONTENTS

INTRODUCTION

Everything you ever wanted to know about fruit is contained within this fascinating book, from information on the various varieties to advice on buying, storing, preparing, cooking and serving. Snippets of historical data are included, as are useful notes on nutrition. The sections are divided by type of fruit for easy reference: Apples, Pears, Quinces and Medlars; Stone Fruits; Berries and Currants; Citrus Fruits; and Exotic Fruits; with a final section on fruits that do not fit into any other category: Melons, Grapes, Figs and Rhubarb. Beautiful photographs help you to identify — and will tempt you to try — hundreds of hitherto unfamiliar fruits.

FRUITS ARE NATURE'S most bountiful and versatile creation. No other foods offer such a variety of colours, textures, scents and flavours. Almost all fruits are pleasing to the senses of sight, smell and taste. Just think of the crispness of an apple, the velvety skin of a peach, the jewel-like colours of redcurrants, the juicy tartness of citrus fruits. There is nothing like the sight of a glorious display of fruit in a market to lift the spirits and whet the appetite. Without colourful, health-giving fruits, our diet would be infinitely more dull.

Fruit is not only good for the soul; it is a supremely healthy food, bursting with natural energy-giving sugars, minerals and vitamins. When energy levels are low, a few grapes, a banana or an apple revitalize us in moments. Fruit provides the perfect guilt-free snack, since most varieties are completely fat-free and contain very few calories. Nearly all fruits have a high proportion of water – between 75 and 90 per cent – which makes them wonderfully thirst-quenching in hot weather. Picture the pleasure of eating a large wedge of chilled watermelon or a

Below: The vibrant seeds from ripe pomegranates can be eaten raw as they are or added to both sweet and savoury dishes.

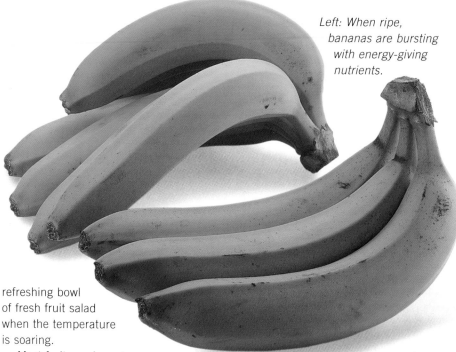

Left: When ripe, bananas are bursting with energy-giving nutrients.

refreshing bowl of fresh fruit salad when the temperature is soaring.

Most fruit can be eaten raw, just as it is (be sure to wash it first), although some varieties may need peeling. Nothing beats a simple dessert of perfectly ripe juicy fruit, perhaps served with a scoop or two of vanilla ice cream or a dollop of cream, or with some good cheese – try crisp apples with a wedge of Farmhouse Cheddar or Lancashire cheese, juicy, ripe pears with either blue Stilton or Gorgonzola, or raspberries and sliced peaches with mascarpone cheese.

All fruits can be served on their own, or used to create sweet and savoury dishes of infinite variety, from pies to puddings, cakes, muffins, ice creams, mousses, soufflés and featherlight fruit-topped pavlovas.

You could easily base an entire meal on fresh fruit without repeating any colours, textures or flavours. The meal might begin with the classic combination of melon with Parma ham, or a refreshing fruit soup, followed by Normandy pheasant with apples and cider, then a platter of cheese, fresh and dried fruit and nuts and finally a tropical fruit salad, a bowl of bright red berries or a lemon tart.

Fruit is enormously rewarding to cook with and is very versatile. Almost all fruits complement each other, so you can create all manner of interesting combinations. Although the recipes in this book concentrate on the use of fruits in sweet dishes, they have an important role to play in savouries too. Tart fruits like gooseberries, rhubarb and cranberries cut the richness of fatty fish like mackerel, and can also enhance the sometimes insipid flavour of poultry. Dried fruits are used extensively in North African and Middle Eastern cooking – the combination of meat and sweet, sticky dates, prunes or

dried apricots is superb. Most fruits also marry well with exotic spices, such as cinnamon, ginger and vanilla, and even those fruits that are relatively bland can be lifted by the addition of a squeeze of lemon or lime juice.

The hundreds of different kinds of fruit can be divided into four main categories: soft fruits, such as raspberries, strawberries, blueberries and red-, black- and whitecurrants; stone fruits, including peaches, apricots, cherries and plums; "pome" fruits of the apple and pear families; and citrus fruits. In addition there are the "one-offs" that do not fit into any other category. These include figs, grapes, melons and rhubarb (which is actually a vegetable, but is always treated as an honorary fruit).

Fruits are no longer the seasonal produce they once were. Nowadays, thanks to sophisticated transportation methods, all types of fruit from every country are available almost all year round. Travellers who have enjoyed exotic produce abroad now find it

Above: Orleans Reinette apples – one of the "pome" fruits.

Left: Watermelons, like other melon varieties, are in a category of their own.

gracing the shelves of their local greengrocer or supermarket, giving less fortunate stay-at-homes a taste of the Tropics. The disadvantage of this is that we no longer wait with eager anticipation for a particular fruit to come into season; somewhere in the world it will be grown year-round. So strawberries, raspberries and peaches have ceased to be exclusively summer treats, but can be bought in almost any season, although they will never taste as good as when freshly picked, and are still always at their best and cheapest in the summer.

There are many other ways of savouring fruits throughout the year. They can be frozen, bottled or preserved in other ways – as juices or liqueurs or macerated in alcohol; canned, dried or candied; or made into jams, jellies, curds, chutneys and relishes. There is no time of year when fruit is not readily available in one form or another, so you need never go without nature's most precious bounty.

EQUIPMENT

Although most fruits can be prepared with the aid of a good sharp knife, a wide variety of special implements is available to make the task easier, safer and more efficient. The following items are very useful – provided you have space for them in your kitchen.

Peeling and Coring

Paring knife The most useful item in any kitchen. Choose a really sharp knife with a short blade and a handle that is comfortable to hold. Always use a stainless steel knife for preparing fruit, as the acids may damage other metals.

Apple corer This utensil removes apple and pear cores in one easy movement. Place over the core at the stem end and push down firmly right through the fruit, then twist slightly and pull out the core and pips.

Apple segmenter Use this handy device to core and slice an apple into twelve even-size segments in one simple operation.

Apple processor Perfect for people with a huge glut of home-grown apples, this hand-cranked implement peels, cores and neatly slices the fruit into rings in seconds. The processor is expensive to buy, but worth it if you have apple trees that bear abundantly.

Above right: Apple corer
Below left: Paring knife
Below right: Apple segmenter

Above: Fixed- and swivel-blade vegetable peelers

Pineapple easy slicer Cores and slices a pineapple in one easy corkscrew-like action. This simple-to-operate utensil is useful for keeping the pineapple shell intact for use as a serving container, but only works with smaller pineapples.

Swivel-blade vegetable peeler Use this tool to pare off the thinnest possible layer of peel or skin so that no nutrients are lost.

Fixed-blade vegetable peeler This type of peeler takes a thicker strip of peel or skin than the swivel-blade version.

Grating and Zesting

Box grater Choose a stainless steel grater with four different grating

Below: Canelle knife and citrus zester
Right: Box grater

Left: Pineapple easy slicer

surfaces and make sure it will stand firmly on a chopping board or in a bowl. Most include a flat blade suitable for slicing lemons or limes.

Citrus zester The row of holes at the top of the zester shaves off thin shreds of zest, leaving behind the bitter pith.

Canelle knife This tool has a tooth-like blade that pares off the zest in ribbons or julienne strips. Combined zesters/canelle knives are available.

Juicing

Lemon squeezer Hand-operated squeezers catch the juice in the base. Basic models can also be used for limes and small oranges. Some have interchangeable heads to accommodate citrus fruits of various sizes.

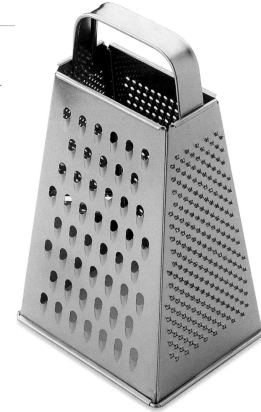

Left: Citrus press
Below: Reamer

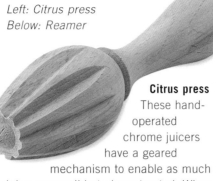

Citrus press

These hand-operated chrome juicers have a geared mechanism to enable as much juice as possible to be extracted. When the handle is pulled forward, the juice is squeezed into a container.

Electric juice extractor These machines will extract juice from other fruits besides citrus. They take up a lot of space, but are invaluable for lovers of fresh fruit juice.

Stoning and Preparing

Cherry stoner The bowl of this implement has a hole through which the cherry stone is ejected when the fruit is pressed. Useful for large quantities.

Grapefruit knife A curved knife serrated on both sides. Run it between the membranes and pulp to release the segments.

Left: Cherry stoner

Below: Grapefruit knife

Grapefruit segmenter This curved implement has a V-shaped blade. Position with the point against the inside of the rind and push down, round and inwards to cut out the segments.

Melon baller Insert this small round scoop into the melon flesh and twist to remove neat balls of fruit. It comes in various sizes and can also be used for other fruits. Tiny ones sometimes double as a cherry stoner.

Preserving

Funnel Essential for pouring hot jams and jellies into jars. Stainless steel funnels will withstand heat better than plastic ones.

Jelly bag A heavy muslin filter bag for straining jellies and juices. Suspend it from the legs of a chair placed upside down or, far better, buy one on a stand.

Preserving pan Especially designed for preserving, this is a thick-bottomed double-handled pan. The heavy base prevents the fruit preserve from burning and sticking.

Sugar thermometer Use this for checking the temperature of a syrup or to determine whether the setting point of a jam and jelly has been reached.

Above: Sugar thermometer
Below: Funnel with strainer

Reamer This wooden device enables you to squeeze the fruit directly into a bowl or pan. Insert into the cut fruit and twist.

Lemon tap A simple gadget that turns citrus fruit into a "juice jug". If only a small amount of juice is required, leave the tap inserted in the fruit to keep the juice fresh between squeezings.

Below: Lemon squeezer

Above: Melon baller

PURCHASING, PREPARING AND COOKING

BUYING FRUIT

Obviously, the best time to buy fruit is when it is fully ripe and at its peak. The exceptions are fruits, such as bananas and pears, that ripen quickly and should therefore be bought at different stages of maturity so that they are not all ready at the same time. You are most likely to find top quality fruits in markets and shops that have a quick turnover of fresh produce, preferably with a daily delivery. Although most fruits are now available almost year-round, they are best and cheapest when in season in the country of origin. Only buy as much fruit as you need at one time so that it remains fresh and appetizing.

PREPARING FRUIT

For some fruits, the only preparation needed is washing or wiping with a damp cloth; others must be peeled or skinned, cored, stoned or seeded. Wash fruit only just before using. If necessary, cut away any bruised or damaged parts.

Firm Fruit

Peeling

Some firm fruits, such as dessert apples and pears, can be eaten raw without peeling. For cooking, peeling is often necessary. Pare off the skin as thinly as possible to avoid losing the valuable nutrients under the skin.

1 Wash the fruit and pat dry using kitchen paper. Use a small, sharp paring knife or a vegetable peeler to pare off the skin in long, thin vertical strips. Pears are best peeled by this method.

2 Alternatively, for apples, thinly peel all round the fruit in a spiral.

Coring

1 To core whole apples and pears, place the sharp edge of a corer over the stem end of the fruit.

2 Press down firmly, then twist slightly; the core, complete with pips, will come away in the centre of the corer. Push out the core from the handle end.

Storing

Storage methods depend on the type of fruit, but there are some basic guidelines:
- Do not wash fruit before storing, but only when ready to use.
- Store fruit at the bottom of the fridge or in the salad crisper.
- Do not refrigerate unripe fruit; keep it at room temperature or in a cool, dark place, depending on the variety (see individual fruits).
- Fragile fruits, such as berries are easily squashed, so spread them out in a single layer on a tray lined with kitchen paper.

Segmenting

1 Halve the fruit lengthways, then cut into quarters or segments.

2 Cut out the central core and pips with a small sharp knife.

Preventing discoloration

Some fruits, such as apples, pears and bananas, quickly oxidize and turn brown when exposed to the air. To prevent discoloration, brush cut fruits with lemon juice. Alternatively, acidulate a bowl of cold water by stirring in the juice of half a lemon. Drop the cut fruits into the bowl immediately after preparing.

Citrus Fruit

Peeling

It is very important to remove all of the bitter white pith that lies just beneath the rind of citrus fruits.

1 To peel firm-skinned fruits, hold the fruit over a bowl to catch the juice and use a sharp knife to cut off the rind.
2 For loose-skinned fruit, such as tangerines, pierce the skin with your forefinger at the stalk end and peel off the rind. Pull off all the white shreds adhering to the fruit.

Segmenting

Use a small serrated knife to cut down

between the membranes enclosing the segments; carefully ease out the flesh.

Grating

Citrus zest adds a wonderful flavour to

many dishes. If it is to be eaten raw, grate it finely, using the fine face of a grater. Remove only the coloured zest, if you grate too deeply into the peel, you will be in danger of including the bitter white pith. For cooking, pare off long, thin strips of zest using a zester.

Garnishing

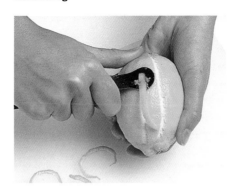

1 To make thick julienne strips of zest, cut lengthways, using a canelle knife.

2 To make twists, slice the fruits thinly, cut to the centre, then twist the ends in opposite directions to make an S-shape.

Soft Fruit

Peeling

Fruits, such as peaches, nectarines and apricots can be peeled with a sharp paring knife, but this may waste some of the delicious flesh. It is better to loosen the skins by dipping them *briefly* in boiling water.

1 Make a tiny nick in the skin.

2 Cover with boiling water and leave for 15–30 seconds, depending on the ripeness of the fruit. Remove the fruit with a slotted spoon and peel off the skin, which should come away easily.

Removing stones and pips

1 To stone peaches, apricots etc, cut all around the fruit through the seam. Twist the halves in opposite directions, then lever out the stone with a knife.

2 To stone cherries, put the fruit in a cherry stoner and push the bar into the fruit. The stone will be ejected.

3 To remove grape pips, cut the grapes in half, then pick out the pips with the tip of a small sharp knife.

COOKING FRUIT

Most fruits can be cooked and in a great variety of ways.

Poaching

Apples and pears, stone fruits, figs, rhubarb and even grapes can be poached, either whole, halved or in segments. The classic poaching liquid is syrup and usually consists of 1 part sugar boiled with 2 parts water for about 2 minutes or until clear. The syrup can be flavoured with lemon, orange or spices, such as cinnamon or vanilla. Red or white wine can also be used for poaching, usually with added sugar. Alternatively, use fruit juice.

Bring the poaching liquid to the boil. Lower the heat and add the fruit. Simmer gently until the fruit is just tender.

Stewing

This method is suitable for all fruits that can be poached.

Cut up the fruit. Put in a saucepan with just enough water, wine or fruit juice to cover. Add sugar to taste. Simmer gently until tender. Only stir if you want the fruit to become a pulp.

Grilling

Any firm fruits can be grilled, with or without sugar. Tropical fruits, such as pineapple and bananas, are particularly good for grilling. For desserts, they can be cut into 2.5cm/1in wedges or chunks and threaded on to skewers to make kebabs. Brush the fruit with clear honey before grilling.

For savoury dishes, halve the fruit or cut into pieces, removing the core if necessary. Brush with melted butter and grill under a medium heat, turning occasionally until tender and browned on all sides.

Baking

Apples and pears; stone fruits, such as peaches, nectarines, apricots and plums; figs and rhubarb can be baked whole or in halves, wedges or slices according to type.

1 Put the fruit in a shallow ovenproof dish, add a little water, and sprinkle with sugar to taste.

2 Top the fruit with small pieces of butter. Bake in a preheated oven at 180°C/350°F/Gas 4 until tender.

Microwave Cooking

All fruits, which can be conventionally cooked, can be microwaved, with excellent results, although the skins on some fruits, such as plums, may not soften sufficiently in the short cooking time. Whole fruits, such as apples should be scored, or they may burst. Place the fruit in a suitable dish, cover and cook on High for the time recommended, or until tender.

Sautéeing

Slice or dice the fruit (peel it or not, as you wish) and toss quickly in hot butter until lightly browned all over. Add sugar and flavourings to taste.

Deep Frying

For fruit fritters, such as pineapple, apple or banana, peel the fruit and cut into chunks.

Heat oil for deep frying to 185°C/360°F or until a cube of dried bread sizzles when it is added to the pan. Coat the pieces of fruit in batter and deep fry until the fritters rise to the surface of the hot oil and are golden brown. Drain the fritters on kitchen paper and sprinkle with sugar.

Puréeing

Fruit can be puréed for sauces, fools, ice creams and sorbets. Some types must be cooked first; others, like berries, can be puréed raw.

1 For berries, wash briefly and push through a fine nylon sieve, using the back of a large spoon or ladle. If you prefer, purée the berries in a food processor, then sieve the purée to remove any pips.

2 For cooked peeled fruit, mash with a potato masher for a coarse purée.
3 For a finer purée, whizz cooked, peeled fruit in a food processor or push through a food mill.

Caramelizing

Fruits look pretty when caramelized. Small fruits like cherries can be used whole. Larger fruits should be cubed.

1 Combine 200g/7oz/scant 1 cup granulated sugar and 60ml/4 tbsp water in a small heavy-based saucepan. Stir over a low heat until the sugar has dissolved. When the mixture boils, add 5ml/1 tsp lemon juice and boil until the syrup turns a deep golden brown.

2 Carefully add 15ml/1 tbsp hot water (protecting your hand with an oven glove as the mixture will "spit") and shake the pan to mix.
3 Spear a piece of fruit on a fork and dip it into the caramel to coat. Leave on an oiled baking sheet until the caramel cools and hardens.

Candying

Also known as crystallized or glacé fruits, candied fruits make a delicious end to a meal. Suitable fruits include citrus (slices and peel), cherries and other stone fruits, physalis and pineapple. For professional results, the candying process is a lengthy one, but this simplified method works well for candied citrus zest or for fruit that is to be eaten within a few days.

1 Cut the fruit into slices or chunks. Make a syrup, using 225g/8oz/1 cup granulated sugar and 150ml/1/4 pint/ 2/3 cup water; follow the instructions under Caramelizing. Immerse the pieces of fruit in the syrup. Leave in a cool, dry place to soak for 2 weeks. Drain.

2 Place the fruit on a rack over a baking sheet. Dry for 3–6 hours in a very low oven (no higher than 50ºC/122ºF). Cool, then store in an airtight container.

Frosting

Try this technique with grapes, red and blackcurrants and cranberries. Eat on the day they are prepared.

1 Leave the fruit on the stalk. Dip in lightly beaten egg white, then roll in caster sugar until frosted all over. Leave to dry before serving.

Drying

Suitable fruits include apples, pears, stone fruits, figs, grapes and bananas. Commercial dehydrators are available, but you can dry the fruit in a low oven.

Prepare the fruit: peel, core and slice apples; peel, core and halve pears; halve and stone peaches or similar fruits. Leave smaller fruits whole. Lay the fruit on clean wooden slatted trays, cut-side up. Dry in an oven preheated to the lowest possible temperature. Cool completely before storing.

Preserving in Alcohol

All fruits can be preserved in alcohol. In the eighteenth century, seafarers discovered that their cargoes of exotic fruits could be preserved in barrels of rum. Dark rum is still the classic preserving spirit, but brandy and other spirits can also be used.

The ideal container is a purpose-made *rumtopf*, but a wide-mouthed preserving jar will do. Start with summer fruits, then add other fruits as they come into season.

1 Wash and dry the fruit. Place in a bowl and cover with an equal weight of sugar. Leave for 1 hour.

2 Tip the fruit mixture into a *rumtopf* or preserving jar. Pour in just enough rum to completely cover the fruit. Cover the jar with clear film and store in a cool, dark place.
3 Continue to fill the jar with fruits as they come into season, using only half as much sugar by weight as fruit; cover the fruit with rum each time. When the jar is full, leave for at least two months before using the fruit.

APPLES, PEARS, QUINCES AND MEDLARS

A bowlful of apples, polished to shiny perfection, is one of life's pleasures — beautiful to behold, delicious and healthy to eat. Pears are almost as popular, with juicy flesh whose scent is almost as tempting as its taste. Quinces are even more aromatic, while medlars are intriguing — not least because they can only be eaten when they are on the verge of rotting. They are all "pome" fruits, with an indentation in the stalk end and the coarse brown remains of a flower at the other, and a tough central core containing a number of brown pips.

APPLES

Ever since Adam bit into the fruit of the Tree of Knowledge, apples have been the stuff of myth and legend. The Ancient Greeks and Romans believed them to be aphrodisiacs, and for the Celts crab apples were a symbol of fertility. In the Middle Ages, the cult of the apple continued in such customs as apple-bobbing at Hallowe'en and wassailing at Christmas.

The most popular of all fruits, apples are also convenient, perfect for eating raw as a nutritious snack and ideal for making into a multitude of hot and cold puddings and desserts. There are thousands of named varieties worldwide, but the choice of those available to buy is, sadly, decreasing year by year. However, because apples are now grown in every temperate country in the world, some varieties can be found in the shops all year round. Delicious as they may be, no shop-bought apples can ever beat the flavour and crisp texture of home-grown apples that have been freshly picked.

Apples come in many shapes and sizes, from tiny cherry-sized crab apples to huge cooking varieties like Howgate Wonder, Reverend W. Wilkes and the unbelievably warty Knobby Russet, which looks remarkably like a huge toad. They can be round, oval, or "cornered", with four distinct corners around the calyx, like the Catshead, which is shaped like the face of a Siamese cat.

Colours range from bright, shiny red through vivid greens, yellows and pale creamy-white to golden russet, while the skins may be ultra-thin or unpalatably thick. As for taste and texture, there is an almost infinite variety – something to suit every palate, from crisp and sour to soft and sweet.

History

Apples have been eaten since prehistoric times, when only wild crab apples existed. The Romans adored apples and were the first people to cultivate the fruit; by the first century AD they were growing at least a dozen varieties throughout the Roman Empire.

Left: Granny Smith apples – first cultivated in Australia in the twentieth century.

The most famous of all apple-growers was the nineteenth-century English nurseryman, Thomas Laxton. With his sons, he hybridized hundreds of varieties of apples, many of which still exist today and bear his name.

The Pilgrim Fathers introduced apples to the New World, planting pips that they had taken with them from England. They proved so popular that in the eighteenth century John Chapman (popularly known as "Johnny Appleseed") planted apple orchards across about 10,000 square miles of North America, using discarded apple pips from cider-making plants. A century later, apple-growing in Australia took off when Mrs Maria Smith cultivated the first Granny Smith apple in her garden in Sydney.

Above: Laxton's Fortune

Below: Braeburn – crisp, juicy apples, which make excellent eating.

Varieties

With over 7,000 named varieties of apples, it would be impossible to list more than a tiny fraction. In any case, only about a dozen varieties are readily available in the shops, although nurseries can supply many more to people who wish to grow apples in their gardens.

Growing your own apples will allow you to enjoy exotically flavoured fruit, like the pineapple-flavoured Pine Golden Pippin or Ananas Reinette, or the Winter Banana, which develops a creamy texture and a banana flavour when laid down. D'Arcy Spice is a small golden apple with the flavours of cinnamon and allspice, while Anisa is one of several aniseed-flavoured apples. Other apples are redolent of melon, strawberries, raspberries, peach, lemon, and even fennel.

Uniquely in Britain, apples are categorized as eating or dessert fruit, or cooking apples. Other countries regard all apples as suitable for both eating or cooking. Of course, there are cider apples as well; many are disagreeably sour, but some are very pleasant to eat.

Below: Beauty of Bath

EATING APPLES

Ashmead's Kernel: These late variety apples were first cultivated in Gloucestershire in the seventeenth century. Their flesh has a good acid/sugar balance and develops a strong, spicy, aniseed flavour in some seasons.

Beauty of Bath A beautiful small flattish green apple extensively flushed with red, with sharp, sweet, juicy flesh. Beauty of Bath apples should be eaten straight from the tree, as they rot almost as soon as they are picked. Consequently, you are unlikely to find this apple in the shops.

Blenheim Orange This apple was discovered growing out of a wall in Blenheim Palace in England in the nineteenth century and was named by permission of the Duke of Marlborough, but it also has sixty-seven synonyms! It is a dual-purpose apple, good for both cooking and eating, with a pleasantly nutty flavour. It is suitable for cooking in dishes, such as apple charlotte and apple crumble, and for serving as a dessert fruit.

Braeburn This crisp, juicy apple with a smooth pale green skin, heavily flushed with red, makes excellent eating. Braeburn apples are grown only in the southern hemisphere, as they need plenty of daylight.

Above: Empire

Above left: Egremont Russet – this sweet crisp apple is delicious served at the end of a meal with a wedge of strong-tasting cheese, such as Farmhouse Cheddar or Lancashire.

Cox's Orange Pippin A greenish-yellow apple of medium size, with some orange-red russetting. The firm, crisp, juicy flesh of this sweet fruit, with its overtones of acidity, make it one of the world's best and most popular apples. Cox's Orange Pippins ar   e excellent for cooking as well as eating raw.

Crispin Large, pale yellowish-green apples with firm and juicy creamy-white flesh and a pleasant mild flavour.

Discovery Bred from the Worcester Pearmain, Discovery was the first apple to be commercially grown in Britain. It is particularly attractive for its highly coloured bright red skin and contrasting hard, crisp white flesh. Best eaten straight from the tree.

Egremont Russet Russet apples have rough, porous skins which allow the water to evaporate out, giving a denser flesh and intensifying the nutty flavour. Egremont Russet is the most readily available. It is golden russet in colour, sometimes with a bright orange flush, and has a crisp texture and very sweet taste. It can be used for eating or cooking and goes superbly with cheese.

Elstar This sweet, crisp and juicy apple is a cross between Ingrid Marie and Golden Delicious. Originally bred in Holland, it is now grown extensively throughout Europe. Picked in mid-autumn, Elstar apples will keep for 3–4 months.

Empire A dark red American apple with a shiny skin, best for eating raw, but suitable for cooking. It has crisp green, juicy flesh and a slightly tart flavour.

Above: Cox's Orange Pippin

Left: Jonagold – these dual-purpose apples have a superb flavour.

Fuji This sweet apple has greenish-yellow skin with a rosy blush and crisp, juicy white flesh. It is also suitable for cooking.

Gala This colourful eating apple from New Zealand has a yellow ground colour flushed with bright orange and red. The yellow flesh is very sweet, juicy and crisp. It is at its best when absolutely fresh. Good for either cooking or eating. **Royal Gala** is similar, but red all over.

Golden Delicious Originally grown from a chance seedling in the USA, this conical, freckled, golden apple has become ubiquitous. At its peak, the cream flesh is juicy and crisp with a mild flavour; unfortunately most commercially grown Golden Delicious are sold when they are under- or over-ripe and are consequently tasteless and mealy in texture. Golden Delicious are suitable for cooking or eating.

Granny Smith First grown in Australia by the eponymous "Granny" Smith, this largish

Right: Golden Delicious

all-purpose apple is bright green, becoming yellow as it ripens. Usually sold under-ripe, it has firm, crunchy flesh and a tart flavour.

Greensleeves This James Grieve/Golden Delicious cross has more flavour than a James Grieve and better acidity. It is an early fruiting variety, which should be eaten immediately after picking.

Ida Red By far the favourite North American apple for making apple sauce. American-grown fruits have a good acid flavour, which is often lacking in the European-grown apples.

James Grieve A Scottish apple raised in Edinburgh in the late nineteenth century, with tart, juicy flesh that bruises easily when handled. James Grieve is good for cooking and eating, but, like most early varieties, it does not store well and should be kept for no more than 2–3 weeks after picking.

Jonagold A hybrid of Jonathan and Golden Delicious, this large round green-tinged yellow apple has creamy

Above: Gala are best eaten very fresh, when the flesh is crisp and juicy.

Left: Katy

Right: Orleans Reinette

white flesh and a superb flavour. It can be used for cooking or eating.

Jonathan This smallish round orange-red North American apple has white, juicy, flesh and a fragrant, slightly acidic flavour. It can be used for cooking.

Katy A highly coloured early apple bred in Sweden from the Worcester Pearmain. Their small size appeals to children, and their flesh is crisp, sweet and juicy. Katy apples are best eaten immediately after picking.

Kidd's Orange Red A New Zealand apple bred from Cox's Orange Pippin. These deliciously crisp apples are highly aromatic, but need many hours of sunshine to develop their full flavour and colour, so they cannot be successfully grown in Northern Europe.

Laxton's Fortune A cross between Cox's Orange Pippin and Wealthy, these apples have yellowish skin heavily tinged with red, and sweet, juicy, lightly aromatic flesh. You are most likely to find them in farm shops.

Laxton's Superb Greenish-yellow and partially covered with red, this all-purpose apple has crisp, very juicy flesh. It is sweet with some acidity.

McIntosh A Canadian apple that is popular throughout North America. It is wonderfully decorative, with deep red waxy skin, which can be polished to a superb sheen, but the skin is quite tough. The pale flesh is melting (and sometimes mushy) with a hint of fresh strawberry flavour.

Orleans Reinette One of the best apples of all, this large orange-flecked russet has a rough skin, but juicy, sweet, aromatic flesh. Orleans Reinette is ideal for cooking and eating.

Pink Lady A pretty Australian cross between Golden Delicious and Lady Williams, this large all-purpose apple has a mild flavour, and is becoming increasing available in supermarkets and greengrocers.

Pomme d'Api Also known as Lady apple, this very attractive fruit has a yellow skin suffused with a bright red blush. Pomme d'Api is a late apple with good keeping qualities.

Red Delicious This North American apple was first grown in the nineteenth century. It has an exceptionally sweet flavour,

*Above:
Pink Lady*

Above: Spartan – a Canadian apple with a tough skin, but delicious, floral-scented flesh.

Left: Grown mostly in the United States, colourful Red Delicious is another apple, with a tough skin that hides juicy, sweet flesh.

but tough skin. Red Delicious apples can be grown in Europe, but not always successfully.

Spartan Another Canadian apple raised in 1926 from McIntosh and Newton's Pippin. It inherits a tough skin from McIntosh, but tastes highly aromatic with a floral perfume.

Worcester Pearmain A conical yellow apple flushed with bright red. The juicy white flesh has a hint of strawberry flavour. Worcester Pearmain are best eaten straight from the tree, but can also be used for cooking.

Above: Worcester Pearmain

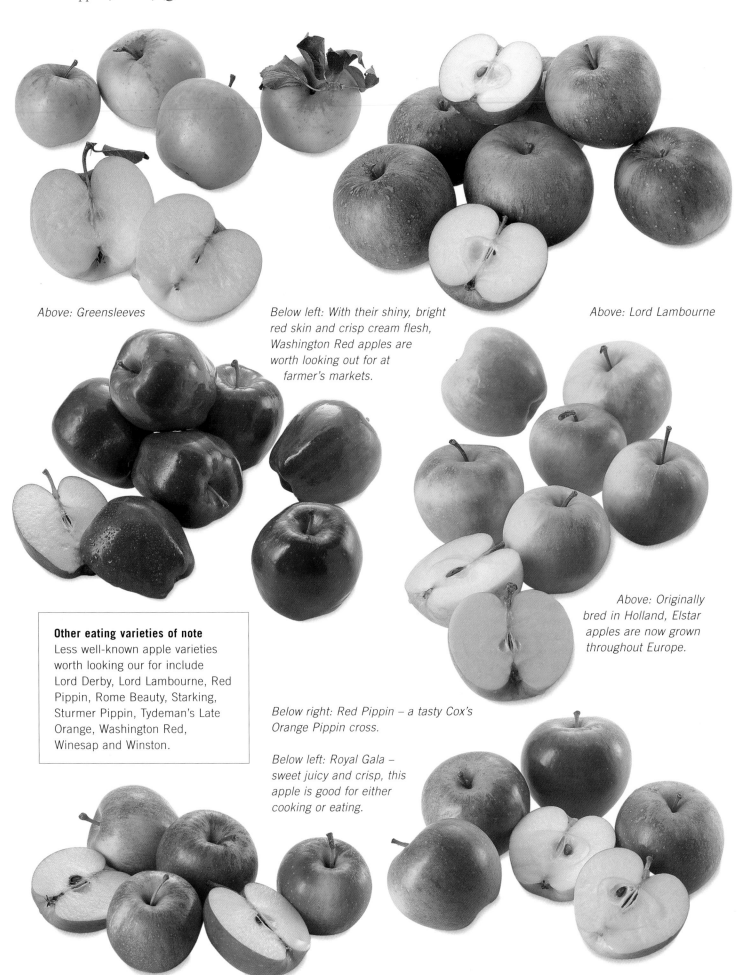

Above: Greensleeves

Below left: With their shiny, bright red skin and crisp cream flesh, Washington Red apples are worth looking out for at farmer's markets.

Above: Lord Lambourne

Above: Originally bred in Holland, Elstar apples are now grown throughout Europe.

Other eating varieties of note
Less well-known apple varieties worth looking our for include Lord Derby, Lord Lambourne, Red Pippin, Rome Beauty, Starking, Sturmer Pippin, Tydeman's Late Orange, Washington Red, Winesap and Winston.

Below right: Red Pippin – a tasty Cox's Orange Pippin cross.

Below left: Royal Gala – sweet juicy and crisp, this apple is good for either cooking or eating.

Above: Bramley's Seedling

Below: Howgate Wonder

COOKING APPLES

Bramley's Seedling The *nonpareil* of cookers, this large, flattish green apple (sometimes faintly flushed with red) has coarse, white, juicy, acid flesh, which cooks into a frothy purée. Bramleys are perfect for baking or as the basis of apple sauce.

Grenadier An irregularly shaped conical apple with yellow skin. The acid flesh is faintly green, firm and juicy. It breaks down during cooking. Grenadiers do not keep well.

Howgate Wonder This apple can grow to an enormous size – in 1997, the world record was achieved with a specimen weighing 1.6kg/3lb 14oz! The juicy white flesh breaks up during cooking and has an uninspiring flavour, so this variety is grown mainly for exhibition.

Reverend W. Wilkes Very large conical apple with pale greenish-white skin. The fine, very white flesh is crisp, juicy and acidic. The apple can be eaten raw, but it is best as a cooker. It keeps well.

Nutrition

Apples were once believed to be the most nutritious of fruits, giving rise to the saying that "an apple a day keeps the doctor away". In fact, they have fewer vitamins than many other fruits (although they contain some vitamins C and A), but are high in pectin and are a good source of dietary fibre. They provide 52 kilocalories per 100g/3¾oz.

Buying and Storing

Choose apples with undamaged skins and never buy bruised fruits. If possible, smell the fruits to determine their fragrance (not easy when they are pre-bagged) and squeeze gently to ensure they are firm. Do not be too seduced by the skin colour of an apple; those gorgeous-looking specimens with thick, vivid red, waxy skins often have woolly, tasteless flesh.

Apples continue to ripen after they have been picked, so their colour and texture may change during storage. For short-term storage, they can be kept in a ventilated polythene bag in the fridge. To store pick-your-own apples, wrap each one in newspaper and place folded-side down in a single layer in wooden or fibre trays. Keep in a cool, dry, dark place and check occasionally to make sure none has gone rotten. A bad fruit will taint all the others, so remove it immediately.

Dried Apples These have a sweet, concentrated flavour and are an extremely useful storecupboard ingredient. Eat them straight from the

Below: Dried apple rings

Drying apples at home

1 Peel the apples, remove the cores and slice the fruit into rings. Soak in salted water for a few minutes to prevent discoloration.

2 Thread the apple rings on to string. Hang them from the ceiling or suspend across the room until they are completely dry.

3 Alternatively, arrange the rings in a single layer on a wire rack on a baking sheet, making sure that they are not touching. Place in an oven set to 70°C/150°F/Gas Low for several hours until dried.

packet as a nutritious snack, add them to home-made muesli or soak them in water, then cook them in sweet and savoury dishes like fruit compotes, apple sauce or casseroles. Dried apples are available commercially, but it is easy to dry your own when there is a glut, and you can choose your favourite varieties. Russets are particularly delicious when dried.

Preparing

Most apples can be eaten with the skin on. To peel, use a vegetable peeler or small, sharp knife, either in a spiral following the circumference of the apple, or peeling downwards in strips from stem to calyx. Peeled apples go brown very quickly; brush them with lemon juice or drop them into water acidulated with lemon juice or cider vinegar immediately.

Cooking

Some apples are only suitable for eating raw, but most can be cooked in such classic sweet dishes as apple pies, crumbles and tarts, baked apples and strudel. Sweet apples combine well with other fruits, like blackberries, quinces and lemon, and dried fruits like raisins or cranberries. Aromatic spices like cinnamon, nutmeg and cloves highlight their flavour. Their high pectin content will help other fruit jellies and jams to set, or they can be made into crab apple jelly, apple cheese and chutney.

Tart apples make excellent accompaniments for game birds, black pudding and sausages, and rich meats like pork, duck and goose. They go well with red cabbage and are a vital ingredient in Waldorf salad.

To bake apples, core them with an apple corer and score around the circumference to prevent the skin from bursting. Stuff with dried fruit, nuts, butter and sugar and bake in a preheated oven at 180°C/350°F/Gas 4 until soft.

To cook sliced apples and rings, sauté in butter and sugar to help them keep their shape. To stew, cook in the minimum amount of water, or with butter and seasonings.

Making apple purée

1 Peel, core and thickly slice the apples, immediately dropping the pieces into a bowl of cold water acidulated with lemon juice or cider vinegar.

2 Barely cover the bottom of a saucepan with cold water. Add the apple pieces and cook to a purée, adding sugar to taste towards the end.

3 If you are using firmer dessert apples, which will not disintegrate to a purée, cook until very tender, then rub through a coarse sieve.

CRAB APPLES AND CIDER APPLES

Crab apples have grown wild in hedgerows for thousands of years and were eaten in prehistoric times. The fruits are smaller and often more colourful than cultivated varieties. Nowadays crab apples are often grown for their ornamental qualities. The fruits can be vivid yellow, green, orange or bright red.

Crab apples are seldom worth eating raw (and may be completely inedible), although some are perfectly palatable for those without too sweet a tooth. You may find larger self-seeded crab apples, which have grown from the pips of cultivated apples that have become wild; these can be eaten.

Thanks to their high pectin content, all crab apples make wonderful jellies, either on their own or mixed with other wild fruits, such as haw berries.

Cider apples are closer to eating apples than crab apples, but usually have a bitter or sour flavour due to their

Below: Crab apples are almost always too sour to eat raw.

high tannin content. There are hundreds of different varieties with wonderful names like Strawberry Norma and Foxwhelp, and each local grower will insist that his is the best. Some, like Tom Putt, are sweet enough to eat; these are used to make sweet cider.

Apple Drinks

Apple juice, cider and apple brandies, such as Calvados, are the main drinks made from apples. Apple juice is made by crushing dessert apples; the best is pressed from a single variety, such as Cox's Orange Pippin or Russet, but most commercial apple juices are made from a mixture of varieties or, worse, from concentrate. Apple juice may be fizzy or still.

Cider may have been brought to Britain by the Phoenicians or the Celts; it has certainly been around for thousands of years. It is a fermented drink made from the juice of cider apples and, depending on the variety of fruit and

pressing technique, can range from sweet and gassy to cloudy and flat. The best ciders are still made by small producers using artisan methods; some of these ciders can be lethally strong. The strongest and crudest cider is scrumpy. It is made from the apples of the poorest quality, but can certainly pack a punch!

Apple brandy is made from fermented and distilled apple juice. The best of all is Calvados, the famous apple brandy from Normandy, which is double distilled and aged in oak. Calvados may only be produced within a defined area; other apple brandies must be labelled *eau-de-vie de cidre* or simply "apple brandy" ("applejack" in North America).

Fermented apple juice can also be made into cider vinegar, which has a strong apple taste and is excellent for making fruit chutneys or adding extra flavour to casseroles containing apples.

Left: Cider – the best is still made by artisan producers.

Right and far right: Calvados and applejack are both types of apple brandy.

PEARS

There are almost as many varieties of pears as there are apples, but only a dozen or so are available in the shops. Pears are related to apples, but are more fragile and are more often eaten raw than cooked. They have fine white granular flesh and a central core containing the pips. Most pears have the familiar shape, wider at the bottom than the top, but some are apple-shaped, while "calabash" pears have an elongated neck, like a gourd. Pears are less vividly coloured than apples, generally varying from bronze to gold, green or yellow, but there are some beautiful red varieties, too.

History

Wild pears are native to Europe and Asia, where they have grown since prehistoric times. They were cultivated by the ancient Phoenicians and the Romans, and they became a royal delicacy for the ancient Persian kings. Their popularity spread so fast that in medieval Italy over 200 varieties of

Below: Beurré Bosc

Right: Anjou pears are sweet, juicy and aromatic.

pear were cultivated. By the seventeenth century, the French were growing 300 different varieties, inspired by Louis XIV's passion for the fruit. There are now said to be more than 5,000 named varieties throughout the world.

Varieties

Cooking pears (which cannot be eaten raw) do exist, but almost all the pears available in the shops are dessert fruit, which can also be cooked. Pears are seasonal, so only a few varieties are available at any one time.

Anjou These large pears have greenish-yellow skin with brown speckles or russetting. The flesh is juicy and sweet. Suitable for eating and cooking.

Beth This modern pear variety resembles Williams Bon Chrétien in flavour and texture, but has the added advantage of being longer keeping.

Beurré Bosc and **Beurré Hardi** These elongated pears have an uneven green-gold skin, which becomes yellow and completely russetted as the fruit ripens. The creamy-white flesh is firm and juicy with a buttery texture (hence the name, which means "buttered"), and the flavour is deliciously sweet and aromatic with some acidity. Both varieties are excellent for eating and cooking.

Beurré Superfin These medium-to-large pears are round conical in shape. Their uneven, almost knobbly skin is pale greenish-yellow, which changes to yellow with bronze russetting as they ripen. The creamy-white flesh is firm and buttery and extremely juicy, with a sweet flavour with a hint of acidity. A truly delicious pear.

Conference First cultivated in Berkshire in 1770, these long, conical pears have remained a favourite in Britain, largely because they keep so well. The yellowish-green skin with extensive russetting turns yellower when the pears are mature. The granular flesh is tender, sweet and juicy. Excellent for eating and cooking.

Doyenné du Comice (also known as **Comice**) This large, roundish pear is one of the finest of all, with creamy white, melting, very juicy flesh and a sweet, aromatic flavour. The thick, yellowish-green skin is covered with speckles and patches of russetting. Doyenné du Comice are best eaten raw, and are delicious with Brie or Camembert.

Forelle A beautiful golden pear with a dark red flush on one side. The grainy flesh is crisp, with a fresh flavour that goes well with cheese, but is at its best when cooked.

Josephine de Malines A French pear, first raised in 1830. The medium-size fruits are round-conical in shape, with

Below: Conference are one of the best-loved English pears.

yellowish-green skin flushed with red and some russetting, The tender flesh can be white or pinkish and is very juicy, with an aromatic flavour. It has good keeping qualities.

Merton Pride An exceptionally sweet and juicy pear with a superb flavour. The conical fruits have yellow skin wih brown freckles.

Onward A cross between Laxton's Superb and Doyenné du Comice, these roundish pears are best peeled before eating as they have ribbed skin. The yellowish-green skin is flushed with red and mottled with pale russetting. The creamy-white flesh is exceptionally good – soft, melting, juicy and very sweet.

Packham's Triumph The first successful Australian pear was produced by Charles Packham in 1896 and remains a favourite. A largish dessert pear, it has a smooth green, lightly russetted skin, which changes to yellow as it ripens. The soft white flesh is succulent and sweet, with a touch of acidity.

Passacrena Very plump, roundish pears with russetted greenish-yellow skin. The flesh can sometimes be rather gritty, but is very juicy and sweet.

Above: Doyenné du Comice, also known simply as Comice, are very juicy and aromatic.

Right: Forelle are ideal pears to use for cooking.

Red Williams These pears have shiny, speckled skins, at first green with a red blush, turning to yellow flushed with red. The flesh is sweet and juicy.

Rocha A Portuguese pear with greenish-yellow skin with russet spotting and brown markings at the stem end. The firm white flesh has a sugary flavour and, unlike many other pears, which pass their prime almost as soon as they reach it, the fruit remains in excellent condition for several days.

Williams Bon Chrétien Known as "Barlett" in the United States, these irregularly shaped pears are generally swollen on one side of the stalk. The speckled skin is golden yellow with russet patches and sometimes a red tinge. The delicious tender flesh is creamy-white and very juicy, and the flavour is sweet and slightly musky. Unfortunately, these superb pears do not keep well. Williams Bon Chrétien are suitable for cooking and eating.

Winter Nelis This roundish medium-size pear has thick but tender greenish-yellow skin with cinnamon brown russetting and sometimes a pink flush. The creamy-white flesh is soft and very juicy, and the flavour is sweet. These pears can be cooked or eaten raw.

Left: Packham's Triumph

Nutrition

Pears contain a small amount of vitamins A and C and some potassium and riboflavin. They provide about 60 kilocalories per 100g/3¾oz.

Pears should always be bought when they are in perfect condition, as they deteriorate quickly. Once past their best, they become woolly or squashy and unpleasant. Test for ripeness by pressing the stem end between your forefinger and thumb; it should give a little, but the pear should still be quite firm. Once ripe, pears should be eaten within a couple of days, or they will "go over". Keep ripe fruit in the bottom of the fridge.

Above: Suitable for both eating and cooking, Williams Bon Chrétien have delicious creamy-white flesh. They don't keep well, so use them as soon as they are ripe.

Below: Juicy, with a red blush, Red Williams make excellent eating.

Above left: The firm-fleshed Rocha will remain in good condition for several days in your fruit bowl.

Dried pears Although dried pears are most often used in winter fruit compotes and savoury casseroles, they have a delicate flavour and are delicious eaten raw. They are readily available in the shops, but it is easy to prepare your own.
Canned pears Pears are among the most successful of all canned fruit and can be used to make almost any dessert that calls for cooked pears. They are often canned in heavy syrup, but are now available in the healthier alternative of apple juice. Purée drained canned pears, flavour them with pear liqueur, lemon or preserved ginger syrup and freeze for a quick and easy sorbet.

Preparing and Cooking

Most pears are eaten raw, by themselves or with a robust cheese, such as Gorgonzola, Parmesan, Stilton or Roquefort. They also make a good addition to winter salads. Whether or not to peel pears before eating raw is a matter of preference, but they should always be peeled before cooking. Pears discolour quickly once they are peeled, so rub the cut surface with a little lemon juice immediately or place in a bowl of acidulated water. For whole poached pears, simply peel,

Right: Dried pears

leaving on the stalk. Use an apple corer to core the pears if you want to stuff them with nuts or dried fruit. Poach in port or red wine spiced with cinnamon, cloves and thinly pared lemon rind, or in a vanilla-flavoured syrup. For sautéed or grilled pears, peel and quarter or halve the fruit and scoop out the cores with a melon baller.

Dessert or cooking pears can also be cooked in compotes, tarts, terrines, trifles and the famous Poires Belle Hélène (poached pears with vanilla ice cream and hot chocolate sauce). They make marvellous fritters and go very well with ingredients, such as nuts and spices, port and marsala. Cooked pears are also excellent in savoury dishes – with game and duck, for example – either made into chutney, or casseroled with game birds or venison. They can be preserved with sugar and vinegar, or pickled with mustard seeds and horseradish. If you are cooking dessert pears, use them while they are still slightly under-ripe.

Pears can also be dried, canned, crystallized and distilled into spirits like *eau-de-vie de poires* and Poire William. The bottle in which this liqueur is sold sometimes contains a whole pear, an apparent illusion as the neck is too narrow to allow the pear to pass. The effect is achieved by placing the bottle necks over the infant fruits on the tree so that each pear grows inside a bottle. When it has ripened, the bottle is topped up with the pear-flavoured liqueur.

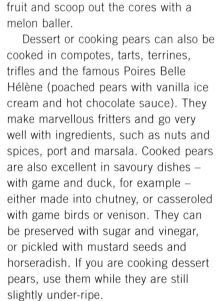

Left: Canned pears

Drying pears

1 Peel the pears and cut them in half lengthways.

2 Scoop out the cores with a small melon baller, removing all the fibrous part of the fruit.

3 Brush them with lemon juice to prevent discoloration. Spread out in a single layer on a rack over a baking sheet and dry in an oven set to 70°C/150°F/Gas Low for several hours until dried.

ASIAN OR NASHI PEARS

There are many varieties of Asian pear, but their characteristics are very similar. Round rather than pear-shaped, the fruits have a golden-brown russet skin and very crisp, white, juicy flesh. The crunchy texture resembles that of an apple but is more granular. It would be a shame to spoil the crisp texture by cooking. Asian pears are best eaten straight from the fridge, to be enjoyed as a "drink on a stalk". They also make excellent additions to fruit salads or savoury winter salads.

HOSUI PEARS

These pears have much the same crunch and juiciness of Tientsin pears, but look more like apples, with greeny-brown mottled flesh, which tastes like a cross between an apple and an unripe pear.

PERRY PEARS

With the demise of the most famous of the sparkling alcoholic pear drinks, perry pears have largely fallen into disfavour. A few small producers still press perry pears into juice, wine or "champagne" perry, but although there

Left: Tientsin pears are best eaten chilled.

are still about 300 known varieties, you will never find these fruit in the shops. Perry pears are smaller than their dessert counterparts. Although they look delicious, they contain large quantities of tannin and taste bitter and astringent, whether they are eaten raw or cooked.

TIENTSIN PEARS

These Asian pears from China and Korea are very similar to Asian Nashi pears in taste and texture. They are available when Asian pears are out of season. They look rather like elongated apples, tapering gently at both ends, The skin is pale yellow, slightly speckled with light brown. The pure white flesh is exceptionally juicy and crunchy – perfect for a hot day. Tientsin pears are best eaten chilled to appreciate their refreshing quality, and make the perfect healthy alternative to ice lollies.

Left: Asian pears are round rather than pear-shaped and their crunchy texture resembles that of apples, too.

QUINCES

These highly aromatic fruits are known as "apple" or "pear" quinces, according to their shape. Unripe fruits have a downy skin, while ripe quinces have the smooth texture of a pear. Raw quinces are inedible, but they make excellent natural air fresheners – a quince kept in the glove compartment will shrivel but not rot, and will fill your car with the most delicious aroma for up to six months.

Above: Quinces may have been the mythical golden apples of Hesperides.

History

Quinces originate from Turkestan and Persia, but are grown all over Europe. It is said that they were the mythical golden apples of the Hesperides and that the golden apple Paris gave to Aphrodite, the goddess of Love, was in fact a quince. To the Ancient Greeks and Romans, quinces were a symbol of happiness, love and fruitfulness. The fruits were widely grown in Britain from the sixteenth to the eighteenth century, but their popularity has declined. In Spain, however, they are still highly prized and are used to make a thick fruit paste called *membrillo*.

Choosing and Storing

Quinces are not readily available in the shops, but you may find them growing in gardens. The skin of ripe quinces should be uniformly golden yellow; unripe fruit may still have patches of down, which can be rubbed off. Quinces keep well – the best way to store them is in a bowl in your kitchen or living room. They will fill the room with their delicious scent.

Preparing and Cooking

Quinces are always cooked. They are prepared in much the same way as pears. For jellies and fruit pastes, the skin is left on as it contributes valuable pectin, as do the pips (the word "marmalade" comes from the Portuguese word for quince, *marmelo*). Quince jelly can be spread on bread or served with pork and game. Quinces can be baked whole like apples or pears, stuffed with a rich mixture of butter, sugar and cream. One or two quinces also make a good addition to an apple pie. Peel and slice the quinces

---

Quince jelly
Makes about 2kg/4½lb

1 Roughly chop 1kg/2¼lb quinces. Put in a large, heavy-based pan with 2 litres/3½ pints/8 cups water.

2 Bring to the boil, then simmer until the quinces are very tender.

3 Pour into a jelly bag set over a bowl; let the juice run through, but do not squeeze the bag or the finished jelly will be cloudy.

4 Measure the strained juice and pour into a large, heavy-based pan. Add 500g/1¼lb/2½ cups preserving sugar for each 600ml/1 pint/2½ cups of the juice. Bring to the boil, stirring until the sugar has dissolved completely. Boil rapidly until setting point is reached.

5 Skim the jelly and pour into sterilized jars. Cover the jars while the jelly is still hot, then label once the jars are cool enough to handle.

(this will be easier to achieve if you parboil them for 10 minutes), then toss them with the apple slices, sugar and cinnamon before layering them in the pie.

In Spain, quince pulp is boiled with sugar to make the fruit paste, *membrillo*, which is then cooled, cut into squares and served with soft cheeses or as a sweet. The French equivalent is known as *cotignac*, while quince cheese is similar, but softer and more spreadable.

Quinces marry well with almost all meats, from poultry to beef and game, and also make a wonderful scented addition to spirits such as vodka, grappa or *eau-de-vie*.

Japonica Quince

As the name suggests, this cultivated quince came originally from Japan. The hard yellowish fruits are virtually inedible raw, but can be cooked and used like quinces. Their perfume is less intense, but they are still sufficiently aromatic to make an excellent addition to pies and tarts. They can also be made into both quince jelly and quince cheese.

Above: Japonica quinces are not edible raw, but they make a wonderful jelly.

MEDLARS

Medlar trees resemble pear trees, but the fruits are quite different. They look rather like large golden brown rosehips with a russetted skin and a distinctive open five-pointed calyx end, for which the French have an indelicate term (*cul de chien*). They are eaten when over-ripe, almost rotten. The process is known as "bletting" and is traditionally achieved by spreading out unripe fruit on straw and leaving it to decay for several weeks, by which time the flesh can be spooned out. To speed up the bletting process, whole unripe medlars can be frozen to break up the cell structure, then left to decay at room temperature. The flesh has a dry, sticky texture. It tastes a little like the flesh of dried dates, but is tarter. Medlars are not to everyone's taste; the nineteenth-century horticulturalist George Bunyard described several different varieties of medlar as "all of equal unpleasantness".

Left: Medlars are nowadays seldom sold in shops, nor eaten much either.

History

Medlars originated in the Transcaucasus, but are found growing wild in Asia Minor and southern Europe. They were cultivated by the Assyrians, who introduced them to Ancient Greece. In Victorian times in England, they were often enjoyed at the end of a meal with the port, but they are seldom eaten nowadays.

Choosing and Storing

Medlars are seldom sold in shops, but are sometimes cultivated or found growing wild. They are extremely hard and, if left on the tree, are unlikely to ripen sufficiently to be eaten. They are therefore picked in their unripe state and left to "blet". A bletted medlar will be soft and yielding to the touch.

Preparing and Cooking

To eat bletted medlars raw, peel back the skin from the five points of the calyx and suck out the flesh, leaving the five pips behind, or scrape it out with a spoon. Unripe medlars can be used with bletted fruits to make medlar jelly, or baked to make a thick sauce that goes well with rich meats. Medlar jelly is made in the same way as quince jelly.

STONE FRUITS

One of life's greatest joys is to bite into a perfectly ripe, juicy stone

fruit and savour the wonderful sweetness of the sticky juices.

Stone fruits herald summer — the season starts with cherries,

continues with sun-drenched peaches and apricots, and ends with

plums, from gorgeous greengages to fat, juicy Victorias. Although

stone fruits (or "drupes") may seem very different, they are all

members of the prunus family and share the characteristics of soft,

juicy flesh and a single stone. Stone fruits are often grown in

greenhouses, but nothing beats the taste of a sun-ripened fruit,

so it is worth waiting until they are in season.

PEACHES

Sometimes known as the "queen of fruits", peaches are certainly among the most beautiful. Their downy, velvety skin is yellow, flushed with red, and they are voluptuously curvaceous – the French call one variety *tétons de Venus* (Venus' breasts).

The most familiar peaches are round or "beaked", with a pointed end, but they can also be flat and disc-shaped. The delicate fine-textured flesh, which can be yellow, white or tinged with red, encloses a heavily ridged stone. In some peaches, the flesh clings firmly to the stone; these are known as "clingstone". In "freestone" fruit, the flesh comes away easily and cleanly from the stone.

Peaches and nectarines originated from the same species and are very similar, except that peaches have fuzzy skin, while nectarines are smooth. So alike are they that peach trees sometimes spontaneously produce nectarines and vice versa.

History

Peaches have been grown in China since the fifth century BC and are regarded as a symbol of longevity and immortality. Even today, some Chinese families place peach trees or branches outside their front doors to ward off evil spirits. Peaches were taken along the old silk routes to Persia where they were discovered by Alexander the Great, who introduced them to the Greeks and Romans; the word "peach" comes from the Latin *Persicum malum* (Persian apple). Immensely popular in Europe, peaches were introduced to America by Christopher Columbus and spread so profusely that they were once thought to be indigenous. Nowadays, so many are grown in Georgia that it is known as the "peach state".

Varieties

Peaches are seldom sold by variety, but by the colour of their flesh – yellow or white. Which you choose is a matter of preference; some people believe that white peaches have the finer flavour.

Above: Mireille, a white-fleshed peach.

Yellow varieties include Elegant Lady, Royal George and Bellegarde. Mireille is a popular white peach. The finest peaches of all are the *pêches de vigne,* small red-fleshed fruits that are grown in vineyards. They do not look particularly attractive, being covered in greyish down, but the flavour is superb. You are unlikely to find them outside markets in France.

Nutrition

Peaches are a source of vitamins A, B and C and provide about 60 kilo-calories per 100g/3¾oz.

Buying and Storing

Peaches do not ripen successfully after picking, so always buy ripe fruit. The fruits should be handled carefully. Press gently to ensure that they are firm, with some "give". Never buy greenish peaches, except for chutney-making, and avoid fruit with bruised skin. Peaches do not keep well. Firm fruit can be kept at room temperature for a day or two to soften; ripe peaches can be kept in the fridge for not more than two days.

Left: Elegant Lady – a popular yellow variety of peach.

Dried peaches These are not as widely available as dried apricots, but are becoming increasingly popular. Use them in compotes and cakes, or eat them on their own. Peaches are also crystallized or glacéed as a sweetmeat.

Canned peaches Available in syrup or apple juice, canned peaches are fine for cooking, but lack the delicate texture and flavour of the fresh fruit.

Above: Dried peaches

Stoning a peach or nectarine

1 Slice through the seam line all around the peach.

2 Twist the two halves in opposite directions to separate them.

3 Lever out the stone with a knife.

Glacé peaches The fruits are coated in a thick syrup, which hardens to a shiny glaze. Glacé peaches are often included in boxes of assorted glacé fruits. They are very sweet, with a melting texture.

Preparing and Serving

A really ripe peach is delicious eaten on its own or in a fruit salad. Peaches combine well with most other fruits and nuts, particularly raspberries, a marriage that inspired Escoffier to create his famous dessert, Peach Melba, in honour of the great singer

Above: Glacé peaches are coated in a thick sugar syrup and are very sweet.

Left: Canned peaches, available in halves or slices, are fine for cooking but lack the flavour of the fresh fruit.

Dame Nellie Melba. Fresh peaches feature in ice cream sundaes and can be used to make luxurious drinks like Bellini (Champagne, peach liqueur and crushed peach pulp) or Champagne cocktails. They are also made into liqueurs and peach wine and brandy.

The fuzzy skin of a peach is not particularly pleasant to eat, so the fruit is best peeled. Nick the fruit, place it in a heatproof bowl and pour over boiling water. Leave for 15–30 seconds, depending on how ripe the fruits are, then drain and refresh in cold water. The skins will peel off easily.

Cooking and Serving

Peaches can be cooked in a multitude of ways – poached whole in vanilla-flavoured syrup or wine; macerated in alcohol; in compotes, soufflés, pies, tarts, pancakes, ice creams and sorbets. They make very good jams and jellies, while spiced peaches are delicious with cured or cold meats. Under-ripe green-tinged peaches can be made into excellent relishes and chutneys.

Peaches are also good, raw or cooked, in salads and are natural partners for gammon and duck. They can be substituted for mangoes in South-East Asian dishes and are particularly good with crab and lobster.

To poach peaches in syrup, put 1 litre/1¾ pints/ 4 cups water in a pan. Add 500g/1¼lb/2 cups granulated sugar, 2 strips of pared lemon rind, a piece of cinnamon and half a split vanilla pod. Bring to the boil, stirring to dissolve the sugar. Boil for about 5 minutes, then add six to eight peeled peaches (whole or halved) and poach gently until tender, turning occasionally. Leave the fruit to cool in the syrup. Peaches make a delicious sweet after-dinner liqueur, Crème de Peche, which can be drunk on its own, or combined with Champagne or sparking white wine to make an unusual cocktail. To make a classic Bellini, put some fresh peach pulp in a Champagne glass, add a teaspoon of peach liqueur and top up with Champagne.

Left: Peach liqueur

NECTARINES

The botanical name for nectarines is *prunus persican*, meaning "Persian plum", although these smooth-skinned fruits are a variant of peaches and natives of China. They taste very similar to peaches, with a touch more acidity. The flesh can be yellow, white or pinkish and is delicate and sweet. Unlike peaches, they do not require peeling, so some people prefer them as a dessert fruit. They can be prepared and cooked in exactly the same way as peaches. Nectarines are sometimes crossed with peaches, but the fuzzy peach skin is generally dominant, so the hybrids are often actually peaches.

Left: Smooth-skinned white nectarines

Nutrition

Nectarines have a lower calorie count than peaches (containing only about 45 kilocalories per 100g/3¾oz). They are a good source of potassium and phosphorus, dietary fibre and vitamins A and C.

Buying and Storing

Like peaches, nectarines do not continue to mature after picking, so choose ripe fruit. The skins should be bright and smooth, with no blemishes or wrinkles. Nectarines can be kept at room temperature or in the fridge for two or three days.

Left: Yellow nectarines

APRICOTS

These round, yellow-orange fruit have velvety skins flushed with pink. The flesh is firm, sweet and fragrant, and contains little juice. The kernel of the stone is edible and is used to flavour jams, biscuits and Amaretto liqueur.

History

Apricots grew wild in China thousands of years ago and were introduced to Persia and Armenia, from where they got their Latin name *Prunus armeniaca*. Alexander the Great brought apricots to Southern Europe; they were prized by the Romans and Greeks, who called them "golden eggs of the sun". They were first successfully cultivated in Northern Europe in the sixteenth century.

Nutrition

Apricots contain the antioxidant beta-carotene, and are a rich source of minerals and vitamin A. An average 65g/2½oz apricot provides only 20 kilocalories.

Left: Ripe apricots are deliciously fragrant.

Above: Turkish sun-dried apricots

Below: Semi-dried apricots

Buying and Storing

Apricots do not travel well, nor do they continue to ripen after picking, so those that you buy may be disappointing. Look for plump fruit with a rich colour and smooth skin. Do not buy dull-looking or greenish fruit, as their flesh will be woolly. Keep apricots at room temperature for a couple of days, or store in a polythene bag in the fridge for up to five days.

Dried and canned apricots Because apricots are so delicate, they are often preserved by drying or canning. The best dried apricots come from Turkey; they are burnished orange and have a rich flavour. Dried apricots can be substituted for fresh apricots and make excellent jams. Use them just as they are in slow-cooked dishes that contain plenty of liquid, like stews and casseroles, but, unless they are semi-dried, soak them in warm water for a couple of hours before using them in sweet dishes.

Preparing and Cooking

Ripe apricots are delicious raw and can be used in fruit salads and platters. Because

Right: Canned apricots

the flesh is dry, they will not disintegrate during cooking, which makes them ideal for tarts, flans and Danish pastries. Apricots can be poached in syrup or sweet white wine and served with yogurt or spice-flavoured ice cream; they are also very tasty when halved, stuffed with crushed amaretti biscuits and baked, or caramelized and served over *pain perdu*. Apricots make wonderful jams and conserves.

Both fresh and dried apricots make frequent appearances in Middle Eastern and North African recipes, where they go particularly well with lamb, poultry and rice dishes.

PLUMS

There are thousands of varieties of plum, all differing in size, shape, colour and flavour. These members of the rose family originate from three main types – European, Japanese and Western Asian. The skins can vary from blue-black to purple, red, green and yellow. They have a long season, and one variety or another is available almost all year round. All plums have smooth skins with a bloom and juicy flesh with plenty of acidity.

Dessert plums can be eaten on their own; they are usually larger than cooking plums (up to 10cm/4in long) and are sweet and very juicy. Cooking plums are drier, with tart flesh that is ideal for pies, flans and cakes.

History

Wild plums originated in Asia at least 2,000 years ago. They were first cultivated by the Assyrians, then adopted by the Romans, who hybridized them with great enthusiasm; the historian Pliny wrote of the huge numbers of plum cross-breeds available. The Crusaders brought plums to Europe, where they became highly prized. Nowadays they are grown in almost all temperate countries.

Varieties

There are over 2,000 varieties of plum, ripening at different times throughout summer and autumn, although only a dozen or so are available in the shops. Japanese varieties are large, round and juicy; they can be purplish-red with orange flesh, or orangey-yellow

Right: Victorias are the most prolific dessert plum.

with yellow flesh. On the whole, dark-coloured plums have bitter skins, while the red and yellow varieties tend to be sweeter. Most dessert plums can be cooked as well as eaten raw.

DESSERT PLUMS

Denniston's Superb An early variety of plum, with medium-size green fruits flushed with red. These plums have an excellent, sweet flavour.

Gaviota These large round plums have yellow skins deeply tinged with scarlet, and sweet, juicy, red flesh. They are best eaten raw.

Marjorie's Seedling These small purple plums with a green flush have bitter skins and sweet, green, almost translucent flesh. They are good for eating and cooking.

Santa Rosa and **Burbank** Large and round, with bright red skins, these two North American varieties of plum are mainly grown in California. They have juicy, deep yellow flesh and a pleasantly tart flavour, which makes them good for both cooking and eating.

Above: Mirabelles – the golden-skinned variety of these small wild plums, which grow on long stalks like cherries, are best cooked.

Victoria The most prolific of all dessert plums, Victorias were first cultivated in 1840 from a stray seedling found in Sussex, England. Since then, these large oval fruits with yellow skins flushed with scarlet, and sweet, juicy flesh have become ubiquitous. They are good for bottling and canning, stewing or eating raw.

Left: Marjorie's Seedling have sweet, almost transluscent green flesh and are good for cooking and eating.

COOKING PLUMS

Beach plums These small plums grow wild along the Atlantic coast of North America, especially near Cape Cod. They have dark purplish-black skins and tart flesh which makes them unsuitable for eating raw, but they make excellent jams and jellies.

Cherry plums or **mirabelles** These very small wild plums are round and grow on long stalks like cherries. They have black, red or yellow skins, which can taste rather bitter, but all have sweet, juicy flesh. These plums can be eaten raw, but are best stewed or baked, or made into jams, sauces and jellies. Golden mirabelles are delicious in tarts and soufflés, and are also made into a plum *eau-de-vie,* called *mirabelle.*

Czar Large, rather acidic dark blue-black plums with golden flesh, these can be eaten raw, but are more usually used for cooking. They are best eaten straight from the tree.

Nutrition

Plums contain more antioxidant than any other fruit. They provide about 40 kilocalories per 100g/3¾oz.

Buying and Storing

Plums are delicate, so make sure that the ones you buy are unblemished. They should be plump and firm, with some "give" (but never squashy), and they should be fully coloured for their variety. Plums should always have a pleasant aroma.

These fruit ripen fast and quickly become over-ripe, so store them in the fridge for only a day or two. For cooking at a

Above: Angelino – the skin colour varies from red to almost black, but the flesh of these plums is always yellow.

Left: Sweet-tasting Avalon plums.

Below: Red-fleshed Spanish Autumn Rose plums.

Quetsch Also known as *svetsch* or *Zwetschen,* these small purplish-black plums have a beautiful bloom. Although their flesh is sweet, they are seldom eaten raw, but are used in Eastern Europe to make plum breads and *pflaumenkuchen,* yeast dough topped with purple plums. Quetsch plums are also used for making *slivovitz* and other plum brandies.

Other varieties of note

Angelino, Autumn Rose, Avalon, Circiela Queen Rose, Reeves Seedling, Stanley and Sungold

later date, plums can be frozen: halve the fruit and remove the stones. Place on trays and open freeze, then pack the fruit into polythene bags and seal.

Preparing and Cooking

Dessert plums are delicious eaten on their own. Dual varieties (suitable for eating and cooking) and cooking plums make excellent pies and tarts, compotes, crumbles, dumplings, sauces, mousses and soufflés. They can be poached, baked or stewed, either whole or in halves or slices. It is not recommended that plums with tough skins are cooked in the microwave, as they will not soften in the short cooking time. Cook plums until just tender; do not let them disintegrate. Plums make tasty ice cream, and the poached fruit goes very well with ice creams flavoured with spices like cardamom, nutmeg and cinnamon.

Plums go extremely well in savoury dishes. The Chinese make them into a thick sweet-sour sauce to serve with Peking duck, lamb or pork. Spiced stewed plums are good with gammon, cured meats, terrines and poultry. Plums add a special flavour to beef or lamb casseroles.

Plums also make superb jams and jellies. They can be preserved in many different

Above: Circiela Queen Rose

Below: Reeves Seedling

Below: Stanley

ways; dried (as prunes), crystallized and candied, bottled or made into wine and liqueurs like *slivovitz* and plum brandy.

Preserved plums There are many ways of preserving plums, the best-known being by drying them as prunes. In Spain, Elvas plums are partially dried, then rolled in granulated sugar. The Portuguese candy sweet greengages, while Carlsbad plums (named after the spa town, now Karlovy Vary) are a speciality of the Czech Republic. These plums (usually Quetsch) are candied in hot syrup until shrivelled, then halved and stuffed into dried damsons. The process gives them a very intense flavour. Carlsbad plums are considered a great delicacy and are packed into attractive wooden boxes.

Soaking prunes

Prunes must be soaked for at least 4 hours before using. Place in a bowl and cover with cold water or tepid weak tea for added flavour. Leave overnight if possible to plump up. For compotes and purées it is not necessary to soak the prunes; cook them directly in wine, water or fruit juice until they are very tender.

Prunes These wrinkled dried purple or red plums can be prepared in various ways. The plums can be left to dry naturally on the tree, but are more often sun-dried. They can also be desiccated in a low oven. The finest variety of "pruning" plum is the Agen, which is grown in France and California. These prunes are sold complete with stones and must be soaked overnight before being cooked.

Left: Chinese plum sauce has a wonderful sweet-sour flavour and is classically served with Peking duck.

Nowadays, stoned no-soak prunes are also widely available, but they tend to be flabbier than the traditional variety. Apart from their famed laxative qualities, prunes have other healthful properites. They are said to be an excellent cure for hangovers, give a great energy boost, and are purported to be an aphrodisiac.

Culinary Uses

Cooked prunes are traditionally served with custard, but they are equally good with thick cream. They make excellent ice cream, especially when combined with Armagnac. Prunes are often used in savoury dishes, particularly in Middle Eastern cooking, and they go extremely well with pork and chicken. They are an essential ingredient in Scottish cock-a-leekie soup. They go well with citrus flavours and can be made into a compote with red wine and orange or lemon zest.

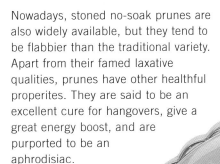

Left: Slivovitz – black Madjarka plums are crushed with their stones and slowly fermented to make this eau-de-vie from Croatia.

Puréed prunes can be sweetened, then spiced up with a little ground cinnamon or nutmeg and served as a sauce with vanilla ice cream.

Below: Californian prunes

Below: French Agen prunes

GREENGAGES

These small members of the plum family have green skins, sometimes tinged with yellow or rose pink, which turn golden as the fruit ripens. There are many varieties of greengage; all have firm flesh and a delicious honeyed flavour. "Transparent" gages have fine, translucent flesh; if you hold the fruit up to the light, you can clearly see the shadow of the stone. These golden gages have a particularly sweet flavour.

History

Wild greengages from Asia Minor were probably introduced to Britain by the Romans, but disappeared from cultivation until Sir Thomas Gage brought them from France in the eighteenth century (and gave them his name). In France, they are known as *Reine-Claude* after the wife of François I, who adored their sweet flavour.

Preparing and Cooking

The deliciously sweet flavour of greengages makes them ideal for eating raw. They can also be gently poached in syrup, puréed for mousses and fools or made into excellent compotes and jam.

Below: Greengages, named after Sir Thomas Gage, have firm flesh with a deliciously sweet flavour.

DAMSONS

These small plum-like fruits take their name from Damascus, which is probably where they originated. They have deep blue-black skins with an attractive bloom. The flavour is very strong and tart, which makes them more suitable for cooking than eating raw. Damsons grow wild in hedgerows, but are also commercially available.

Preparing and Cooking

Damsons can be stewed and used in pies, tarts, ice creams and fools, but they are most commonly used for bottling or for jams and jellies. Once cooked with sugar, they develop a pleasantly spicy flavour. A traditional old English sweetmeat is damson cheese, very thick fruit pulp boiled with sugar to make a solid jam similar to quince cheese, which can be eaten with bread and butter or biscuits.

The tart flavour of damsons makes them particularly suitable for savoury dishes, such as pork or lamb casseroles. The fruit can also be made into wine or damson gin.

Above: Once cooked, damsons have a pleasantly spicy flavour.

Damson cheese

Damson cheese is a traditional English country dish with a very distinctive flavour, which is an acquired taste. The "cheese" is potted and aged for several months before being eaten. To make 2.5kg/5½lb damson cheese, put 1.5kg/3½lb damsons in a saucepan, barely cover with water and simmer until the flesh is so tender that it falls off the stones. Sieve the pulp, weigh it and return it to the pan with three-quarters of its weight in soft light brown sugar. Boil until the jam is clear, skimming the surface frequently. Pot the jam in oiled straight-sided containers, seal and leave in a cool dark place for at least two months. Serve with bread and butter, and eat with a knife and fork.

BULLACES

The small round plums known as "black bullaces" have bluish-purple skins and mouth-puckeringly acid flesh. So-called "white" bullaces are pale greenish-yellow. They can be found throughout Europe in late autumn growing in thorny hedgerows long after the other wild fruits like sloes and blackberries have finished. Although very tart and virtually inedible when raw, bullaces can be cooked with sugar to make pies and tarts. They are also good for jams and other preserves.

Right: The pale greenish-yellow fruits, known as "white" bullaces are almost inedible raw, but can be cooked with sugar to make delicious jams and jellies or a filling for pies.

SLOES

Sloes are the fruit of the blackthorn, a thorny shrub, which grows wild throughout Europe (hence its botanical name, *prunus spinosa,* which means spiny plum). These small wild fruits resemble tiny plums. The blue-black skins have a slight bloom. The flesh is highly astringent and cannot be eaten raw. Sloes ripen late and can be picked from the hedgerows in autumn, but they only become edible after the first frosts. They can be made into jams, jellies, sloe wine and liqueurs, but their chief claim to fame is that they are the principal ingredient of the irresistible sloe gin.

Make sloe gin as soon as the fruit is ripe,

and with any luck you'll have a bottle ready in time for Christmas. For each 750ml/1¼ pint bottle of gin, you will need 250g/9oz/2 cups sloes and 130g/4½oz/generous ½ cup caster sugar. Wash the sloes and prick them all over with a darning needle. Pack

them loosely into a perfectly clean flagon or bottle, add the sugar and top up with gin. If you like, add two or three drops of almond essence and shake well. Seal and leave for at least three months before drinking, shaking the bottles three times a week. If pricking the sloes seems too much trouble, freeze them for several hours to crack the skin. Purists however allege that this compromises the flavour of the gin.

Left: Sloes are small wild fruits, which grow in hedgerows throughout Europe. They are best picked in late autumn, after the first frosts.

CHERRIES

Cherry trees in blossom are one of the great delights of spring, followed in summer by clusters of bright shiny fruit hanging in pairs from long, elegant stalks. The skin of these small round stone fruits can vary in colour from pale creamy-yellow to deepest red or almost black. The firm juicy flesh can be sweet or sour, depending on the variety, of which there are hundreds. Cherries are categorized into three main groups: sweet (for eating), sour (for cooking) and hybrids such as the nobly named Dukes and Royals, which are suitable for eating raw or cooking.

History

The original wild sweet cherries, known as *mazzards,* were found in Asia Minor and were cultivated by the Chinese 3,000 years ago. Mazzards were known to the Ancient Egyptians, Greeks and Romans, and still exist today. Sour cherries were brought to Rome from Greece and all modern varieties derive from these early specimens.

Varieties

Sweet cherries fall into two main groups: **bigarreaus,** with firm, crisp flesh, and **geans** or **guines,** with a softer texture. Today, there are also many hybrids. Sour cherries range from almost sweet to bitter and tart; they are full of flavour and are mainly used for preserving or in the manufacture of liqueurs.

SWEET CHERRIES

BIGARREAUS The best-known of these are the **Napoleons,** large pale yellow cherries tinged with light red. Their crisp fragrant flesh is slightly tart. **Bing** cherries are large, heart-shaped deep red fruit with a superb flavour. They are widely grown in North America. **GEANS/GUINES** These fruits have soft, juicy flesh and come in many colours. **Black Tartarian** are deep purplish-black ·from the skin right through to the stone. **Early Rivers** have dark purple skins and flesh, and very small stones. They are fragrant, sweet and juicy. **Ranier** has golden skin with a pink blush. The famous Swiss black cherry jam is made from intensely dark guines.

Above: Bright red Colney cherries.

Left: Napoleons are one of the sweet cherry varieties, with slightly crisp, tart, fragrant flesh.

Left: Widely grown in North America, sweet Bing cherries have a superb flavour.

SOUR CHERRIES

Most sour cherries are too tart to eat, but are ideal for cooking. The two main types are **morello** and **amarelle**. Morellos have dark juice, and amarelles have light, almost colourless juice. The small, dark red morello cherries (known in France as *griottes*) are inedible raw, but are delicious preserved in either brandy or syrup.

Montmorency These are bright red cherries with a sweet-sour flavour. They have given their name to a range of dishes, which include the fruit, from duck to gâteaux and ice creams.

English cherries are small, bright orange-red fruit with soft translucent flesh. They are mainly used for preserving in brandy.

Above: Dried sour Montmorency and Bing cherries

Left and below: Maraschino cherries may be bottled with their stalks.

Right: Morello cherries, which are often preserved in brandy.

Maraschino cherries

These small wild fruit from Dalmatia are *damasca* or *amaresca* cherries. They are distilled into a colourless sweet, sticky Italian liqueur called Maraschino. The familiar bottled Maraschino cherries beloved of barmen were originally damasca cherries preserved in Maraschino liqueur; nowadays, the vibrant red fruits sold as "maraschino" tend to be ordinary cherries tinted with artificial colouring and steeped in syrup flavoured with bitter almonds. Check the label before buying.

Nutrition

Cherries contain vitamins A and C and some dietary fibre. Their calorie content varies with the type; sweet cherries provide about 77 kilocalories per 100g/3¾oz, while the same quantity of sour fruit provides about 56 kilocalories.

Buying and Storing

Choose plump cherries with shiny, unblemished skins. It is best to buy them still on the stalk. As a rule of thumb, pale cherries are very sweet, while dark cherries tend to be more acidic; if possible, taste before you buy.

Unwashed cherries will keep for a few days in the fridge; wash them just before serving. They can also be removed from their stalks and frozen.

Preparing and Cooking

Sweet cherries often need no preparation other than washing and are best eaten on their own or in fruit salads. They make unusual sweets when left on the stalk and dipped into melted dark chocolate. Stoned fresh cherries make a delicious filling for sponge cakes and pavlovas, or an attractive decoration for gâteaux and desserts. There is no reason not to cook with sweet cherries, but they may not have much flavour, due to their low acidity. Although fresh cherries can be served as they are, for cooking they should be stoned.

Cherries can be preserved by drying in the sun or in a low oven, by preserving in sugar or in brandy. Candied – or glacé – cherries are a popular ingredient in baking.

Dual-purpose and sour cherries can be cooked in tarts, pies, compotes and sauces. They go well with sweet spices, citrus flavours and chocolate; the classic combination of cherries and chocolate is found in Black Forest Gâteau. In Eastern Europe, they are made into a sweet-sour soup or pickled in spiced vinegar as an accompaniment for rich meats. Cherries go well with all game and are classically served with duck. Amarelle and morello cherries are used for making jam and preserves, or for crystallizing as glacé cherries.

Below: Brightly coloured, sweet and sticky glacé cherries are a popular baking ingredient.

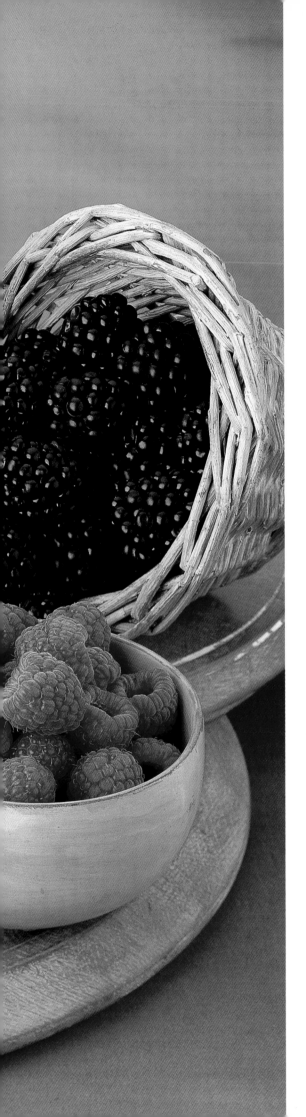

BERRIES AND CURRANTS

Small wonders — that sums up the splendour of berries.
The glowing colours and delectable flavours of strawberries and
raspberries, gooseberries, currants, loganberries and blackberries
(to name but a few of the many varieties) give us immense
pleasure. Whether you brave the brambles or pick up a punnet
at your local supermarket, these wonderful treats
are there for the taking.

STRAWBERRIES

For centuries, strawberries have been the most highly prized soft fruit. A sixteenth-century enthusiast, on tasting his first strawberry, summed up their eternal appeal: "Doubtless God could have made a better berry, but doubtless He never did". Nowadays, greenhouse-grown strawberries are available all year round, but these fruits are at their seductive best when grown outdoors.

History

Cultivated strawberries derive from the small wild fraises des bois, tiny fragrant woodland fruits that grow in all temperate countries and which were transplanted into kitchen gardens as early as Roman times. By the fourteenth century, the French had become strawberry enthusiasts, but it was another hundred years before the first bowls of strawberries and cream were served in England, at a banquet given by Cardinal Wolsey in 1509.

The cultivated strawberries we enjoy so much today were developed in the nineteenth century from small scarlet wild strawberries from Virginia. These were crossed with the larger yellow Chilean pine strawberries, which the aptly named French Captain Frézier (the French word for strawberry is *fraise*) had brought to Brittany in 1712. Once the perfect balance of flavour and size had been achieved, enthusiasm for cultivated strawberries blossomed and they remain one of the world's favourite fruits.

Varieties

Strawberries come in many different sizes, colours and shapes, ranging from conical to globular to oval or heart-shaped. New varieties are constantly being developed.

Left: Fraise de Bois liqueur is a wild strawberry version of crème de fraise.

Above: These tiny wild woodland fruits, fraises des bois, have a lovely perfumed flavour.

Below: Cultivated strawberries like these are now one of the world's favourite fruits.

Below: Fragrantly scented and vanilla-flavoured white fraises des bois.

Above: Gorella – conical-shaped and deep red when ripe.

Left: Cambridge Favourite – medium-size strawberries that are popular with both commercial growers and gardeners.

Below: Elsanta have a great flavour.

FRAISES DES BOIS

The smallest wild strawberries are the **Hautbois** varieties, whose tiny red fruits taste wonderfully fragrant. **Alpine** strawberries are generally a little larger and less juicy, with a highly perfumed flavour. Yellow and white varieties look less appealing, but have a delicious flavour of vanilla.

SUMMER STRAWBERRIES

Cambridge Favourite Medium-size berries with an attractive colour and flavour, this variety is indeed a favourite with strawberry-growers large and small.
Elsanta Largish, firm berries with attractive glossy flesh and an excellent sweet flavour.
Elvira These Dutch strawberries were developed in the 1970s. The oval berries are a deep glossy red.
Gorella A deep red conical berry with paler red flesh. This is an extremely consistent variety.
Perpetual and remontant strawberries As their name implies, these late-season strawberries go on to fruit continuously throughout the autumn. Although they are juicier than summer berries, they are not as sweet, so are better for cooking than other varieties. They can be picked while they are still green and made into jams, sauces and compotes.

Preparing strawberries

1 Wipe the strawberries with a piece of damp kitchen paper.

2 Hold the strawberry between your thumb and forefinger and twist off the green frill and stalk. Try to remove the central hull in the same movement.

Below: Chocolate-dipped strawberries make a delectable after-dinner treat, or a delightful decoration for chocolate cakes and desserts.

Nutrition

Strawberries are rich in vitamins B and C and contain considerable amounts of potassium, iron and fibre. 100g/3¾oz strawberries provide fewer than 30 kilocalories.

Buying and Storing

Size and colour are not necessarily indications of quality. Some smaller, greenish varieties taste succulent and delicious. Try always to buy locally grown fruits and check those at the bottom of the punnet, making sure they are not squashed or mouldy.

Strawberries should ideally be eaten the day they are bought. If this is not possible, keep the berries in the fridge for a day or two, covering them with clear film to prevent them from drying out and from permeating other foods with their scent. Remove from the fridge at least an hour before you serve them.

Frozen strawberries are never as good as fresh, as the texture collapses after freezing, but they are fine for sauces and ice cream. To freeze whole strawberries, sprinkle with a little sugar and pack in a single layer in a plastic box, or open freeze on a tray, then pack in a rigid container. Puréed strawberries can be frozen with or without added sugar.

Preparing and Serving

It is best not to wash strawberries, as they easily become waterlogged. If they are very dirty, wipe them gently.

Really ripe strawberries need no other accompaniment than cream or crème fraîche and perhaps a little sugar. Improbable though this may sound, a grinding of black pepper or sprinkling of balsamic vinegar will bring out the flavour of the fruit. Strawberries are seldom improved by cooking, although they make delicious jam. They are best used in their raw state in such desserts as strawberry tartlets, shortcake and pavlovas. They have an affinity with chocolate and make a fine decoration for chocolate terrines and mousses, or they can be dipped into melted chocolate and served as petits fours.

To "dress up" strawberries, macerate them in red wine, Champagne or orange juice. The classic dish, Strawberries Romanov, simply consists of fresh strawberries macerated in orange juice and orange liqueur. Puréed strawberries can be served as a coulis or made into ice creams and sorbets.

Arbutus (tree strawberry)

The arbutus is a tall shrub, whose bright red fruits look like strawberries, but have a different taste. The sweet spiky berries have a soft, slightly mushy texture and a faint flavour of vanilla. You will not find arbutus berries in shops, but the shrubs can be found growing in Europe, as far north as western Ireland (where they are known as Killarney strawberries), and in the United States and China. The berries are unexciting to eat raw, but are used to make jellies and liqueurs.

RASPBERRIES

Perhaps surprisingly, raspberries are a member of the rose family, as you might guess if you have ever been pricked by a raspberry thorn. Native to hilly areas of Europe and Asia, they grow best in a cool, damp climate and can be found even in Alaska. The deep red (or sometimes yellow) jewel-like fruits have a sweet, intense flavour, and indeed many people prefer them to strawberries.

History

Wild raspberries have been eaten since prehistoric times, but, perhaps because they were so plentiful in the wild, the fruits were not cultivated until the Middle Ages. Nowadays, in colder climates, raspberries are cultivated from native European raspberry varieties, while in North America, they derive from an indigenous species better suited to the drier, hotter conditions that prevail there.

Varieties

Although there are many different varieties of raspberry, and new ones are constantly being developed, those sold in shops and markets are not identified specifically. Gardeners have their own favourites:

Heritage is a late-fruiting variety with outstanding flavour.

Malling Jewel, which fruits in mid-season, is a heavy cropper.

Wild raspberries You will often find these tiny, fragrant fruits growing in

Above: Raspberries – deep red fruits, with a wonderfully intense flavour.

Above: Arctic raspberries, grown in the chilly climes of Alaska.

Below: Yellow or golden raspberries are worth seeking out, since they have a delectable flavour.

cool, damp areas of woodland. They are full of pips, but their exquisite flavour makes up for this deficiency.

Yellow and golden raspberries Clear golden berries, not widely available, but worth seeking out for their fine flavour.

Nutrition

Raspberries are a valuable source of vitamin C, potassium, niacin and riboflavin, and dietary fibre. They contain 25 kilocalories per 100g/3¾oz. Raspberry juice is said to be good for the heart, while the leaves have long been renowned for their beneficial effects during childbirth; raspberry leaf tea is said to prevent miscarriages, ease labour and help the uterus to contract after the birth.

Buying and Storing

Raspberries are ripe when they are brightly and evenly coloured. They are always sold hulled, but if you are picking your own, they should slide easily off the hulls. When buying raspberries in a punnet, check the bottom to make sure it is not stained red or leaking – a sure sign that the fruit is soft and past its best.

If possible, always eat raspberries the day they are bought or picked; if necessary, they can be stored for up to two days in the bottom of the fridge, but bring them out at least an hour before serving.

Raspberries freeze very well; whole berries emerge almost as good as before. Open freeze the fruit in a single

Left: Raspberry vinegar makes a sharp, yet refreshingly fruity addition to home-made salad dressing.

layer on a baking sheet, then pack into rigid cartons. Less than perfect raspberries can be puréed and sieved, then sweetened with a little caster sugar or icing sugar before being frozen.

Preparing and Serving

Do not wash raspberries unless this is unavoidable; they are seldom very dirty, and washing will ruin the texture and flavour. All you need do is gently pick off any bits of leaf or stalk.

Good raspberries have such a wonderful flavour that they are best eaten on their own, with a little sugar and cream. They go well with other fruits, like oranges, apples, pears, figs and melon. In the classic dish, Peach Melba, raspberries are used as a coulis to coat a lightly poached peach. They also make delicious fillings for pastries, pavlovas and tartlets, and, because they look so attractive, they are ideal for decoration.

Raspberries can be crushed with a little icing sugar, then pushed through a nylon or stainless steel sieve to make sauces, coulis or bases for ice creams and sorbets. They can be cooked in pies; apple and raspberry is a classic combination. They are rich in pectin, so make excellent jams and jellies. Raspberry vinegar is delicious and makes delectable dressings and sauces.

Preparing a raspberry coulis

1 Put the raspberries in a bowl and crush to a purée with a fork.

2 Tip the purée into a sieve set over a clean bowl. Rub through, using the back of a large spoon.

3 Sweeten to taste with icing or caster sugar and stir well.

CLOUDBERRIES

These deep golden relatives of the raspberry grow on boggy land in the cold northern climates of Scandinavia, Siberia, Canada and even the Arctic Circle. Because they lack warmth, the berries ripen slowly, allowing the flavour

Left: Popular in Scandinavia, cloudberry jam makes a colourful topping for chocolate mousse or soufflé.

to develop to an extraordinary intensity and sweetness, almost like honeyed apples (Canadians call cloudberries "baked apple berries"). These unusual berries are particularly highly prized in Scandinavian countries, where they are made into excellent jams and desserts, and also into wonderful fruit soups.

Cloudberries are also distilled into a nectar-like liqueur, which tastes delicious with bitter chocolate. The berries have a particular affinity with chocolate; try topping a chocolate mousse or soufflé with a spoonful of cloudberry jam.

Above: Brightly coloured cloudberries have an amazingly intense flavour.

BLACKBERRIES AND DEWBERRIES

These two relations of the raspberry and the rose are virtually indistinguishable, the main difference being that blackberries are larger and grow on thorny upright bushes or brambles, while dewberries trail. The shiny purplish-black berries are made up of a number of segments (drupelets), each containing a hard seed. They grow wild almost everywhere in the world, but are also cultivated to give a larger, juicier berry with better keeping properties. Buying cultivated blackberries, however, is not nearly as much fun as picking your own from the hedgerows.

Below: Large, cultivated blackberries

History

Archeological excavations show that man has eaten blackberries since Neolithic times. The Ancient Greeks prized them as much for the medicinal properties of their leaves as for the fruit, and they have remained popular throughout the centuries. Not everyone appreciates the qualities of wild brambles, though; after they had been introduced to Australia by the early settlers, they were declared a noxious weed in some areas!

Nutrition

Blackberries are rich in dietary fibre and vitamin C and are often used to make health drinks. They also contain some calcium, phosphorus and potassium. Blackberries typically contain about 30 kilocalories per 100g/3¾oz.

Choosing and Storing

Whether you pick or buy blackberries, they should be plump and tender, but not wet or mushy. Look for large, shiny fruit, and if you are buying a punnet check that the underside is not stained. Legend has it that blackberries should not be picked after September, or the Devil will be in them and they will taste impossibly sour.

Blackberries do not keep well. If you cannot eat them immediately, store them for no more than one day in the bottom of the fridge.

Preparing and Cooking

If you must wash blackberries, do so just before serving and drain them well on kitchen paper.

Freezing blackberries

Blackberries freeze well. Open freeze perfect specimens in a single layer on a baking sheet, then pack into rigid containers. Damaged berries can be puréed and sieved, then sweetened with sugar or honey.

Above: Wild blackberries – also known as brambles.

*Right: Crème de mûre –
this richly flavoured
blackberry liqueur is
seldom drunk on its own.
It is more often used as
a colourful flavouring
for cocktails.*

*Left: Dewberries – a
smaller, but very
similar fruit to
blackberries, which
grow on long
trailing branches.*

Blackberry Kir Royale

Ripe, juicy blackberries
are best eaten just as
they are, with sugar and
cream. They make a
tasty addition to
breakfast cereal or a
fruit salad. Blackberries
can be puréed and
sieved to make
coulis, ice cream,
sorbets and fools.
They make delicious
jam or bramble jelly
and are the classic
partner for apples in
a pie or crumble.
There is no need to
cook them before
using them in a pie
filling or a pudding.

*Left: English Bramble
liqueur*

*Above: Dewberry flowers, which appear
before the fruits develop.*

Blackberries go well with many other
fruits besides apples, and can be used
in savoury game dishes. Use them to
flavour spirits, such as vodka or *eau-de-
vie,* or make a cordial to combat a cold.
Commercially produced *crème de mûre*
(blackberry liqueur) enhances the
flavour of any dessert that incorporates
fresh uncooked blackberries.

For a delicious variation on the
classic Kir Royale, which is
usually made with crème de
cassis (blackcurrant liqueur),
pour a little crème de mûre into
a champagne flute and top up
with Champagne or sparkling
white wine. Alternatively, to make
an exceptionally luxurious
cocktail, put some blackberries in
a champagne flute, add a dash of
orange liqueur, such as Cointreau,
and top up with Champagne or
sparkling white wine.

HYBRID BERRIES

There are a wide variety of raspberry/blackberry crossbreeds. Some of these occurred naturally, like the loganberry; others have been cultivated to produce a more robust or better-flavoured fruit. All these hybrids can be cooked and frozen in the same way as raspberries or blackberries.

Loganberries The first loganberry appeared in 1881 at Santa Cruz in California in the garden of Judge J.H. Logan. It was a natural hybrid, probably derived from a cross between a native dewberry and a raspberry. Since then, loganberries have been

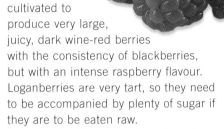

Right: Tayberries were bred in Scotland.

cultivated to produce very large, juicy, dark wine-red berries with the consistency of blackberries, but with an intense raspberry flavour. Loganberries are very tart, so they need to be accompanied by plenty of sugar if they are to be eaten raw.

Youngberries These dewberry/loganberry hybrids resemble a dark red, elongated blackberry, but taste rather like a sweeter loganberry.

Boysenberries An even more elaborate hybrid – a cross between a youngberry and a raspberry, but resembling a large reddish-purple blackberry.

Left: Large, sweet boysenberries are mostly used to make jam.

Boysenberries are sweeter than loganberries and can be eaten raw, although they are more often used to make jam.

Tayberries Tayberries are arguably the finest hybrids of all. Bred in Scotland, they are a cross between the American blackberry Aurora and a tetraploid raspberry. They grow on long, spiny canes. The bright red, elongated berries have a slightly tart, aromatic flavour and although they can be eaten raw, tayberries are better cooked.

Tummelberries are similar to tayberries, but fruit later in the season. Other, similar crossbreeds include **sunberries** and **wineberries.**

Above: Loganberries, which look more like reddish blackberries, have an intense raspberry flavour.

Left: Dark red youngberries are a hybrid of the dewberry and loganberry, but taste rather like a sweeter version of loganberry.

MULBERRIES

Mulberries grow on magnificent dome-headed trees, which can often be very ancient and grow up to 10m/30ft across, so they are rarely found in small modern gardens! Silkworms feed on the leaves, but the berries are left to drop to the ground as they ripen and have a delicious, slightly musky flavour. Luscious black mulberries taste very good but beware – they stain everything with which they come into contact. Legend has it that rubbing a stain created by a ripe mulberry with an unripe mulberry (if you can reach one) will remove it.

Right: Mulberries taste very good, but the juice stains terribly.

History

Black mulberries are native to Western Asia. They were known to the Ancient Greeks, but it was the Roman emperor Justinian who deliberately encouraged their propagation as part of an enterprise in silk production.

In the sixteenth century, it was discovered that silkworms preferred to feed on the white mulberry leaves, and many of these trees were planted in Europe in the vain hope of stimulating a silk trade. Some of these white mulberry trees still survive today.

Varieties

White mulberries are actually pinkish or pale red. There is also an American red mulberry, whose leaves turn beautifully yellow in autumn.

Black mulberries are considered finer than the white variety. The elongated, dark wine-red berries resemble loganberries.

Preparing and Serving

Ripe mulberries can be eaten just as they are, with or without the addition of cream and are usually sweet enough not to need sugar. They also make a good addition to summer pudding.

Over-ripe fruit is best used for jams, jellies and sauces. Mulberries make excellent ice creams, fools and sorbets. Mulberry sauce goes well with richly flavoured roast meats, such as game, duck and lamb.

HUCKLEBERRIES

These berries, which gave their name to Mark Twain's famous character Huckleberry Finn, are quite similar to blueberries, but have a tougher skin and hard internal seeds. They have a sharper flavour than blueberries, but can be eaten and cooked in exactly the same way.

Another variety of huckleberry is the **tangleberry**, which grows on the coast of North America. These purplish-blue berries are sweeter than huckleberries and have a subtle tang of the sea.

Right: Huckleberries, which are similar to blueberries, have fairly tough skins and a sharp flavour.

BLUEBERRIES AND BILBERRIES

Blueberries and bilberries (also known as blaeberries, whortleberries or whinberries) are both small, round blue-black berries with a silvery bloom. They grow on shrubs on inhospitable, peaty moors and uplands. The flavour is mild and sweet and the texture firm.

American blueberries are generally larger and sweeter than bilberries. Nowadays, they are often cultivated, resulting in large, perfect berries that sometimes lack the distinctive flavour of the wild fruit.

Nutrition

Blueberries and bilberries are a source of vitamin C, iron and dietary fibre. They provide about 60 kilocalories per 100g/3¾oz.

Buying and Storing

The best blueberries and bilberries are those you pick yourself. If you buy them, look for plump berries of uniform size. Reject shrivelled specimens, or those without the characteristic bloom. Unwashed berries will keep for up to a week in the bottom of the fridge.

Blueberries and bilberries can be frozen just as they are, provided they are in a sealed bag. Alternatively, poach them in a little lemon-flavoured syrup and then freeze.

Right: Blueberries – mild and sweet flavoured.

Above: Dried blueberries are available in specialist food shops and greengrocers. They make a tasty addition to home-made fruit cakes and muesli, and are delicious scattered into fresh fruit salads or over breakfast cereal.

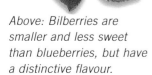

Above: Bilberries are smaller and less sweet than blueberries, but have a distinctive flavour.

Preparing and Cooking

Blueberries and bilberries have soft seeds, so they can be eaten raw. Simply rinse and drain them first. However, they are more usually baked in pies or muffins, or used as a jam-like topping for cheesecake. To cook, make a light sugar syrup and flavour it with lemon, orange and cinnamon or allspice, and poach the berries until tender.

Blueberry Pie is a classic dessert, as is Blueberry Grunt, which consists of blueberries stewed with lemon and spice, baked with a dumpling-like topping. Blueberries can also be made into a sauce to serve with game.

ELDERBERRIES

Although you can seldom buy elderberries, you will find them growing all over the countryside throughout the summer. First come the creamy-white flowerheads, whose flavour goes very well with gooseberries. These are followed by flat, wide clusters of small, almost black berries with a sweet, slightly sickly taste.

History

Elderberries have grown in Europe and Asia since prehistoric times. The bushes themselves were little loved, perhaps because of their unattractive smell, but the berries provided sustenance for the poor. People often used elderberries as a fabric dye and to make wine; later the berries were used to add colour and extra flavour to thin, cheap wines.

Nutrition

Elderberries are an excellent source of vitamin C.

Choosing and Storing

Never pick elderberries growing close to a road, as they will be contaminated by dust and pollution. Good elderberries should be shiny and black. For elderflower syrup, choose creamy flowerheads that are fully open, but whose petals have not begun to drop. Use both flowers and berries as soon as possible after picking.

Below: Elderberries can be cooked with other fruits in pies, tarts and fools or used to make jellies and sauces.

Preparing and Cooking

Use a fork to strip the berries off the stalks. Elderberries can be cooked in the same way as redcurrants or other berries. Flowers should be shaken to dislodge any insects or loose petals and briefly rinsed in cold water.

Sprigs of elderflowers can be dipped in batter to make fritters, or made into a flavoured syrup. The berries can be made into jellies, or used to bulk out other berries in pies, tarts and fools. Elderberries can be made into a savoury sauce for pork and game. They are often used to make vinegar, and are excellent for making wine.

Elderflowers can be made into a refreshing summer drink. To make eight 750ml/1¼ pint bottles, you will need about 12 large elderflower heads. Choose blossoms that are fully open, but not shedding their petals, and wash thoroughly. Place in a large pan and pour over 7 litres/12 pints boiling water. Add 250g/9oz caster sugar, 2 thinly sliced lemons and 120ml/4fl oz/½ cup white wine or cider vinegar. Stir and leave to macerate in a cool place for three days, stirring twice a day. Strain the liquid and pour into sterilized wine bottles. Cork very firmly and leave for at least a week before drinking.

Left: Elderflowers can be made into fritters and intensely flavoured drinks.

Stripping elderberries

Hold the stalk in one hand and run a fork through the berries.

ROWANBERRIES

These bright orangey-red berries are the fruit of the mountain ash. They grow in large clusters and are a great favourite with wild birds. Rowanberries are not available commercially.

Nutrition

Rowanberries are very rich in vitamin C and pectin.

Preparing and Cooking

The best known use for rowanberries is in a glorious deep orange jewel-like jelly with a bittersweet flavour, which goes particularly well with rich meats and game. Rowanberries are also used to add colour to sweet apple dishes, such as pies and crumbles, or they can be made into compotes and sauces. Cook them in the same way as other berries. They cannot be eaten raw.

Right: Rowan berries can be made into a vibrant jelly.

ROSE HIPS

These are the seed pods of roses, and appear after the plants have finished flowering. They vary in colour from orange to deep red and make a beautiful sight in autumn in gardens and hedgerows. Hips contain extremely hairy seeds, which must be removed before they can be eaten.

Nutrition

Rose hips are so rich in vitamin C that in wartime Britain they were picked by both children and adult volunteers and used in vast quantities to make bright pink rose hip syrup for pregnant women and babies. A single rose hip typically contains twenty times more vitamin C than an orange.

Right: Rose hips are enormously rich in vitamin C.

Preparing and Cooking

Very ripe rose hips can be eaten raw, but they do not taste particularly pleasant. Plump rose hips can be made into a bittersweet jelly to serve with poultry or game, or sweetened with sugar or honey and boiled to a syrup. Rose hips can also be used to flavour vinegar, and make an attractive garnish for salads.

Before cooking rose hips, top and tail them, cut them in half and scoop out every trace of the seeds and prickly hairs. If making jelly or syrup, strain the liquid twice through a double layer of muslin.

HAWS

The fruit of the hawthorn or May tree, the white spring blossom is followed by these small, wine-red berries with a bitter, pungent taste.

Preparing and Cooking

Haws cannot be eaten raw, but make a delicious jelly when combined with crab apples. Elderberries can be added to the mixture to make a hedgerow jelly. Haws also make a good sauce for rich meats and game.

Right: Wine-red haws are pretty to look at, but have a bitter, pungent taste.

GOOSEBERRIES

The gooseberry, a botanical cousin of the blackcurrant, is native to Europe and North America. The fruits, which grow on dauntingly spiny bushes, come in many varieties – hard and sour, succulently soft and sweet, smooth and hairy – and in a range of colours, from vivid green to luscious purple.

History

Gooseberries were popular all over Britain well before Tudor times, when they grew wild in many kitchen gardens. The Tudors served them in savoury sauces and in all manner of sweet dishes. They were first cultivated in the sixteenth century and became so popular that in the nineteenth century competitors formed gooseberry clubs to see who could grow the biggest berry (some are reputed to have been grown to the size of a bantam's egg).

For some reason, their popularity did not spread abroad; even today the French use them only in a sauce to cut the richness of oily fish. There is no specific French word for gooseberry; it shares its name with the redcurrant and is known as *groseille de maquereau* ("redcurrant for mackerel").

Varieties

Gooseberries have a very long season. Early gooseberries are usually bright green and rather hard. They cannot be eaten raw, but taste wonderful cooked. These are followed by the softer, mid-season fruits, which are not generally identified by variety when sold in supermarkets and greengrocers, but which you may find in gardens and farm shops.

Early Sulphur A very early variety with golden, almost transparent berries and a lovely sweet flavour.

Goldendrop As attractive as its name, this small round yellow gooseberry has a fine rich flavour, which makes it ideal for eating

raw as a dessert fruit. Ready to pick in mid-summer.

Langley's Industry A large red hairy berry with a lovely sweet flavour. Ideal for the less green-fingered gardener, it will grow vigorously anywhere and can be picked early for cooking, or left to ripen fully on the bush to eat raw like grapes.

Above: Huge, deep-red London berries are sweet enough to eat raw.

Leveller A mid-season, yellowish-green berry with a sweet flavour.

London This huge mid-season berry is deep red or purple. For thirty-seven years, between 1829 and 1867, it was the unbeaten British champion in major gooseberry competitions! These dessert gooseberries can be eaten fresh, just as they are.

Left: Green gooseberries – these early-cropping fruits cannot be eaten raw, but are delicious cooked.

Right: Fully ripe red gooseberries are quite sweet enough to be eaten just as they are.

Nutrition

Gooseberries are high in vitamin C and also contain vitamins A and D, potassium, calcium, phosphorus and niacin. They are rich in dietary fibre and provide only 17 kilocalories per 100g/3¾oz.

Buying and Storing

Choose slightly unripe green gooseberries for cooking. Check that they are not rock hard. Dessert varieties should be yielding and juicy (if possible, taste before you buy). Gooseberries will keep in the fridge for up to a week.

To freeze whole gooseberries, top and tail them and open freeze on baking sheets. Pack the frozen berries into polythene bags. Alternatively, purée and sieve them, sweeten and freeze in rigid containers.

Below: You may find Leveller berries, which have a lovely sweet flavour, in garden centres, pick-your-own farms and farm shops.

Preparing

For recipes using whole gooseberries, wash, then top and tail them (this is not necessary if you are making jam or jelly, or are going to sieve the cooked fruit).

Cooking

Gooseberries are rich in pectin, particularly when they are slightly unripe, which makes them ideal for jams and jellies. Their tartness makes an excellent foil for oily fish and rich poultry or meat.

Cook gooseberries very gently with a little water and sugar to taste until all the fruit has collapsed. If you like, flavour them with cinnamon, lemon or herbs. A few fennel or dill seeds will enhance a gooseberry sauce for fish.

In England, the first gooseberries of the season were traditionally used to make a Whitsun pie. They also make a good filling for suet pudding or crumble.

Worcestershire berries

A North American species of gooseberry that grows on a bush with evil spines. The small purplish-red berries are hardly much bigger than blackberries, but have the distinctive veining of gooseberries and a gooseberry flavour. Worcestershire berries can be eaten raw or cooked.

Topping and tailing gooseberries

1 Hold the gooseberry between your forefinger and thumb.
2 Snip off the stem and flower end with sharp scissors or trim with a knife.

Puréed, sieved and mixed with whipped cream, they make the perfect fruit fool. Gooseberries have an extraordinary affinity for elderflowers, which come into season at the same time as the early fruit and add a delicious muscat flavour to the berries.

Below: Sweet-tasting Early Sulphur are golden and almost translucent.

CRANBERRIES

These tart, bright red berries grow wild on evergreen shrubs in peaty marshland all over northern Europe and North America. They are closely related to blueberries and bilberries, but are much more sour and are always served cooked. **Cowberries** and **lingonberries** are very similar, but smaller.

Cranberries are sometimes known as "bounceberries", since they were traditionally tested for firmness by being bounced seven times. Any which failed the bounce test were too squashy and were therefore discarded. Because of their waxy skins, cranberries keep for much longer than other berries, which helps to explain their popularity.

History

For centuries before the first settlers arrived in America, the native American Indians prized wild cranberries for their nutritional and medicinal value, and used them to make a dye for fabric and for decorative feathers. Although cranberries were already known in Britain, the Pilgrim Fathers found that the American berries were larger and more succulent.

Right: Bright red cranberries can be used in sweet and savoury dishes.

Below: Dried cranberries

Cranberry sauce

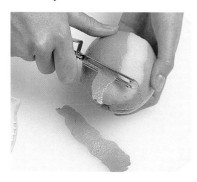

1 Thinly pare an orange with a swivel-bladed vegetable peeler, taking care to remove only the zest. Squeeze the juice and put it in a saucepan with the zest.

2 Add 350g/12oz/3 cups cranberries and cook gently for a few minutes until the cranberry skins pop.

3 Stir in caster sugar to taste and simmer for 5 minutes. Stir in 30ml/2 tbsp port (optional). Pour the cranberry sauce into a bowl, then cool and chill before serving.

They called them "craneberries" because the pink blossoms resembled a crane's head, or possibly because the cranes, which lived in the marshlands, were partial to the berries.

Cranberries featured in the first ever Thanksgiving feast in 1620 and have been a traditional part of the celebrations ever since. Commercial cultivation began in the nineteenth century, and nowadays cranberries are available frozen, canned, dried, as juice and in jellies and relishes.

Nutrition

Cranberries contain vitamins C and D, potassium and iron. They were considered to be a good protection against scurvy. They are naturally very low in kilocalories (but need sweetening to make them palatable).

Buying and Storing

Look for plump, firm, bright red berries and make sure that those at the bottom of the pack are neither squashed nor shrivelled. Fresh cranberries will keep in the fridge for four weeks, or they can be frozen in polythene bags and used without being thawed.

Preparing and Cooking

Cranberries can be used in sweet or savoury dishes. Their most famous incarnation is as cranberry sauce, which is served with turkey or red meat and game. Their distinctive tartness even adds zest to firm-fleshed fish. The berries are high in pectin, so they make excellent jams and jellies. They combine well with orange and apple, and can be mixed with blackberries and raspberries to make an autumnal variation on summer pudding.

Cranberries should be stewed slowly with sugar to taste and a little water or orange juice until the skins pop. Dried cranberries can be used in the same way as raisins. Cranberry juice can be mixed with soda water and white wine or grape juice to make a refreshing drink. It is also good with orange juice and vodka.

Cranberry and chestnut stuffing

The traditional Christmas accompaniments of cranberries and chestnuts can be combined to make the perfect stuffing for turkey or other poultry. To make about 450g/1lb (enough to stuff a 4.5–5.5kg/10–12lb bird), soften 115g/4oz finely chopped onion in 25g/1oz butter in a saucepan. Stir in 175g/6oz unsweetened chestnut purée and 30ml/2 tbsp cooked cranberries or chunky cranberry sauce. Season to taste with salt and pepper and mix thoroughly. Take the pan off the heat and stir in 225g/8oz fresh white breadcrumbs. Coarsely crumble or chop 115g/4oz cooked chestnuts (canned chestnuts are fine) and fold into the stuffing mixture. Leave to cool completely before stuffing the bird.

Below: Cranberry juice and soda makes a refreshing drink.

BLACKCURRANTS, REDCURRANTS AND WHITECURRANTS

These native European berries, with their glowing colours, make a beautiful sight in summer, hanging like tiny bunches of grapes on the bush. Each berry contains a mass of small seeds. Currants can be eaten whole, but because they are highly acidic, this is seldom the preferred option.

History

Currants grow wild all over Europe and even as far north as Siberia. For some inexplicable reason, they were not cultivated by the Romans, but became popular only in the sixteenth century, when they were prized for their health-giving properties.

Nutrition

All currants, particularly blackcurrants, are very rich in vitamin C. Blackcurrants are used in cordials, throat sweets and other remedies designed to ward off colds; in the past, they were often used as a cure for quinsy. They are also high in pectin.

Buying and Storing

Choose plump, firm currants with shiny skins. They will keep in the fridge for several days. They can be frozen very successfully: strip the currants from the

Below: Buffalo currants are a type of blackcurrant with larger berries.

Right: Blackcurrants grow wild all over Europe. The fruits have a tart flavour and are usually cooked.

stalks, then rinse and drain them. Freeze in rigid containers. Sweetened or unsweetened blackcurrant purée also freezes well.

Preparing

Strip the currants from the stalks, unless this has already been done. If you wish, pick off the calyx tops before cooking the currants by pinching them between the nails of your forefinger and thumb. This is a tedious process, and is seldom necessary.

BLACKCURRANTS

Although they are often combined with other currants in cooking (as in summer pudding), blackcurrants are different from other types. They have tougher skins and, unlike other currants, which grow on old wood, they

fruit on new wood. Both the bushes and the currants themselves are highly aromatic and the fruits have a luscious tart flavour.

Cooking

Blackcurrants can be added raw to fruit salads if they are not too tart, but are usually cooked in a little water, with sugar to taste. Simmer until just tender – do not overcook them or they will lose their fresh flavour. Blackcurrants make wonderful jams and jellies and combine well with soft cheeses, rich meats and game. To serve blackcurrants with meat, sauté them lightly in butter, adding a

Stripping currants off the stalk

Hold the bunch of currants by the stem and strip off the berries with the tines of a fork.

Right: Whitecurrants are less tart than other currants and can be eaten raw.

pinch of sugar. They adapt well to other flavourings, such as mint and lemon, and are used to make the liqueur *crème de Cassis,* which is the basis for *Kir Royale* and similar drinks.

REDCURRANTS

Redcurrants can be eaten raw. Small bunches look very decorative if frosted with egg white and caster sugar. They are an essential ingredient for summer pudding and make a good addition to creamy desserts, such as crème brûlée. For a refreshing summer drink, purée 450g/1lb/4 cups redcurrants with 500ml/18 fl oz/2 cups water and sugar to taste, then press the purée gently through a sieve placed over a jug. Serve with sparkling water or soda water, or add a dash of vodka or gin.

The most familiar use of redcurrants, however, is in the jewel-like redcurrant jelly that goes so well with lamb and venison. Cumberland sauce (for game, ham and rich meats) is made by heating redcurrant jelly with lemon zest, port and sometimes mustard.

WHITECURRANTS

These beautiful, translucent, silvery-golden currants are an albino strain of redcurrants. They are less tart than other types and can be eaten raw. They look wonderfully decorative frosted with egg white and sugar. **Pink currants** are an even more attractive variety, with a beautiful pink flush.

Above: Redcurrant jelly

Left: Redcurrants are an essential ingredient for summer pudding.

Redcurrant jelly

1 Put the redcurrants (as many as you have) in a preserving pan with just enough water to cover. Simmer for 8–10 minutes or until the currants are very soft.

2 Strain through a jelly bag, then measure the liquid. Pour it back into the pan and add 350g/12oz/1½ cups granulated sugar for every 600ml/1 pint/2½ cups liquid. Stir over a medium heat until dissolved.

3 Boil briskly for 10 minutes or until setting point is reached, skimming off any scum as it rises to the surface. Pour the jelly into sterilized jars, seal and label.

CITRUS FRUITS

No family of fruits seems to store up sunshine more successfully than citrus fruits. Golden oranges and tangerines, yellow lemons, deep green limes — their glowing colours light up a room, and the wonderful scent of their essential oils tempts the tastebuds. Wonderfully versatile, they can be juiced, enjoyed just as they are or used in both sweet and savoury dishes. All citrus fruits have tough, bitter peel that is highly scented and contains aromatic essential oils. Inside, the fruit is segmented and encloses juicy flesh, with a more or less acid flavour. The fruits ripen on the tree and do not continue to develop after picking, so they have excellent keeping qualities.

GRAPEFRUIT

One of the largest citrus fruits, grapefruit can vary in diameter from 10–18cm/4–7in. Most have deep yellow skins, but the flesh can range from very pale yellow (confusingly called "white"), through rosy pink to deep pink (known as "ruby"). Generally speaking, the pinker the flesh, the sweeter the grapefruit will be.

History

Grapefruit are descended from the original West Indian **pomelo** or **shaddock**, a large sour fruit (the pomelos sold today are a cross between a grapefruit and a shaddock). These fruits were brought to Europe from the West Indies in the seventeenth century and are now grown in every sub-tropical country of the world.

Varieties

The main varieties of grapefruit are white, pink or ruby, but you may also find the green-skinned **Sweetie,** whose flesh, as the name implies, is so sweet that it needs no sugar.

Nutrition

One of the most filling fruits, yet very low in calories (about 43 kilocalories per 100g/3¾oz), grapefruit are an excellent source of dietary fibre and vitamin C; one fruit provides one-and-a-half times the adult daily requirement.

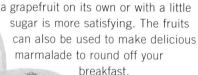

Above: Sweetie is a very sweet variety of grapefruit that needs no sugar.

Buying and Storing

Choose fruits that feel heavy for their size; they will be juicy. The skin can be thin or thick, depending on the variety, but it should be plump and firm; if it is puffy and coarse, the flesh will be dry. Avoid grapefruit with bruised or damaged skin. You cannot ripen grapefruit once they have been picked, but they can be kept in a cool place or in the fridge for a week or more.

Preparing and Serving

Grapefruit are best eaten raw and chilled, although in the 1960s it was fashionable to sprinkle them with brown sugar or brush with melted butter and caramelize them under the grill. They constitute the perfect breakfast food; perhaps the easiest way to enjoy them is freshly squeezed into a glass, but half a grapefruit on its own or with a little sugar is more satisfying. The fruits can also be used to make delicious marmalade to round off your breakfast.

Grapefruit can be used to start or finish a main meal. The tart flavour goes well with

Above: White grapefruit have pale yellow flesh.

Segmenting grapefruit

1 Cut the grapefruit in half and remove the pips.

2 Using a curved, serrated grapefruit knife, cut between the skin and flesh.

3 Using a small, sharp paring knife, cut carefully between the membrane that separates the segments. Start at the centre, work out to the skin, then around the segment and back to the centre again.

4 Finally, cut out the central core of the grapefruit with a sharp knife and remove the membrane.

seafood; grapefruit segments mixed with prawns and avocado make a refreshing starter. They combine well with smoked fish and poultry, and segments are sometimes served as a garnish to cut the richness of liver or sweetbreads. The segments can also be used in fruit salads, mousses and sorbets. Grapefruit juice makes an unusual addition to salad dressings, and the peel can be candied to be used in cakes or coated with chocolate as a sweet with after-dinner coffee.

Left: The flesh of pink grapefruit can range from rosy pink to deep pink. As a rule of thumb, the pinker the colour, the sweeter the grapefruit.

Below: Chocolate-coated grapefruit peel – a delectable sweet treat.

POMELOS

Although they resemble grapefruit, true pomelos are not a hybrid of the grapefruit, but a species in their own right. They are sometimes known as "shaddocks" after the sea captain who brought them from Polynesia to the West Indies. They are much larger than grapefruit, with thick yellow dimpled skin, pinkish-yellow flesh and a sharp, refreshing flavour, which often needs a little sugar to make it palatable.

Below: Pomelos sold today are a smaller, rounder and smoother-skinned cross between the original pomelo or shaddock and grapefruit.

UGLI FRUIT

Despite its large size, baggy shape and mottled green skin, the Ugli is a hybrid of the grapefruit, orange and tangerine. It may not be the beauty of the citrus family, but the flavour is sweet and delicious – a cross between grapefruit and tangerine. The peel can be candied like grapefruit.

LEMONS

Arguably the most useful of all fruit, the distinctively shaped lemon can be very large or quite small, with thick or thin, smooth or knobbly skin. The skin contains aromatic essential oils, and a good lemon will perfume the air with its fragrance. The juicy, pale yellow, acid flesh enhances almost any other food and never fails to awaken and refresh the tastebuds.

History

Originally from India or Malaysia, lemons were introduced into Assyria where they were discovered by the soldiers serving Alexander the Great. They took them back to Greece, where the lemons were used as a condiment and for medicinal and cosmetic purposes. The Crusaders brought lemons to Europe from Palestine, and their cultivation became widespread. Like limes, lemons became invaluable as a protection against scurvy and were carried by sailors on every sea voyage.

Nutrition

Rich in vitamin C and very low in calories, lemons only provide about 22 kilocalories per 100g/3¾oz.

Buying and Storing

Choose lemons that are firm and heavy for their size. Smooth-skinned lemons are best for juicing and cooking, while the knobbly skinned varieties are easier to grate. Lemons become paler as they ripen and lose some juiciness and acidity, so avoid light yellow fruit; look instead for deep yellow specimens with glossy unblemished skins. Do not buy lemons with patches of mould, or those with hard, shrivelled skins.

Lemons have often been treated with diphenyl, an ethylene gas that keeps the skins yellow and fresh-looking. If you are going to use the lemon rind, buy untreated or "unwaxed" fruit.

Lemons do not ripen once picked. They can be kept in a cool room or the fridge for at least a week.

Preparing and Cooking

Although few people would choose to eat a lemon raw, these citrus fruits are infinitely versatile. Their high ascorbic acid (vitamin C) content prevents oxidization, so lemon juice is often brushed over cut fruit or white vegetables, such as potatoes, celeriac or artichokes, to stop them from turning brown. Lemons can be distilled into alcoholic drinks, such as *limoncello,* a sweet *digestivo,* which is served straight from the freezer.

Every part of the lemon can be used in sweet and savoury cooking, from the juice to the zest. Lemon wedges are traditionally served as an accompaniment to fish dishes, particularly fried fish; their acidity counteracts the fattiness of all fried

Left: Smooth-skinned lemons are best for juicing and cooking.

Zesting or grating a lemon

1 Choose an unwaxed lemon. Hold it firmly in one hand.

2 Scrape a zester down the length of the lemon to pare off fine slivers of zest.

3 Chop the pared zest finely with a sharp knife if desired.

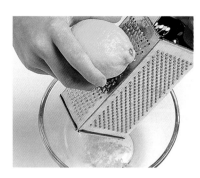

4 For grating, choose a knobbly skinned lemon if possible. Grate it on the fine side of a grater, taking care to remove only the yellow zest. Work over a bowl, or, if you prefer, work over a piece of foil – this makes it easy to transfer the grated rind to a bowl or pan with the aid of a pastry brush.

foods. Lemon slices are a popular addition to tea and cold drinks, or can be used to garnish any number of sweet or savoury dishes. Whole lemons can be preserved in salt and are widely used in North African dishes, such as Moroccan *tagines*.

Lemons give a wonderful flavour to sweet dishes. They can be used for jellies, jams and lemon curd or cheese and make refreshing mousses, sorbets and ice creams.

Lemon juice Lemon juice can be drunk on its own, with added sugar or as a refreshing long drink, such as lemonade. It enhances the flavour of most other foods and can be used as a healthy substitute for salt. Use it in dressings, sauces and marinades; marinating fish for a long time in lemon juice will even "cook" the fish without heat, as in the South American dish

Below: Lemon juice enhances the flavour of most other fruits.

Above: Knobbly-skinned lemons are easy to grate.

ceviche. Lemon juice will also tenderize meat. A few drops added to the cooking water helps poached eggs to coagulate, and a couple of spoonfuls will turn fresh cream into soured cream.

Lemon juice has non-culinary uses, too. It acts as a bleach and can be used as a household cleaner or cosmetically, to whiten the skin or lighten blonde hair.

Lemons yield more juice if they are warmed before squeezing; roll them between the palms of your hands for a minute or two, cover with boiling water or microwave on High for 30 seconds before squeezing. Do not squeeze lemons too hard, or the juice will become bitter.

Lemon zest and peel
The essential oils in lemon zest have an aromatic flavour that enhances many dishes. The zest can be obtained by grating or peeling into strips with a zester or canelle knife. Use it as a flavouring for butter, sauces, custards, mousses, cakes, biscuits and tarts. For a milder lemon flavour, rub a lump of sugar over the surface of a lemon so that it absorbs the oils, then add the sugar cube to a sauce or pudding.

Lemon peel (including the white pith) contains pectin, which helps to set jams and jellies. Strips of peel (minus pith) can be added to casseroles, or candied to serve with coffee or to add to cakes and puddings.

CITRON

A lemon or pear-shaped citrus fruit originally from China, citrons are large fruit, sometimes up to 20cm/8in long, with thick, knobbly, greenish skin. They give very little juice, but this can be used like lemon juice. Citron flesh is very bitter and unpalatable, but the attractive green peel can be candied and used like candied lemon peel; it develops a lovely translucency. The peel can also be used for marmalade and jams. In Corsica, citrons are used to make a liqueur called *Cédratine*.

Right: Citrons are large fruit with bitter, unpalatable flesh.

LIMES

Limes are the smallest members of the true citrus family. They have thin, fairly smooth, green skins and a highly aromatic, acid flavour. Unlike lemons, limes will grow in tropical regions and are an essential ingredient of South-East Asian, Mexican, Latin American and Caribbean cooking.

History

Limes originated in India. Attempts were made to grow them in Mediterranean countries, but they proved insufficiently hardy. They do very well in Egypt, however, where they are more plentiful than lemons. They are widely grown in the West Indies, and it was from these islands that supplies came for the British Navy, to supplement the sailors' rations and help to prevent scurvy. Limehouse, in London's docklands, takes its name from the warehouses where the fruit was stored.

Varieties

There are basically three types of lime:
Tahitian Large limes, with pale fine-grained pulp and a very acidic flavour.
Mexican Smaller fruit with bright green skin and a very aromatic flavour.
Key Lime Pale yellowish-green fruit, very juicy with a strong, sharp flavour. Not surprisingly, these are the main ingredient of Florida key lime pie.

Nutrition

High in vitamin C, limes contain some potassium, calcium and phosphorus, and provide about 20 kilocalories per 100g/3¾oz.

Right: Limes have a sharper flavour than lemons.

Buying and Storing

Limes are the most perishable of all citrus fruit and quickly dry out and develop brown patches on their skins. Choose unblemished fruits that feel heavy for their size and avoid those with yellowish skins, as they may have lost some of their tanginess. Store limes in the fridge for up to a week.

Preparing and Serving

Limes can be used in the same way as lemons, but will add a sharper flavour, so use fewer of them. Classic *ceviche* is made by marinating chunks of white fish in lime juice until they turn opaque. Freshly squeezed juice is used in rum punches, margaritas and daiquiris, or commercially made into a cordial.

Strips of lime zest can be buried in caster sugar to add a delicious fragrance. A few drops of lime juice squeezed over tropical fruit, such as papayas, melons and prickly pears will do wonders for the flavour. In Caribbean and Latin American cooking, limes are cooked with fish, poultry and meat, while in South-East Asia they are made into pickles and chutneys to serve with curries.

Limes can be made into jams and jellies and add a special zing to marmalade. One of the world's great desserts is Florida key lime pie, which is similar to a lemon meringue pie. Lime blossoms are dried and made into infusions or used to flavour ice creams and mousses.

> **Paring and cutting julienne strips of citrus rind**
> **1** Wash and dry the lime, lemon or orange. Using a swivel-blade vegetable peeler, peel downwards to remove long strips of rind. Do not include the bitter white pith.
> **2** With a small sharp knife, square off the strips.
> **3** Cut them lengthways into fine julienne strips.

KAFFIR LIMES

These are not true limes, but belong to a sub-species of the citrus family. Pale green and gnarled, the fruits have a haunting, scented citrus bouquet, but unfortunately the flesh is inedible. In Thailand and Indonesia, the finely grated rind is sometimes used in cooking, but it is the leaves that are most useful in culinary terms. When torn or shredded, they impart a distinctive flavour to soups, fish and chicken dishes, and curries.

Right: Kaffir limes are not eaten, but the finely grated rind is used in South-East Asian cooking.

KUMQUATS

Kumquats are not true citrus fruits, but belong to a similar species, *fortunella*. Their name comes from the Cantonese *kam kwat,* meaning "golden orange". The small, elongated fruits are about the size and shape of a large olive, with thin orange rind that is edible. The rind is sweeter than the sour pulp and the two parts eaten together provide a delicious sour-sweet sensation.

Nutrition

Kumquats are a source of vitamins C and A and have some calcium, phosphorus and riboflavin. They provide about 65 kilocalories per 100g/3¾oz.

Buying and Storing

Look for unblemished fruit with taut orange rind. Kumquats can be kept in the fridge for up to a week.

Preparing and Cooking

Kumquats can be eaten whole, just as they are, or sliced into miniature rings and used in winter salads and fruit salads. They taste superb poached in syrup, and can also be bottled with sugar and alcohol and served whole or chopped with ice cream, duck, red meats or cheese. They make delicious marmalade and jam and can be used in cake and biscuit mixes. For unusual petits fours, dip whole kumquats into melted bittersweet chocolate.

Kumquats combine well with bitter salad leaves like chicory and frisée and make excellent stuffings for poultry.

Limequats

These are, as the name suggests, a cross between limes and kumquats. Limequats are bright green with thin, edible skins, but they are extremely sour, so cannot be eaten raw. They should be cooked or preserved like kumquats and can be served in the same way.

Whole kumquats can be cooked with fish, poultry and white meats, and spiced kumquat preserve is a Christmas treat.

Left: Not true citrus fruits, kumquats can be eaten whole – skin and all.

BERGAMOTS

These small yellow citrus fruit are seldom found in their natural state. They are best known for the essential oil contained in the rind, which is used in confectionery and perfumery, but most famously as a highly distinctive flavouring for Earl Grey tea. Bergamot oil is used in the barley sugar made in the French town of Nancy. The fruit can also be made into delicious and unusual marmalade.

Right: Seldom used for cooking, bergamots are best-known for their essential oil, which gives Earl Grey tea its unusual, aromatic scent and flavour.

TANGERINES OR MANDARINS

Sometimes known as "easy peelers", tangerines or mandarins are part of a large family of small citrus fruit. They resemble slightly flattened oranges with loose orange skin and have a fragrant aroma, which is inextricably bound up with Christmas. Who can forget the childhood delight of finding a tangerine in the toe of a Christmas stocking? The tangerine family all have aromatic skins, which can easily be detached from the segments (unlike oranges and lemons) and segments that separate easily. The flesh is sweet and perfumed, but often contains a large number of pips.

History

As the name suggests, tangerines or mandarins almost certainly originated in China and were brought to Italy in Roman times by Arab traders. Like oranges, they were regarded as a

Right: Easy to peel, satsumas have a refreshing tart flavour.

symbol of luxury and prosperity. They are now grown throughout North Africa and the Mediterranean.

Varieties

The names of many types of tangerine are commonly interchanged, so you may find a bewildering variety of fruits that are essentially the same.

Clementine The smallest of the tangerines, with bright orange skin and no pips. This, and their sweet, aromatic flesh, make clementines the most popular tangerine variety. They are sometimes sold with the leaves still attached, which makes them particularly attractive.

Mandarin Most commonly sold canned, tiny peeled tangerine segments are sold as mandarin oranges, although they are usually satsumas. The deliciously sweet, vibrant segments make an attractive decoration for a dessert.

Satsuma These largish tangerines from Japan have loose skin and a refreshing, rather tart flavour. Satsumas contain very few pips.

Right: These tangerines, grown in Italy, have sweet flesh, but often contain a large number of pips.

Making tangerine shells

1 Choose attractive, well-shaped fruit. Cut off the top of each to make a lid.

2 Carefully scoop out the segments with a teaspoon, a few at a time. Scrape out any pith or membrane, taking care to avoid breaking the skin. Fill the shells with iced tangerine pulp.

Right: Clementine is the smallest and most popular variety of tangerine.

Ortanique Also known as "honey tangerines" because of their delicious sweetness, ortaniques are a hybrid, which can be found growing on the same trees as tangerines or oranges.

Tangelo These are a cross between a tangerine and a grapefruit, and have the easy-peeling qualities of the former. Tangelos are irregularly shaped and have a refreshing, tart flavour, rather like an orange.

Minneola Another tangerine–grapefruit hybrid, minneolas can be recognized by the distinctive bulge at their stalk end. They have bright orange skin and are very easy to peel. The sweet, juicy flesh has no pips.

Nutrition

All tangerines and their hybrids are extremely good sources of vitamin C and beta-carotene. They provide about 40 kilocalories per 100g/3¾oz.

Buying and Storing

Many varieties of tangerine have loose, puffy skins, which are no indication of quality. Choose fruits that feel heavy for their size; they will contain more juice. Avoid fruits with damaged skins and, if you are buying pre-packed fruits, check that none is mouldy or it will quickly taint all the others.

Tangerines do not keep as long as other citrus fruit, but can be stored in the fridge for up to a week.

Canned mandarin oranges are a very useful store cupboard item. Use them in trifles, chocolate slices and on cheesecakes. Children love them set in orange or mandarin jelly.

It is also possible to buy canned peeled whole mandarins in syrup – the lazy cook's answer for a simply sensational dessert. Just make a caramel sauce, add the drained fruit and decorate with some fresh orange or mandarin zest. A dash of orange liqueur gilds the lily.

Preparing and Serving

All varieties of tangerine can be used in the same way as oranges. The peel is as useful as the flesh, and the zest can be candied or used to flavour sweet liqueurs. Strips of peel can be dried and used in savoury stews or included with herbs to make a bouquet garni.

Tangerine segments can be eaten on their own. Dipped in melted chocolate or crystallized, they make a delicious after-dinner sweet. Tangerine juice adds a distinctive flavour to marinades for pork and poultry; combine it with oriental aromatics like five-spice powder, ginger and soy sauce.

ORANGES

Below: Navelina oranges contain a tiny embryonic fruit.

Despite their name, oranges are not always orange; they can also be yellow or mottled with red. The size can vary too – an orange can be as large as a football or as small as a cherry – and the flavour can range from sweet to intensely sour. Orange trees are beautiful all year round. Their dark glossy evergreen leaves give off a wonderful citrus scent. The beautiful waxy white, star-shaped flowers also have an intense aroma, which is captured in orange blossom water. The fruits turn from green to bright orange or yellow, making a striking contrast with the leaves.

Like other citrus peel, orange rind contains essential oils, which are used in cooking and perfumery.

History

Oranges originated in China. They were probably known to the Ancient Greeks and may have been the mythical Golden Apples of the Hesperides. If so, they would have been bitter oranges, which were the only variety

Right: Cointreau – flavoured with the peel of bitter oranges.

known at the time. Over the centuries, traders took oranges to India and Arabia and thence to the Mediterranean region. When the first oranges reached Europe, they were so rare that they became a symbol of opulence, to be offered as luxury gifts; the Medici family adopted five oranges as their coat of arms. The oranges were too precious to be eaten raw (in any case, they would have been too sour), but were made into preserves. The first sweet oranges to arrive in Europe were brought from India by traders in the seventeenth century. They became popular throughout Europe and were served in theatres as refreshments – hence Nell Gwynn's appearance in the history books.

Varieties

Oranges fall into two groups: sweet oranges, which can be eaten raw, and bitter oranges, which cannot.

Sweet oranges

Sweet oranges can be divided into four main categories, which are available at different times of the year.

Navel and **Navelina** These seedless oranges take their name from the navel-like protuberance at the end, which contains a tiny embryonic fruit. They have thick, pebbly skins and very sweet, juicy flesh. The skin is particularly good for making candied peel.

Blonde These pale-skinned winter oranges include **Jaffa** and **Shamouti**. The large fruit have thick skins that are easy to peel. The flesh is crisp and juicy. If you are lucky, you may find **Salustianas oranges**, which are full of juice and contain no pips.

Blood oranges These small oranges have red-flushed skins and jewel-like flesh, which can range from golden to deep ruby red. These are the best oranges to use for sorbets and desserts, where colour is important. They are an essential ingredient of *sauce Maltaise*,

Peeling and segmenting oranges

1 Using a serrated knife, cut a thin slice from each end of the orange to expose the flesh.

2 Cut off the peel in a circular motion, removing the white pith.

3 Hold the fruit over a bowl to catch the juice. Cut each segment between the membranes.

4 Squeeze out all the juice.

Below: Seedless Navel oranges have very sweet juicy flesh.

an orange-flavoured mayonnaise, which takes its name from the sour but juicy Maltese blood orange.

Late oranges These include **Valencia** oranges, which have smooth, thin skins and contain few or no pips; they are the world's most popular variety. They have pale flesh and are very juicy, with a sharp flavour. Valencia are the best oranges for juicing.

Bitter oranges

As well as the sweet oranges, there are bitter oranges.

Seville or **Bigarade** cannot be eaten raw, but are used for making marmalade, jams and jellies. Vast numbers are grown in Seville, but surprisingly the Spaniards never make marmalade; almost all their oranges are exported to Britain. Seville oranges are used in the classic *sauce bigarade*, which is traditionally served with roast duck. In

the south of France, these oranges are crystallized and the blossoms are distilled to make aromatic orange flower water. The aromatic oils from the peel are used to flavour such liqueurs as Grand Marnier and Cointreau. Bitter oranges have a very short season and are only available in January.

Nutrition

An orange provides twice the adult daily requirement of vitamin C, and is high in dietary fibre. The average fruit provides about 50 kilocalories.

Buying and Storing

Choose firm oranges that feel heavy for their size – these will be juicy. Never buy oranges with damaged, shrivelled or mouldy skin. Oranges keep well; they can be stored at room temperature or in the fridge for up to two weeks. The juice and grated zest can be frozen.

Right: Bitter Seville oranges have a very short season – they are only available in January.

Right: Valencia oranges are the world's most popular variety of orange and are the best variety for juicing.

Candied orange peel

1 Choose thick-skinned oranges. Wash and dry well. Peel the oranges with a swivel vegetable peeler.

2 Using a sharp knife, cut the peel into thin julienne strips.

3 For each orange, bring to the boil 250ml/8 fl oz/1 cup water with 115g/4oz/½ cup granulated sugar. Add the strips of orange peel, half-cover the pan and simmer until the syrup has reduced by three-quarters. Leave to cool completely.

4 Sift icing sugar in a thick, even layer over a baking sheet. Roll the candied peel in the sugar. Dry in a cool oven. Store the peel in a jar; it will keep for 2–3 months.

Preparing and Serving

Oranges are best eaten in their natural state, but can be used in an almost infinite variety of desserts, pastries and sweetmeats: fruit salads, mousses, soufflés, ice creams, sorbets and granitas, and, perhaps most famous of all, *crêpes Suzette*. They can be squeezed for juice, in which case keep the rind to use in other ways (grated zest can be ground with caster sugar for sprinkling on breakfast cereals or for use in cakes or custards, for example). The juice can be drunk or used in a marinade for poultry or fish. Fresh sliced oranges combine well with spices like cinnamon, ginger and cardamom, and a sprinkling of distilled orange flower water enhances their flavour dramatically. Candied orange peel is good in cakes, biscuits and Christmas pudding. Crystallized quartered orange slices make an attractive decoration for desserts and cakes.

Oranges go well in savoury dishes. Combine them with watercress, beetroot or chicory and thinly sliced raw red onion for a refreshing salad, or glaze carrots in orange juice and butter. Add orange juice and zest to tomato sauces and soups, or add strips of pared rind to hearty fish soups and

Right: Blood oranges

Duck in bitter orange sauce

The acidity of bitter oranges is the perfect foil for the richness of duck. For *caneton à la bigarade*, pare the rind of a Seville orange, removing only the zest. Cut this into julienne strips. Squeeze the orange and set the juice aside. Roast a duck, then keep it hot. Drain off the fat from the roasting tin, then deglaze the tin with a little white wine. Add 300ml/ ½ pint/1¼ cups rich chicken stock and the orange juice, reduce until syrupy, then add the orange zest, season and simmer for about 5 minutes. Beat in 25g/1oz/2 tbsp cubed chilled butter. Carve the duck and pour over the sauce. Garnish with peeled orange segments.

meat or poultry casseroles. Peeled orange slices are also good with liver and fish (especially trout and salmon).

EXOTIC FRUITS

Thanks to modern transportation methods, tropical fruits are no longer merely the stuff of travellers' tales. Rambutans, carambolas, guavas, passion fruit and pomegranates are stocked on greengrocers' shelves, alongside recent rarities, which have now become commonplace, such as mangoes, fresh dates and kiwi fruit. Most supermarkets now label tropical fruits with preparation and serving suggestions, so it is easy to venture into the realms of the exotic.

BANANAS

Bananas are surely the best-known tropical fruit and one of the most healthy and versatile. Neatly packaged in their attractive easy-peel skins, hygienically enclosing the sweet, creamy-white, floury flesh, bananas are the perfect convenience food.

The banana plant, whose elongated, fan-like leaves can grow to over 3.6m/ 4yd long, is actually an enormous herb. "Hands" of up to 200 bananas point upwards through the leaves like fingers.

Above: Bananas, shown here in their unripe state, grow upwards in bunches on a huge plant that is actually a giant herb.

History

Bananas originated in South-East Asia and have grown in the Tropics since ancient times. There is a theory that the fruit of the Tree of Knowledge in the Garden of Eden was actually a banana; certainly, a banana leaf would have protected Adam's modesty more effectively than a fig leaf. Before man began to cultivate bananas, the fruits contained so many bitter black seeds that they were almost inedible.

Varieties

Hundreds of different varieties of banana flourish in the Tropics, from sweet yellow pygmy fruit to large fibrous plantains and green bananas, which can only be used for cooking.

The most common varieties of sweet banana are the long, curved yellow

Left: Lady Finger or Sugar bananas are tiny – often no more than the length of a lady's finger!

dessert fruit, which develop a speckled brown skin as they ripen. The most widely available of these is Cavendish, but unless you are an expert it is practically impossible to differentiate between individual varieties.

Lady Finger or **Sugar** These are tiny finger bananas, often no more than 7.5cm/3in long. They have creamy flesh and a very sweet flavour.

Apple These yellow bananas are also very small. They have golden flesh and when very ripe have a faint taste and aroma of apple.

Right: Perhaps the best-known tropical fruit, easy-to-peel yellow bananas, which come in a variety of sizes, are the perfect convenience food.

Right: When very ripe, small Apple bananas have a faint taste and aroma of apple.

Red bananas These bananas from Ecuador have brownish-red skins and smooth, yellowish-pink, sweet flesh with a creamy texture. Their colour makes it hard to assess the exact degree of ripeness, so they can sometimes prove rather disappointing. Allow a few blackish patches to develop on the skin before eating.

Green bananas Large green bananas are only suitable for cooking. They have crisp flesh and are often used as a substitute for potatoes, although they have a blander flavour. Fried green banana rings are good in curries.

Plantain These fruits resemble large bananas, but are flatter in shape. They have firm, pinkish flesh, which is less sweet than that of dessert bananas, but contains more starch. They are almost always used in savoury dishes and can be cooked like potatoes. Very firm plantains can be peeled, then sliced wafer-thin and deep fried like potato crisps. As plantains ripen, their flesh becomes darker and sweeter and the fruit can be used in desserts.

Right: Small (as here) or large, red bananas have the same sweet, creamy flesh.

Nutrition

Bananas are extremely nutritious, being rich in potassium, riboflavin, niacin and dietary fibre. Bananas also contain vitamins A and C and some calcium and iron. They have a high energy value (99 kilocalories per 100g/3¾oz) and are good for growing children and athletes. They are also excellent for low-salt, low-fat and cholesterol-free diets.

Buying and Storing

Bananas are harvested unripe and stored in a humid atmosphere to ripen slowly. Unripe bananas are green all over; these are inedible. Fruit with green-tinged ends are slightly under-ripe, with a crisp texture and refreshing taste. Perfectly ripe bananas are uniformly yellow; as the fruit continues to ripen, brown speckles appear on the skin until it is covered with brown mottling. By this stage, the flesh is soft and sweet and is best for mashing. Once the skin has become brown all over, the banana is too ripe to eat; the flesh will have collapsed, but it can still be used for cooking. Do not buy bananas with damaged skins, or those that are too ripe. Unlike other fruit, they will continue to ripen rapidly at home. Never store them in the fridge, as the skins will blacken. Kept in a fruit bowl, bananas will hasten the ripening of other fruit.

Dried bananas Drying intensifies the sweetness of bananas. Dried bananas are dark brown, sticky and extremely sweet. They are usually eaten as a highly nutritious but calorific snack, but can also be added to winter fruit salads or savoury stews.

Canned bananas Oriental food stores sell whole baby bananas, sometimes complete with blossom, canned in heavy syrup. Only for those with a very sweet tooth!

Preparing and Cooking

Peel bananas just before using, removing the white threads from the flesh. Slice the bananas and, if not serving immediately, brush with lemon juice to prevent discoloration.

Dessert bananas are delicious eaten raw, but cooking brings out the sweetness and enhances the flavour. Raw bananas can be made into ice cream, milk shakes and trifles. Sliced bananas can be added to fruit salads or used to garnish sweet and savoury dishes. In Indonesia and the Far East, they are served as an accompaniment to rice dishes such as *nasi goreng* and curries. They combine well with other tropical ingredients, especially brown sugar, coconut, exotic fruits like pineapple, passion fruit and mango, and rum.

Bananas can be baked in their skins, then split and served with melted butter and lemon juice. Alternatively, cook them over the dying embers of a barbecue until the skins turn black. Split them, sprinkle with rum and serve with double cream. Another rich dessert is banoffi pie, a very sweet concoction of bananas and toffee. A less sweet, but equally delicious combination is grilled bananas wrapped in bacon. Banana fritters are always popular; cut the fruit into chunks, coat in batter and deep fry, or wrap in filo

Above: Dried bananas are dark brown, sticky and very sweet.

pastry, brush with melted butter and deep fry. Mashed bananas make deliciously moist cakes and teabreads.

Green bananas and plantains are starchier than sweet bananas and contain less sugar, so they are served as a vegetable. They can be boiled, baked, mashed, fried or grilled, and are an essential ingredient of many African and West Indian dishes. Banana leaves are often used as a wrapping for savoury fillings and add a pleasant aromatic flavour to both chicken and fish.

Peeling plantains

1 Using a sharp knife, top and tail the fruit. Cut in half horizontally.

2 Slit the plantain skin with a sharp knife, along the natural ridge. Take care not to cut through the flesh.

3 Ease up the edge of the skin and run your thumb tip underneath to lift up the skin. Lift off and discard the skin.

Right: Plantains are almost always used in savoury dishes and can be cooked like potatoes.

BABACOS

The babaco is a hybrid of the papaya. Pointed at the stem end and blunt at the other, this large five-sided fruit reveals a soft white core when halved. When unripe, the waxy skin is pale green, maturing to yellow. When ripe, the pale orangey-pink flesh is succulent and juicy, with a faint aroma of fresh strawberries, and the flavour resembles that of a rather bland papaya.

History

The babaco is native to Ecuador. European botanists discovered it about seventy years ago, and it is now widely grown in New Zealand, and in the Channel Islands.

Nutrition

The fruit contains valuable enzymes that help to digest fat and proteins and can be used to tenderize meat. It is a good source of vitamin C.

Buying and Storing

Babacos keep well. Yellow fruit are ready to eat straight away and should be stored in the fridge, where they will keep for about five days. Pale green babacos can be kept for a few days at room temperature until yellow and ripe.

Preparing and Cooking

Babacos can be sliced, skin and all, and eaten raw. The delicate flavour can be livened up with lemon or lime juice and sugar. The flesh can be diced and used raw in salads, or squeezed to make a refreshing juice. Babacos can also be poached in syrup and served as a dessert with cream, custard or vanilla or stem ginger ice cream, but you will need to flavour the syrup with lime juice and aromatics. On a savoury note, the fruit makes excellent sauces, chutneys and relishes. Stewed babaco can be served as an accompaniment to roast chicken, pork and ham.

Babaco for breakfast

For a deliciously different breakfast experience, try serving your favourite cereal with chilled cooked babaco. Make a syrup by boiling equal quantities of water and sugar with the juice of a lemon or lime and a split vanilla pod, a cinnamon stick or a grating of nutmeg. Dice the babaco (there is no need to peel it) and poach gently in the syrup for about 10 minutes, until tender. Chill well before using.

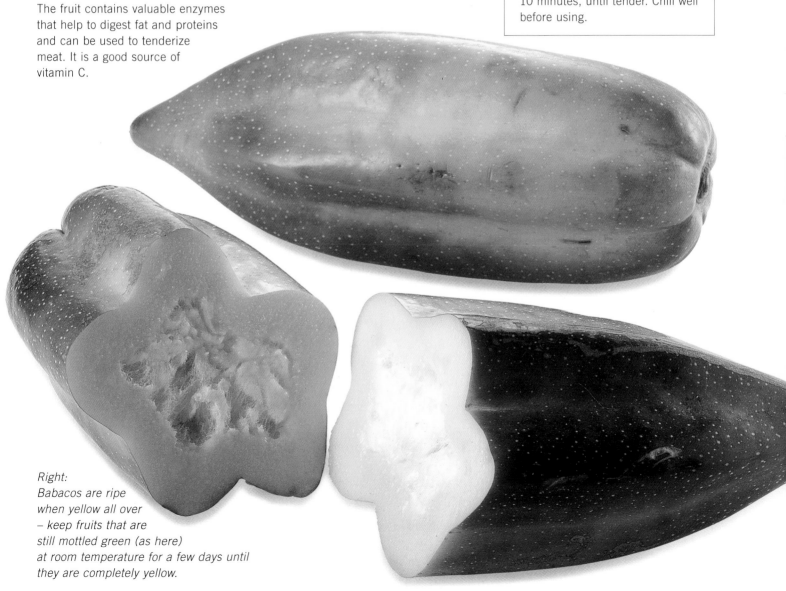

Right:
Babacos are ripe
when yellow all over
– keep fruits that are
still mottled green (as here)
at room temperature for a few days until
they are completely yellow.

BREADFRUIT

The fruit of a very tall tree, these large round to egg-shaped fruits weigh from 300g/11oz to 3kg/6½lb. They have thick, warty, greenish skin and white starchy flesh with a bread-like texture, which sometimes contains up to 200 edible seeds and sometimes none at all. Breadfruit form part of the staple diet in the Tropics.

History

Native to the Pacific and East Indies, breadfruit came to fame in the famous 1787 mutiny on the *Bounty*, when, during the voyage to the West Indies, Captain William Bligh gave the last remaining fresh water to his precious cargo of breadfruit in preference to the crew. After being cast adrift, and enduring immense hardship, the overbearing captain arrived in Timor and was again sent out to collect breadfruit, earning himself the name "Breadfruit Bligh".

Nutrition

Breadfruit is very starchy. It is high in fibre and contains small amounts of vitamin C and folic acid.

Below: Breadfruit

Preparing and Cooking

Breadfruit are normally eaten as a vegetable. When really ripe, they can be eaten raw, but they are more usually cooked. They can be peeled and boiled, roasted or fried like potatoes, or baked whole in the oven.

CARAMBOLAS

Native to Indonesia and the Moluccas, carambolas or star fruit are now widely available in supermarkets. The uncut yellow or pale amber fruit has a waxy skin and is cilindrical in shape, with concave sides and five ridged edges; it resembles an elongated Chinese lantern. When the fruit is sliced crossways, the slices are perfect star shapes, which are wonderful for decorative purposes. Although the fruit often tastes less exciting than it looks, it is refreshing and juicy to eat.

History

Carambolas originated in the Malay Archipelago, between South-East Asia and Australia, but they are now also grown in Africa, Brazil, the West Indies and the United States.

Nutrition

Carambolas are a good source of vitamin C, and contain some potassium, niacin and phosphorus. They provide about 50 kilocalories per 100g/3¾oz.

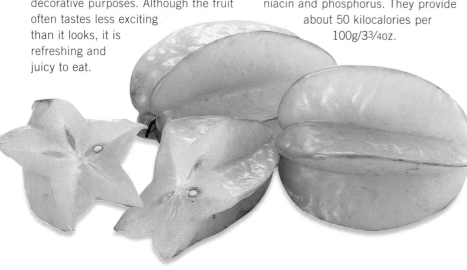

Buying and Storing

Some carambolas have more flavour than others; there is no way of telling before you taste, so they are best used as an attractive decoration or in conjunction with other exotic fruits. Choose firm, undamaged fruits and hope for the best. They will keep in the fridge for up to a week.

Preparing and Serving

A good carambola will be sweet and tangy enough to eat on its own, complete with skin. Slice the fruit crossways and, if you wish, cut out the flat central seeds with a sharp knife. The fruits are generally eaten raw as part of a fruit salad, or made into jams, but they can also be poached in a syrup enlivened with lime juice.

Left: Carambolas make a wonderful garnish. When cut crossways, the slices are perfect star shapes, hence its other name – star fruit.

CHERIMOYAS, CUSTARD APPLES ᴬᴺᴰ SOURSOPS

Native to South America and the West Indies, cherimoyas are the fruit of shrubs belonging to the annona species. The large heart-shaped or oval fruit is made up of many corpels, or concave sections, with scaly yellowish-green or tan skin, rather like a pine cone or a half-prepared globe artichoke. Inside, the fruit has creamy-white, custard-like flesh with a sweet-sour flavour (hence its name) reminiscent of pineapples and bananas, and large black seeds.

Varieties

There are many different varieties of cherimoya, of which custard apples and soursops are the most widely available.
Custard apples These are heart-shaped or oval and can weigh up to 450g/1lb.

Below: Heart-shaped soursops have a tangy, acidic flavour.

They have light tan or greenish quilted skin, which develops brown patches as the fruit ripens; the flesh is particularly mellow and custard-like.
Soursop Also called prickly custard apples or bullock's hearts, soursops are the largest of this group of fruits. They have dark green skins covered in numerous short spines. The white juicy flesh has a tangy, acidic flavour, which gives the fruit its descriptive name. Once ripe, soursops rapidly ferment and become inedible.

Nutrition

Cherimoyas are high in vitamin C and iron, and provide 92 kilocalories per 100g/3¾oz.

Buying and Storing

Cherimoyas are fragile, so choose compact fruit with unblemished skin and tightly packed corpels; once these have separated, the fruit is past its best. Press gently to check that the fruit has a slight "give". Cherimoyas should be eaten as soon as possible after buying, but can be kept in the bottom of the fridge for a day or two. Unripe fruit should be kept in a brown paper bag at room temperature until they are ready to eat.

Preparation and Serving

All types of cherimoya can be eaten fresh. Simply cut the fruit in half

Above: Custard apples have delicious mellow flesh, which is soft – almost like custard (hence their name).

lengthways and scoop the flesh straight from the shell with a spoon, discarding the inedible seeds. For a special treat, add a dollop of cream.

Cherimoya flesh makes a delicious fruit sauce when blended with bananas and cream, or it can be blended with four times its volume of water to make a refreshing drink; stir in sugar to taste. The fruits can also be made into jams, jellies and sorbets.

CURUBA

Also known as the "banana passion fruit", the curuba is like an elongated passion fruit, with soft yellowish skin. The orange pulp has a sharp flavour and needs a little sugar to make it palatable. The skin can be peeled off in the same way as a banana. Curubas marry well with other tropical fruits and can be used in the same way as you would passion fruit.

Right: Curuba have a sharp flavour and can be used like passion fruit.

DATES

Dates are the fruit of the date palm, which grows in sub-tropical and desert areas throughout North Africa, the Arab States, California and Australia. The finger-shaped fruit grows in clusters of several dozen at the top of the tall trees, ripening from green to burnished brown. Date palms are prolific; the average annual yield of a single palm is 50kg/110lb.

Until a few years ago, only dried dates were available outside their native lands, but now fresh dates are exported, although only a few of the many varieties reach the shops.

History

Dates are one of the world's oldest cultivated fruits. It is probable that the Babylonians grew them as long as 8,000 years ago; certainly records show that they have been cultivated for over 5,000 years. In early times, the date palm was regarded as the "tree of life". Every part of it was used; the buds and fruit were eaten or dried and ground into flour, the sap was drunk, the fibres were woven and the date stones were used as fuel or fodder for donkeys and camels. Even today, dates are still known as the "bread of the desert".

Left: Boxed halawi dates.

Above: Date Palms grow throughout North Africa, the Arab States, California and Australia.

The Ancient Greeks and Romans were also fond of dates and often combined them with meat in their cooking.

Varieties

Of the many varieties of date, only a few are exported, and these are seldom sold by name. The most popular variety is the golden brown *deglet noor* ("date of the light") from North Africa and Israel; you may also find the very sweet *halawi* or the fragrant *khaleseh,* which can be recognized by its orange-brown skin. The finest dates are the large crinkly-skinned *medjool* from Egypt and California, whose flesh is intensely mellow and sweet.

Nutrition

Dates are extremely nutritious. They contain more natural sugar than any other fruit and deliver a substantial amount of dietary fibre and potassium, as well as providing many vitamins and mineral salts. They provide 144 kilocalories per 100g/3¾oz.

Buying and Storing

Fresh dates These should be plump and moist, with a smooth skin and a slightly crunchy texture. They are sold loose or in punnets. Dates are ripe when they are burnished brown. Unripe dates are more golden; they can be eaten in this state, but the flesh will be crisp and less honeyed than ripe dates. To ripen, keep the dates at room temperature. Fresh dates can be frozen whole, but check that they have not been previously frozen (they almost always have been).

Semi-dried dates These are sold in a cluster on the stem. They have wrinkled skins and a chewy texture.

Dried dates These are the old familiar Christmas favourites, sticky and intensely sweet, and are often sold sitting on a frilly doily inside a long box decorated with palm trees and camels. Since the advent of fresh dates, their popularity has declined. Dried dates are also sold pressed into blocks for use in cooking. Some oriental supermarkets stock tiny, wrinkled red dates and smoky black dates with the flavour of a bonfire, which are only suitable for cooking. Semi-dried and dried dates will keep for months, but do not store them near strong-smelling foods like onions, as they absorb odours.

Below: Dried deglet noor dates in their familiar long box.

Stuffed dates

1 Cut the dates in half and pick out the stones.

2 Fill the cavities of the dates with cream cheese and sandwich the halves together.

3 Alternatively, mould a little marzipan to fill the cavities, roll the date halves in granulated sugar and top each with a walnut half.

Right: Dried dates pressed into a block. For cooking, this type of date may need to be softened in hot water before using.

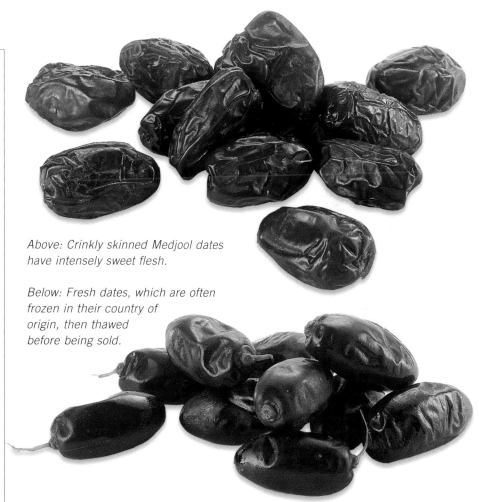

Above: Crinkly skinned Medjool dates have intensely sweet flesh.

Below: Fresh dates, which are often frozen in their country of origin, then thawed before being sold.

Preparation and Cooking

Fresh dates can be eaten just as they are. If you prefer to peel them, gently pinch the skin at the stem end until the fruit pops out. They can be stoned and filled with plain or coloured marzipan or nuts, or rolled in sugar to serve as decorative petits fours.

Fresh dates also make good additions to fruit salads and winter compotes. Surprisingly, they are also good in savoury dishes; in North Africa, they are used in *tagines* (fragrant stews) and curries, or as a sauce or stuffing for fish, meat or poultry.

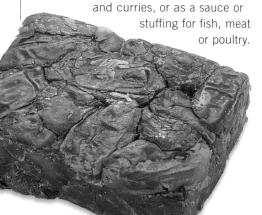

Above: Dried Chinese dates are only suitable for cooking.

Dates have a particular affinity with cheese. Serve them on a cheese board, or halve and stone them and sandwich together with cream cheese.

Dried dates are good in moist cakes and hot sticky puddings, and combine very well with nuts, particularly walnuts and almonds. For cooking, dried dates should be stoned and chopped, using scissors dipped in hot water.

DRAGON FRUIT

Dragon fruit, or pitihayas, come in both yellow and pink versions. Pink dragon fruit are large, fuschia-pink fruit about 10cm/4in long, covered with pointed green-tipped scales, rather like the leaves of a globe artichoke. Inside, they are spectacularly beautiful, with translucent pearly-white flesh dotted with a mass of edible black seeds, which add an appealing crunch. The flesh is sweet and refreshing, with a slightly acidic melon-like flavour. It has the texture of kiwi fruit.

Yellow dragon fruit look more like prickly pears or mini-pineapples. They taste exactly like the pink variety.

Nutrition

Dragon fruit are rich in vitamin C and dietary fibre.

Buying and Storing

Yellow dragon fruit are ripe when golden all over. Both pink and yellow varieties should yield when gently squeezed in the hand. Best eaten as soon as they are ripe, but the fruits can be kept in the fridge for up to three days.

Preparing and Serving

Dragon fruit are best eaten on their own, sprinkled with lemon or lime juice to enhance the flavour. They should be served chilled. Cut them in half lengthways, then scoop out the flesh from the shell. The shells can be used as unusual serving dishes.

Above: Brightly coloured dragon fruit have sweet refreshing flesh.

DURIANS

The disgusting, all-pervading, sewage-like smell is legendary and has given rise to the alternative name: civet fruit. When ripe, the flavour of the flesh, however, is delicious.

Durians are large fruit, which can weigh up to 4.5kg/10lb. Round or oval, they have a woody, olive green outer layer covered with stubby, sharp spikes, which turns yellow as they ripen. They consist of three to five segments containing aromatic creamy-white flesh with the texture of rich custard; the flavour is sweet, a little like strawberries, with a creamy after-taste. The large brown seeds are edible if cooked.

History

Durians originated in Malaysia or Borneo and from there spread to South-East Asia in prehistoric times. Despite their unspeakable smell, they have always been considered an aphrodisiac.

Nutrition

Durians are starchy fruits. They contain a small amount of fat and are a good source of potassium and vitamin C.

Buying and Storing

It is essential to eat durians very fresh; don't attempt to store them, however briefly, or your house will smell of blocked drains. Never buy fruit with damaged skin, or the smell will be

unbearable. Do not buy durians abroad and attempt to bring them home, as they are banned by most airlines! Take care not to drip juice on to clothing or table linen as it stains indelibly. Despite all these dire warnings, don't be put off trying this exotic fruit, it really does taste wonderful.

Preparing and Serving

Durians are best eaten raw. Use a large sharp knife to slit the skin at the segment joints, press out the segments and scoop out the flesh and seeds with a spoon. The rich, custardy flesh can be eaten just as it is, or puréed to make ice cream or milk shakes. Durian flesh is also used for making jam and cakes, and is available canned. The richness of the pulp also makes an excellent foil to hot, spicy foods like curries and chilli dishes. Durian seeds can be roasted or boiled and eaten like nuts.

Left: The horrible, all-pervading sewage-like smell of Durians is legendary, however, when ripe, the flavour of the flesh is delicious.

FEIJOAS

Although a distant member of the guava family, feijoas resemble small slightly pear-shaped passion fruit, with a dark green skin that yellows as the fruit ripens. The thin, tough skin protects a soft jelly-like pulp containing tiny hard seeds, which are edible. Despite its alternative name of "pineapple guava", the feijoa tastes more like an aromatic strawberry. Treat it like guava.

History

Originally from South America, the feijoa takes its name from the Portuguese botanist Dom da Silva Feijoa, who discovered it in Brazil. It is also nowadays cultivated in New Zealand.

Nutrition

Feijoas are an excellent source of vitamin C and are rich in iodine. They provide 20 kilocalories per 100g/3¾oz.

Right: Feijoas taste a little like aromatic fresh strawberries.

GINUP

The bright green dimpled skin of the ginup gives rise to its alternative name of "Spanish lime", but it is related to neither the lime nor the lychee, which it resembles in flavour. Ginups are small round tropical fruits, about 3cm/1¼in in diameter, which grow on trees in bunches like grapes. The tough green skin protects a jelly-like pink pulp containing a large central seed. The flesh is juicy and sweet, with a slightly acidic note. Despite its pale colour, ginup juice stains horribly and if you get it on your clothes or table linen, it will never come out.

GRANADILLAS

Granadillas, or grenadillas, are the largest members of the passion fruit family and can weigh several pounds. In their unripe state, these large specimens are used as vegetables, but they are seldom exported. The granadillas you will find in the shops are smooth, round, orange-skinned fruits, with greyish pulp containing small hard seeds. They look more attractive than passion fruit, but taste less fragrant. Granadillas can be eaten and used in exactly the same way as passion fruit.

Right: Granadillas

GUAVAS

Similar in shape to pears or plums, guavas can be as small as 2.5cm/1in or as large as 10cm/4in in diameter. They have thin, pale green skins, which turn light yellow as they ripen; the flesh varies from white through to deep pink or salmon red. It contains a number of flattish, hard but edible seeds. Guavas are highly scented with an aromatic sweet-acid flavour, not unlike that of quinces.

Guavas are available tinned in syrup and made into sweet fruit drinks.

Varieties

There are several varieties of guava, the most common being the familiar yellow fruit. Strawberry or cherry guavas are smaller, with reddish-purple skins.

Nutrition

Guavas are exceptionally rich in vitamin C and are a good source of niacin, potassium and dietary fibre. They provide 62 kilocalories per 100g/3¾oz.

Preparing and Cooking

Ripe guavas are delicious eaten raw. They can be poached in syrup, but must be simmered gently as the flesh easily disintegrates. The flesh can be puréed to use in ice creams and sorbets, or made into jams and jellies (alone, or with other fruits) or sweet drinks. Like quinces, they have an affinity with apples; a few slices of peeled guava added

Preparing guavas

To eat guavas raw, cut in half and squeeze over a little lime juice. Scoop out the flesh from the skin.

to an apple pie or apple sauce impart a special fragrance.

Guavas can also be used in savoury dishes and are particularly good in a sauce for duck or game birds. They make an interesting addition to salads, and can be stuffed with cream cheese and served as a starter.

Above: Guavas are delicious eaten raw.

JACKFRUIT

Jackfruit are related to breadfruit. The large, irregularly shaped oval fruits can weigh 20kg/44lb, but you will only find smaller specimens in the shops. They have a rough, spiny skin, which ripens from green to brown, and each fruit contains large white edible seeds. Ripe jackfruit have a pungent, musty odour.

History

Jackfruit come originally from the rainforests of India and Malaysia, and are now grown in Asia, Africa, America and Australia.

Preparing and Cooking

Ripe jackfruit can be peeled and eaten raw; the pulp is

sweet and rather bland. They are better boiled, roasted or fried, to be served as a vegetable or in a curry. The seeds can be eaten boiled, fried or roasted like chestnuts.

Below: Jackfruit are huge – they can weigh up to 20kg/44lb.

JAMAICAN PLUMS

Also known as "hoy" or "hog" plums, golden apple, limbu and mombin, this fruit belongs to the same family as the mango and is grown in the West Indies, Central and South America, South-East Asia and India. The golden yellow, to deep red and purple fruits are small, about 4cm/1½in long and 2.5cm/1in in diameter. They grow several to a branch and, like mangoes, have soft skin and contain a large central stone. The firm, yellow flesh, which is juicy, deliciously fragrant and sweet, is more akin to pineapple or apple than mango. The distinctive flavour has a slightly acidic tang. Unfortunately, these fruits are fragile and do not travel well, but you may find them in Indian shops. Jamaican plums can be eaten raw, sweetened with a little brown sugar or sprinkled with rum or liqueur and served with cream. They combine well with other fruits in a fruit salad, and can also be poached, pickled or made into jams, jellies and sorbets. They make a good addition to curries.

Right: Unripe Jamaican plums

JUJUBES

Also known as Chinese jujubes, apples or dates, these small greeny-brown fruits and have been cultivated in Northern China for more than 4,000 years and are now grown extensively in India (where they are known as bec or bor), Asia, Southern Europe and more recently in Northern America and Australia. Jujubes, which ripen in the autumn, can be oblong, egg-shaped or round. They have crisp pearly-white flesh enclosing a single stone, with the sweet flavour and texture of an unripe pear. Most fruits are deep brown when ripe, but can be bought while still firm, but orange-red with just a hint of brown and left at room temperature for a day or two to ripen. They can be eaten raw, stewed with orange juice, candied or made into jams and jellies.

Left: Jujubes

KIWANOS

This strange-looking fruit is also known as horned melon, horned cucumber and jelly melon. The oval fruits have thick, bright golden-orange skin covered in sharp spikes. The skin conceals a bright green, jelly-like flesh encasing edible seeds, rather like a passion fruit, with a subtle taste of cucumber, banana and lime.

History

Originally from Africa, kiwanos are now grown commercially in New Zealand, Portugal and the United States.

Preparing and Cooking

Cut the fruit in half, then spoon the pulp straight from the shell. It makes a refreshing drink or it can be added to fruit salads or cocktails. The shells can be used as serving dishes. Blend the pulp with natural yogurt, honey and vanilla ice cream to make an unusual milk shake.

Right: With their spiky skin, kiwanos resemble strange miniature prehistoric monsters.

KIWI FRUIT

These cylindrical fruit, 7.5–10cm/3–4in in length, are covered with a light brown fuzzy skin, which looks very dull in comparison with the beautiful bright green interior, with its crown of tiny edible black seeds arranged around a white core. The flavour is delicate, yet refreshing and tangy.

History

Kiwi fruit were formerly known as Chinese gooseberries, in recognition of the fact that they originated in the Yangtze Valley. They are now extensively grown in New Zealand, Australia, South America and even Italy and France.

Nutrition

A single kiwi fruit contains more than a day's vitamin C requirement for an adult, plus vitamin E, and provides only 50 kilocalories per 100g/3¾oz.

Buying and Storing

Choose plump, unwrinkled fruit with unblemished skins. Kiwis are ripe when they yield to gentle pressure like a ripe pear; however, hard, unripe fruit can easily be ripened at home. Store at room temperature, but not in a bowl with other fruits, since the enzymes

Right: Kiwi fruit are delicious eaten raw – scoop out the flesh with a teaspoon.

in kiwi fruit cause them to ripen very quickly. Firm, unripe kiwis will keep for several weeks if stored in a cool place.

Preparing and Serving

The skin of a kiwi fruit is edible, but the fuzzy texture is not particularly pleasant, so it is best to peel the fruit with a small sharp knife. For the most attractive effect, slice kiwis horizontally.

When *nouvelle cuisine* was in its heyday, slices of kiwi fruit appeared as a garnish for almost every dish, however inappropriate. Kiwis are certainly decorative, but they are good eaten as a fruit in their own right. They make an attractive addition to fruit salads, open fruit tarts and pavlovas, or can be puréed to make a sorbet or coulis. They go well with

white meats, Parma ham, poultry and fish, especially salmon and shellfish.

Kiwi fruit contain enzymes that make an excellent meat tenderizer. Rub the peeled skin or slices of kiwi into both sides of a cheaper cut of meat and leave for 20 minutes; the meat will become tender enough to grill.

The same enzymes, however, will prevent gelatine from setting and will curdle milk products, so do not attempt to make ice cream with raw kiwi. Cooking destroys the enzymes, but also the delicate flavour and texture.

KUBOS

Looking rather like wine-red guavas, kubos are pear-shaped fruit with thick bitter skin and refreshingly sweet, slightly tangy, creamy-white flesh

spattered with tiny, edible, crunchy black seeds. The texture is a little like that of an unripe pear. To eat, cut the fruit in half lengthways and scoop out

the pulp with a spoon, or spoon the pulp over ice cream. The flesh can be combined with other fruits and makes a good addition to fruit salads.

LONGANS

Distant relatives of the lychee, longans are small, round, undistinguished-looking fruit. The brittle light brown skin encloses translucent, jelly-like flesh around a single large inedible stone.

They taste similar to lychees, but have a pleasant peppery tang. Longans are grown throughout South-East Asia and China where they are particularly popular; the Chinese name means

"dragon's eye". Fresh longans can be peeled and eaten like lychees, on their own or in fruit salads, sweet-and-sour dishes and stir-fries. Oriental food stores sell longans canned in syrup.

LOQUATS

Native to China and South Japan, the loquat is one of the few sub-tropical fruits that belong to the apple and pear family, and is sometimes known as a Japanese medlar. The name comes from the Cantonese *luk-kwyit*, meaning "rush-orange", which describes the colour of the loquat's flesh. The fruits are small and plum-shaped, with apricot-coloured skin and white or yellowy-orange flesh surrounding inedible brown stones. They have a sweet scent and a delicate mango-like flavour, which is greatly enhanced by a squeeze of lime or lemon juice.

Buying and Storing

Ripe loquats are speckled with brown patches; perfect, apricot-like fruit are

Right: Loquats are one of the few sub-tropical fruits that belong to the apple and pear family.

still unripe. These can be ripened at home by being kept in a fruit bowl for a few days.

Preparing and Serving

Loquats can be eaten raw, complete with skin, or poached in a light syrup. They go well with other fruits, like

apples, pears and peaches, and make a wonderful ice cream to accompany these fruits. Loquats make good jams, jellies and chutneys (leave in a few of the seeds to impart a bitter almond flavour); they can also be cooked with brown sugar and wine vinegar to make a sauce for poultry.

LYCHEES

The leathery, scaly, reddish skin or "shell" of the lychee encloses pearly white, translucent flesh that is firm and jelly-like. This sweet, fragrant flesh is wrapped around a large, shiny, inedible brown seed. Canned lychees are on sale

– and are often served as a dessert in Chinese restaurants – but they have none of the fragrance and subtlety of the fresh fruit.

History

Lychees have been cultivated in China for thousands of years. They have been considered a symbol of romance ever since a concubine of one of the Chinese emperors insisted on having teams of horses carry lychees hundreds of miles across country for her pleasure.

Nutrition

Lychees are rich in vitamin C. They provide about 65 kilocalories per 100g/3¾oz.

Buying and Storing

Choose lychees whose shells are as pink or red as possible. Greenish fruits are under-ripe, while brown fruit are

Left: Lychees

past their prime. Although the shells act as protection, lychees quickly dry out, so do not buy too many at a time and eat them as soon as possible after purchase. They will keep in the fridge for up to a week.

Preparing and Serving

Fresh lychees are best eaten raw as a refreshing end to a meal. Diners simply remove the shells, then nibble or suck the flesh off the stones.

Lychees can also be stoned and added to fruit salads, or poached in lemon-scented syrup and served chilled, alone or with ice cream or other poached fruits. For an unusual appetizer, serve stoned fresh lychees stuffed with cream cheese and nuts.

Use these succulent fruits in savoury dishes too – they are good in Chinese sweet-and-sour dishes and also in salads (particularly when combined with avocado). They also make an interesting accompaniment to cold meats like pork and duck.

MANGOES

Among the most delicious and luxurious of all tropical fruits, different varieties of mangoes are grown throughout the Tropics, from the Caribbean to Africa, South-East Asia, Australia and India. Although they come in many different shapes, sizes and colours, mangoes are typically curved oblong fruits with green, pinkish-gold or red skin and glorious orange, highly perfumed flesh surrounding a very large, hairy, inedible flat stone. The meltingly soft flesh is always juicy and sweet, although it sometimes has an acid overtone. Some mangoes have fibrous flesh; others are succulent and buttery. Certain varieties are said to have a flavour of mint, lemon, banana or pineapple, but in reality mangoes have their own distinctive taste, unlike any other fruit.

Below: Mangoes have meltingly soft flesh that is juicy and sweet.

History

The history of the mango goes back over 6,000 years and is closely connected with Hinduism. Buddha was said to have been presented with a mango grove so that he could rest in its shade. Mangoes are native to Malaysia and India, and they form part of the local legend and folklore. The name comes from the Tamil *man-key* ("fruit of the tree"). Nineteenth-century traders introduced the fruit to the West Indies, Africa and South America.

Varieties

There are over 2,500 varieties of mango. They can be round-, oval-, heart- or kidney-shaped and can weigh between 150g/5oz and 675g/1½lb. All mangoes are green when unripe, but some remain green when they ripen, while others turn golden or bright red, or a combination of these colours.

Popular varieties include the **Alphonso** or **Alphonsine** from India, which has supple, buttery flesh and a heady, sweet flavour. West Indian varieties include the small **Julie** and the round, juicy **Bombay**. Cultivated varieties like **Parvin, Kent** and **Tommy Atkins** have thinner skins than wild mangoes and are less fibrous. **Ruby mangoes**, from the Gambia, have an excellent flavour but are rather fibrous. To eat one of these glowing red fruit, squeeze it gently between your hands, then pierce the skin and suck out the juice.

Nutrition

Ripe mangoes are rich in vitamins, especially A and C, and are a good source of beta-carotene. They provide about 59 kilocalories per 100g/3¾oz.

Buying and Storing

Colour is not necessarily an indication of ripeness in a mango; some remain solidly green when ripe. Buy unblemished fruit with no black blotches on the skin, as these indicate that the fruit is over-ripe and will have mushy flesh. The best test of a mango is its aroma, which should be highly perfumed. The fruit should be just yielding when gently pressed.

Mangoes will ripen at home if left in a warm place. To hasten ripening, place them in a brown paper bag with a banana or kiwi fruit. Eat the mangoes as soon as they are ripe.

Canned mangoes Mango slices are available canned in syrup. These are extremely sweet and are best drained before eating. They can be puréed to make a coulis or ice cream.

Above: Parvin

Preparing a mango

1 Place the mango narrow side down on a chopping board. Cut off a thick lengthways slice, keeping the knife as close to the stone as possible. Turn the mango round and repeat on the other side. Cut off the flesh adhering to the stone and scoop out the flesh from the mango slices.

2 To make a "hedgehog", prepare the mango as above and score the flesh on each thick slice with criss-cross lines at 1cm/½ in intervals, taking care not to cut through the skin.

3 Fold the mango halves inside out and serve.

Right: Thin-skinned Tommy Atkins mangoes.

Dried mangoes

These can be added to chutneys and relishes, or mixed with other dried fruits in cake and teabread recipes.

Preparing and Serving

Mangoes are so delicious that they are best savoured in their raw state, perhaps with a squeeze of lime or lemon. The main disadvantage of this is that they are extremely difficult to eat elegantly. Indeed, it is said that the only way to eat them is in the bath. The secret of retaining a modicum of dignity is to remove the stone before attempting to eat the juicy flesh.

Whichever way you cut a mango, some flesh will always be left clinging to the stone. On no account waste this – wait until no one can see you, then cut off the skin and suck the aromatic pulp off the stone for a real treat!

Mangoes make an exotic addition to fruit salads and can be puréed to make sorbets and ice creams. They go well with other tropical flavours, like passion fruit and rum. They are excellent served with cured meats like Parma ham or smoked chicken, and make a refreshing accompaniment to spicy dishes and curries. Prawns or other shellfish combine well with mango.

Ripe mangoes can be mixed with chillies to make a delicious *salsa*, while unripe green fruit are traditionally used to make mango chutney and pickles, which go well with cold meats and curries. In the West Indies and Asia, unripe mangoes are used as a vegetable and are baked or stewed with chicken and meat dishes.

Right: Kent, another of the 2,500 varieties of mango.

MANGOSTEENS

Despite their name, mangosteens have nothing to do with mangoes. Nor are they related to lychees, although their pearly white flesh looks very similar.

Mangosteens are apple-shaped with rather leathery, reddish-brown skin, which is deep purple when ripe. The flesh is divided into five segments, each containing a large seed. The segments are enclosed in dark pink pith, which should be removed before eating. Mangosteens have a sweet, refreshing flavour, rather like that of a plum, but more highly perfumed.

History

Mangosteens are indigenous to South-East Asia. The trees are slow to grow; it is fifteen years before they bear fruit. They are now grown commercially in parts of Thailand, Central America and Australia.

Preparing and Serving

The flavour of mangosteens is too fragrant and delicate to be impaired by cooking. Eat them just as they are, or add to fruit salad. Peeled mangosteens look spectacular surrounded by a ribbon of strawberry or raspberry coulis.

Above: Mangosteens have a highly perfumed flavour. Eat the pearly white fruit segments just as they are, or add them to fruit salad.

Serving a mangosteen

1 Using a small sharp knife, cut the skin around the equator of the shell, then lift off the top half of the shell and spoon out the flesh.

2 Alternatively, cut the mangosteens in half and scoop out the flesh with a spoon.

MARACOYAS

Also known as yellow passion fruit, maracoya is a largish fruit with vibrant green, thick shiny skin that turns yellow as it ripens. Inside is a mass of translucent orange pulp enclosing hard grey seeds, just like a passion fruit, but sharper and less aromatic. Use in exactly the same way as passion fruit, adding plenty of sugar.

Right: Maracoyas

PASSION FRUIT

Passion fruit takes its name from its exotic flower, which is said to symbolize the Passion of Christ. Native to the Americas, these round or oval fruits have a leathery purplish-brown skin (some, like those from Brazil, are yellow in colour), which wrinkles when the fruits are fully ripe. Inside, the edible seeds are surrounded by intensely fragrant, translucent, greenish-orange pulp with a distinctive sour-sweet flavour and a wonderful scent. The fruits can be as small as a cherry or as large as an orange, but the ones most commonly available in the shops are about 7.5cm/3in long.

Left: Passion fruit

Nutrition

The fruits contain vitamins A and C and are a good source of dietary fibre. They contain 34 kilocalories per 100g/3¾oz.

Buying and Storing

Choose fruit that feel heavy for their size, with firm, slightly wrinkled skins. Very wrinkly passion fruit with extremely dark skins will have dried out. Passion fruit can be ripened at room temperature; do not keep them in the fridge. The pulp can be frozen in ice cube trays, then packed into plastic bags. The juice is sold in cartons.

Preparing and Serving

The simplest way to eat passion fruit is on its own; cut the fruit in half and scoop out the pulp and seeds with a spoon. Both are edible, but the pulp can be sieved to make a smooth coulis or refreshing drink. Passion fruit enhances the flavour of all other fruits and makes a delicious topping for a pavlova or cheesecake.

Sieved pulp can be made into ice creams and sorbets, or added to yogurt. Passion fruit jelly goes well with roast meats, or it can be spread on bread or toast. The juice makes an excellent marinade for rich meats like venison and game birds.

PAPAYAS

The papaya, or paw-paw, is native to tropical America, but it is now grown in most tropical or sub-tropical regions of the world. The large pear-shaped fruits grow to about 20cm/8in in length. Some varieties remain green when ripe, but most turn deep yellow or orange. Papayas have beautiful deep salmon-pink flesh, with an abundance of grey-black seeds in the central cavity, which are edible. The soft, juicy, sweet flesh tastes like a cross between melons and peaches.

Right: Papayas

Nutrition

Papayas are rich in vitamin A and calcium, and contain large quantities of the enzyme papain, which breaks down protein and can be used to tenderize meat. Papain also makes these fruit very easy to digest. They provide about 45 kilocalories per 100g/3¾oz.

Buying and Storing

Choose uniformly yellow fruit. Sniff them; they should have a delicate scent. Papayas bruise easily, so do not buy any with damaged or shrivelled skins. If the fruit is not ripe, check the skin around the stem end; it should be yellow, otherwise the papaya will never ripen. Ripe papayas should be eaten immediately. Fruit that is not quite ripe should be left at room temperature until soft and yellow. The flesh can be cubed or puréed and frozen.

Preparing and Serving

Simply cut the papaya in half lengthways and scoop out the seeds from the cavity. You can eat them (they have a peppery flavour), but they are not particularly pleasant. Squeeze a little lime or lemon juice on the flesh before serving.

Papayas can be used in the same way as melons, served solo with a good squeeze of lime, or sprinkled with ground ginger and served with cured meats like Parma ham or smoked chicken. The cubed flesh can be added to fruit salads, piled on top of pavlovas, made into ice creams and sorbets, or served with yogurt and preserved ginger. It also goes well with savoury dishes like seafood and chicken curries. Finely chopped papaya is perfect with chillies in a fresh *salsa*. The skins can be used to tenderize cheaper cuts of meat. The papain, however, prevents gelatine from setting, so do not attempt to make a fruit jelly, cold soufflé or mousse with papaya.

Slightly unripe papayas can be used in salads, while fruit that is still hard is ideal for relishes and chutneys. Large fruit can be stuffed like marrows and baked as a vegetable dish.

PERSIMMONS

Persimmons, also known as "kaki" or "date" plums, arouse strong feelings. People either love them or loathe them. When fully ripe these fruits, which originated in Japan, are exceptionally beautiful; the name means "food of the Gods". They resemble large orange tomatoes, but have a wide, pale brown calyx and translucent, inedible skin. At their best, they have very sweet, honeyed flesh; unripe persimmons, however, are almost inedible, horribly sour and astringent.

Nutrition

Persimmons, rich in vitamin A, yield potassium, calcium and iron. They contain about 30 kilocalories per 100g/3¾oz.

To dry persimmons

Peel the fruit, leaving the calyxes and stems intact. Arrange on a rack over a baking sheet and dry in a very low oven. The sugar which is naturally present in the persimmons will crystallize on the outside. Dried persimmons taste like a mixture of dried figs, prunes and dates. They can be used in place of these fruits and added to cakes and puddings.

Above: Persimmon

Buying and Storing

Persimmons should be plump and extremely soft and pulpy, with undamaged skins. A perfect specimen will look as though it is about to burst, but this is exactly as it should be. Handle with great care and eat immediately, or store briefly in the bottom of the fridge. To ripen, place in a brown paper bag with a banana.

Preparing and Cooking

The fruit are best eaten raw; slice off the top and spoon out the flesh. Serve with cream or yogurt, use to make mousses, custards and ice creams or purée the flesh to make a sauce for ham, pork and game. Slightly unripe fruit can be poached in syrup or peeled and cooked like apple sauce.

Sharon fruit

Developed in the Sharon Valley in Israel, this non-astringent variety of persimmon can be eaten while still firm and does not require peeling. Sharon fruit are less highly flavoured than persimmons, and benefit from a squeeze of lemon or lime juice, but are treated in much the same way. They can be added to salads and make an attractive garnish for avocado vinaigrette.

PEPINOS

This beautiful fruit, with its smooth golden skin heavily streaked with purple, is sometimes called a "tree melon". Native to Peru, the pepino is a relative of the tomato, potato and aubergine family (*Solanacae*), but looks rather like a melon. The pale yellow flesh is quite tart, with a flavour suggestive of lemon, pineapple and melon. The sweet seeds of this fruit are edible.

Nutrition

Pepino fruits are rich in vitamin C, and also yield some vitamin A. They contain about 25 kilocalories per 100g/3¾oz.

Preparing and Serving

Pepinos can be peeled and eaten raw, but they are best poached with sugar or honey to counteract their acidity. Serve the fruit like melon, add pepino cubes to fruit salad or serve with vanilla ice cream.

Right: Pepinos

PHYSALIS

Sometimes also known as "Cape gooseberries", physalis are distantly related to tomatoes, peppers, aubergines and potatoes, although you would never guess this by looking at them. The small, orange-gold berries are encased in a papery beige husk, similar to a Chinese lantern. They have a rather tart, mildly scented flavour reminiscent of a ripe dessert gooseberry with a hint of strawberry.

History

Although physalis are native to South America, the fruits seem to have been known to the Greeks as early as the third century AD. Physalis were introduced to England in the eighteenth century, but did not become popular until two centuries later. The early settlers in South Africa cultivated physalis in the Cape of Good Hope, which gave rise to their common name, Cape gooseberries.

Preparing and Serving

Physalis are delicious eaten raw; the inedible papery husk is simply peeled back and used as a "handle", leaving the luscious berries free to be devoured as they are or dipped in fondant icing or melted chocolate. As such, they are very popular as petits fours and make attractive decorations for cheesecakes, pavlovas and gâteaux.

Physalis can also be cooked – they make the most delicious-tasting jams and jellies.

Above: Physalis

Dipping physalis in fondant icing

1 Peel back the papery husk like petals and fold into "wings".

2 Holding each physalis by the husk, dip into warm fondant icing.

3 Transer to a plate lined with non-stick baking paper and leave to cool.

PINEAPPLES

Pineapples are probably the most recognizable of all fruit. In fact, they are multiple fruits consisting of dozens of lozenge-shaped protuberances, each one being the fruit of a single flower, which together make up a single pineapple. Resembling a large pine cone topped with a spiky grey-green plume of leaves, a whole pineapple makes a spectacular addition to a fruit platter. The warm, distinctive aroma of the fruit is also very pleasing.

Pineapples are very versatile fruit, their sweet, acidic taste lending itself to sweet and savoury dishes.

History

Native to South and Central America, pineapples had been cultivated for centuries before Christopher Columbus discovered them on his voyage to the West Indies in 1493. Astonished by the extraordinary appearance and flavour of the fruit, he brought some back to Europe, where they were regarded with wonder and awe. Due to their rarity and high cost, they became a symbol of hospitality, and stone pineapples often featured on the gateposts of houses to welcome guests.

The first pineapples, ripened in glasshouses, were presented to Louis XV of France, whose passion for the fruit made them even more highly prized. Pineapples are now grown in every tropical region of the world.

Varieties

There are hundreds of pineapple varieties, ranging from very large to miniature fruits. They are seldom sold by name, although **Sweet Gold** is becoming familiar in some stores and markets. The colour of the skin varies from orange to greenish-yellow, while the degree of juiciness and sweetness depends upon the season.

Nutrition

Pineapples, which are rich in both vitamin C and dietary fibre, provide about 46 kilocalories per 100g/3¾oz. They contain bromelain, an enzyme that aids digestion, so are the perfect

Above: Crystallized pineapple

Left: Large, small and baby pineapples

Making pineapple wedges with plumes

1 Place the fruit upright, hold it firmly and slice it in half vertically with a sharp serrated knife, cutting down through the plume into the flesh. Cut each piece in half again to make four wedges.
2 Run a small sharp knife between the rind and flesh. Slice off the core on each wedge, then slice the fruit into neat pieces, leaving these in place.

fruit to finish a rich meal. The enzyme breaks down protein so can be used to tenderize meat, but will prevent gelatine from setting.

Buying and Storing

Choose a plump pineapple that feels heavy for its size, with a fresh, stiff plume. To test for ripeness, gently pull out one of the bottom leaves; it should come out easily. Avoid lifeless-looking, bruised or withered fruit with browning leaves. Use the fruit as soon as possible after purchase. Do not store whole pineapples in the fridge, although peeled, sliced or cubed pineapple can be chilled in an airtight container for up to three days. Fresh, peeled and sliced pineapple is available and should also be kept chilled.
Dried and crystallized pineapple Both can be eaten as a snack or used to make cakes and puddings.
Canned pineapple Chunks and rings are available in syrup or juice. They are useful store cupboard items, but lack the aromatic flavour of fresh pineapple. Crushed pineapple is also available.

Preparing and Cooking

Pineapples are delicious on their own, served in wedges or rings. Some people like to add a splash of Kirsch, but a good pineapple should need no enhancement (although, surprisingly, a grinding of black pepper does wonders for the flavour). They go very well with other fruits; a hollowed-out pineapple shell complete with plume makes a spectacular container for fruit salad or tropical fruit sorbets.

Sliced pineapple can be made into a variety of hot desserts. Sauté in butter and brown sugar, make crisp fritters or combine with other fruits on skewers to make grilled fruit kebabs.

Tropical flavours, such as ginger, vanilla, cinnamon, allspice, coconut and rum go extremely well with pineapple. Perhaps the most famous combination of pineapple, coconut and rum is the pina colada cocktail.

Pineapples' refreshing sweet-sour flavour makes them perfect for savoury dishes and they are often used in Chinese cooking. Traditionally, pineapple is cooked with gammon and pork, but it also goes well with lamb, poultry and fish, particularly in spicy dishes and curries.

Below: Dried pineapple can be eaten as a snack or chopped to use in cake and pudding recipes.

Peeling a pineapple

1 Cut the pineapple across into slices of the desired width.

2 Use a small, sharp knife to cut off the rind.

3 Hold each slice upright and cut out the "eyes".

4 Remove the central core of each slice with an apple corer.

POMEGRANATES

This attractive, apple-shaped fruit has leathery reddish-gold skin and a large calyx or crown. Inside is a mass of creamy-white edible seeds, each encased in a translucent sac of deep pink or crimson pulp and held together by segments of bitter, inedible, yellow membrane that extend outwards to the skin. These seeds gave the fruit its name, which means "grain apple". Eating a pomegranate is quite hard work, as each fleshy seed must be picked out individually, but their delicate, slightly tart flavour and refreshing, juicy texture make the effort worthwhile. Be warned, however, that pomegranate juice stains indelibly.

History

Originally from Persia, pomegranates have been linked with many cultures and religions for centuries and have been a symbol of fertility since ancient times because of their numerous seeds. Venus, the goddess of Love, was said to have given pomegranates as presents to her favourites.

Until the Renaissance, pomegranates were used mainly for medicinal purposes in Europe, although they have always featured in the cooking of Middle Eastern countries. Nowadays, they are widely cultivated, from France, Spain and Israel to America and all over Asia.

Nutrition

Pomegranate seeds are rich in vitamin C and are a good source of dietary fibre. They provide about 72 kilocalories per 100g/3¾oz.

Buying and Storing

A pomegranate that feels heavy for its size is likely to be full of juice. Choose glossy fruit and avoid those whose skin looks hard and dry. They will keep in the fridge for up to a week. Dried pomegranate seeds are used in Middle Eastern cooking.

Preparing and Serving

If you have the patience, pomegranates are fun to eat raw; cut them open and pick out the seeds with a pin. Either suck out the juice and discard the

Below: Inside pomegranates is a mass of seeds, each encased in deep pink pulp.

Preparing a pomegranate

1 Cut off a thin slice from one end.

2 Stand the fruit upright. Cut downwards through the skin at intervals, using a small sharp knife.

3 Bend back the segments and use your fingers to push the seeds into a bowl.

4 Remove all the bitter pith and membrane.

Extracting pomegranate juice
Heat the fruit for 30 seconds on High in a microwave, then roll gently on the work surface to burst the seeds. Make a hole in the bottom, stand over a jug and let the juice drain out, squeezing the pomegranate occasionally. Another method is to put the seeds in a sieve set over a bowl and crush gently with the back of a ladle or wooden spoon.

seeds or eat the jelly-like cells, seeds and all. The seeds make a decorative addition to fruit salads and can be used as a pretty topping for creamy desserts, ice cream or cheesecake. They have a particular affinity with almonds and make a jewel-like garnish for couscous. In India and Pakistan, the seeds are used in meat dishes.

Pomegranate juice Extract the juice very gently, using a hand-held lemon squeezer; electric or mechanical juicers will crush the seeds and make the juice bitter. The juice is delicious in refreshing long drinks, such as pomegranate-flavoured lemonade, or it can be used to make a syrup to colour and flavour alcoholic drinks and cocktails. Commercially produced pomegranate syrup is called *grenadine*.

The juice can also be used for sorbets and sauces, and makes a delicious pink jelly for savoury dishes, particularly those from the Middle East. Use it to marinate pheasant, turkey or chicken, or to make a sauce for chicken or turkey, which can then be garnished with pomegranate seeds.

PRICKLY PEARS

Sometimes known as "Indian figs", prickly pears are the fruit of a cactus. They certainly live up to their name, the skin being covered in tiny, painful prickles. Prickly pears are generally 7.5cm/3in long, with greenish-orange skin and orangey-pink flesh with a melon-like texture. The flavour is sweet and aromatic. The small seeds can be eaten raw, but become hard when they are cooked.

Buying and Storing

Prickly pears are orangey-yellow when ripe. Choose unblemished fruit and ripen it at room temperature if necessary.

Preparing and Cooking

Prickly pears are usually peeled and eaten raw with a squeeze of lime or lemon and perhaps a little cream.

Prickly pears go well with other fruit and are good in fruit salads. They can be made into jams or mixed with oranges to make an unusual marmalade. Mix raw sieved pulp with ginger to make a sauce for gammon or cooked ham, or serve slices of prickly pear instead of melon with cured meats like Parma ham. Try adding stewed prickly pear segments to a fruit compote, or make a sauce or ice cream with the sieved purée. Candied or crystallized slices of prickly pear can be used to decorate cakes and desserts.

Right: Prickly pears have a sweet and aromatic flavour.

Preparing prickly pears

1 The prickles are usually removed before the fruits are sold, but if not, wearing gloves, scrub each fruit with a stiff brush.

2 Using a sharp knife, cut a thin slice from each end of the prickly pear, then make a shallow cut just through the skin from end to end on either side of the fruit.

3 Peel off the skin.

RAMBUTANS

Rambutans are related to lychees and are sometimes known as "hairy lychees". Originally from Malaysia, but now grown in tropical Central America and South-East Asia, they are larger than lychees (about 5cm/2in in diameter) and look quite different, but have a similar texture. The taste is similar, too, but slightly sharper. Rambutans resemble small hairy animals, their reddish-brown leathery skins being covered with soft curly spines or hairs.

Preparing and Serving

Rambutans can be used in exactly the same way as lychees. To prepare, cut around the equator of the rambutan with a sharp knife, penetrating the skin only. Lift off the top half of the skin, leaving the fruit on the half shell, like an egg in a (rather hairy) egg cup. They can be added to fruit salads, served with ice cream (coffee ice cream is particularly compatible) or made into jams or jellies, but are best eaten on their own. For an unusual appetizer, wrap peeled and stoned rambutans in Parma ham and serve speared on cocktail sticks. Rambutans are also available canned in syrup.

Above: Rambutans

SAPODILLAS

The unprepossessing appearance of this drab oval fruit from Central America belies its delicious taste, which resembles that of vanilla-flavoured banana custard. Inside the rough, light brown skin of the ripe fruit, the honey-coloured flesh is sweet and luscious, with a core containing inedible, hard black pips.

Right: Sapodillas are sweet and luscious – like vanilla-flavoured banana custard.

Buying and Storing

Ripe sapodillas should have wrinkled brown skins and "give" slightly when pressed. Unripe fruit has smooth skin with a greenish tinge. Avoid this – unripe fruit is full of tannin and the flesh is unpleasantly grainy and mouth-puckeringly unpalatable. Instead, leave the fruit to ripen for up to a week in a fruit bowl. Ripe sapodillas can be kept in the fridge for up to a month.

Preparing and Serving

Sapodillas can be eaten just as they are – simply cut them in half, scoop out the flesh and discard the pips. A squeeze of lime or lemon enhances the flavour. The flesh can be mashed and stirred into cream or custard, or made into ice creams, fools and mousses. It can be added to cakes and teabreads and makes an unusual pancake filling. Mix puréed sapodilla flesh with home-made mayonnaise or lime vinaigrette to make a sauce or dressing to be served with cold fish or chicken.

The milky sap of the sapodilla tree is used to make chicle gum, the main component of chewing gum.

SNAKE FRUIT

Also known as salak, this large member of the lychee family acquired its nickname from its beautifully patterned scaly brown snake-like skin. The creamy flesh is divided into four segments, each enclosing a very large inedible brown stone. The flesh is denser and less juicy than a lychee and has a distinctive apple flavour. Although the hard shells protect the fruit, the flesh quickly dries out, so eat them as soon as possible after purchase.

Snake fruit can be peeled and eaten just as they are, or added to fruit salads. They are delicious poached in a light lemon- or vanilla-scented syrup and served chilled, alone or with vanilla ice cream or sorbet as a refreshing end to a meal.

Right: Snake fruit – so named because the patterned, scaly brown shell resembles snake skin.

TAMARILLOS

Also known as "tree tomatoes", tamarillos look like large egg-shaped tomatoes with thick, smooth, wine-red skins. Each fruit has two lobes containing a multitude of black seeds.

Buying and Storing

Tamarillos with a greenish tinge will be unripe. Ripe fruit is bright purplish or orangey-red and is soft to the touch. The fruit will keep in the fridge for several days.

Preparing and Cooking

Tamarillos can only be eaten raw when they are completely ripe. At this stage the flavour is tangy, sweet and sour, while unripe fruit has a quite unpleasant tannin taste.

To enjoy tamarillos at their best, cut them in half, sprinkle with a little sugar and leave overnight in the fridge. The next day, scoop out the chilled pulp with a spoon. Do not attempt to eat the skin, which is horribly bitter. Remove it by plunging the fruit into boiling water for about a minute, then slipping it off, or peel the fruit with a sharp vegetable peeler or knife.

Raw tamarillos can be used in fruit salads or puréed and made into jam and ice cream. They can be stewed or dredged with brown sugar and grilled. They make excellent chutney and a delicious sweet-sour sauce to go with fish or poultry.

Above: Tamarillos are members of the same family as tomatoes, aubergines and potatoes.

MELONS, GRAPES, FIGS AND RHUBARB

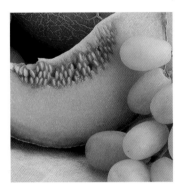

Some fruits are in a class of their own. Melons, grapes and figs have little in common, apart from the fact that they are all fruits, and rhubarb cannot even lay claim to that characteristic: it is technically a vegetable. Without these treasures, however, the food world would be a poorer place. Melons are the cool fruits, grapes the sybarites' choice, figs the sweetest treats and rhubarb the perfect excuse for custard!

MELONS

Sweet melons are members of a large family of fruits and vegetables which grow on trailing vines and include cucumbers, squashes and marrows. They come in a huge number of varieties (possibly thousands) and range in size from a single portion to melons which are large enough to provide a dozen servings. They have a hard, often beautifully patterned rind and very juicy, refreshing flesh enclosing a central cavity filled with a large number of pale, pointed, edible seeds.

History

Melons originated in Africa or Asia and have been known in China for at least 3,000 years. These early melons were bitter, rather like cucumbers, and could not be eaten raw. Hybridization resulted in sweeter fruits, which the Moors brought to Spain from Persia or Africa. They were taken to Italy, and by the fifteenth century reached France, where they were propagated

enthusiastically by the Avignon popes. Christopher Columbus took melons to the New World; when his men had eaten the fruit, they discarded the seeds, which produced large melon crops. These popular fruits are now grown in most warm parts of the world.

Varieties

Melons fall into two main categories – summer fruit, which includes all those varieties with cross-hatched skin that looks like brown netting, and winter melons, which have smooth or finely ridged pale or bright yellow rind and delicate, pale flesh, which can be rather lacking in taste.

Summer melons

Cantaloupe This summer melon takes its name from the Italian town of Cantalupo near Rome, where the fruits were grown in profusion on the papal estate. Most cantaloupes are slightly elongated with craggy pale green or golden rinds, marked into segments, and have aromatic orangey-yellow flesh.

Charentais Charentais have smooth, grey-green rinds and very fragrant orange flesh. A ripe charentais gives off a heady, delicious aroma. Most charentais melons are grown around Cavaillon in France, and are sometimes sold under this name. The French writer Alexandre Dumas so loved these melons that he offered the municipality of Cavaillon all his published and future works in exchange for a life annuity of twelve melons a year.

Galia A relative of the Ogen, Galia is a round melon with a raised pattern of fine netting on the skin. The skin turns from green to golden as it ripens, and the fragrant flesh is green and juicy.

Musk melons These summer melons, also known as "nutmeg" melons, are round or oval, with a raised pattern of lacy netting on the rind. The skins can be green or orange, and the sweet, highly aromatic flesh ranges from orangey-pink to pale green. They take their name from the Romans' habit of sprinkling the fruit with powdered musk to accentuate the flavour. Musk melons are often hothouse-grown.

Ogen A hybrid developed in Israel, this Cantaloupe melon has a smooth pale green skin, marked with green or orange lines, which turns golden when the fruit is ripe. The juicy flesh is sweet and aromatic.

Pineapple or **khoob melons** These large oval melons have orangey-yellow netted skin and beautiful, juicy orange flesh, which has the aroma and faint flavour of pineapple.

Above: Ein d'Or, one of the winter melons, has golden skin and delicately flavoured flesh.

Winter melons

In addition to the winter melons listed below, there are the golden **Ein d'Or** and the **Piel de Sapo,** with rough-ridged, dark green skin and green-to-orange flesh. Its name means "toad's skin".

Casaba is a walnut-shaped melon with ridged, deep yellow skin and pale creamy flesh.

Crenshaws are pointed at the stem end and have smooth golden skins. They have the best flavour of all winter melons, with sweet juicy salmon-pink flesh and a pleasantly scented aroma.

Honeydew is the most common winter melon. Sadly, its name is often more flavoursome than its taste.

Watermelons *See separate entry below.*

Nutrition

Melons have a very high water content, so are low in calories (30 kilocalories per 100g/3¾oz). The more orange the flesh, the more beneficial carotenes it contains.

Left: The aromatic orangey-yellow flesh of Cantaloupes is delicious served with cured meats.

Buying and Storing

Melons should feel heavy for their size and give off a pleasant, sweet aroma; they should not smell too musky, as this is a sign that they are over-ripe. Gently press the stalk end with your thumb; it should "give" slightly, but check that the fruit has not started to rot. The rind should be thick and unblemished with a good colour for its type.

To ripen a melon, keep it at room temperature. Ripe melons are best kept in a cool, airy place. The fridge is fine, but wrap the melon in clear film or a polythene bag first, or the smell will permeate other foods. Melon balls or cubes can be frozen in rigid containers for up to three months, either as they are or in a light syrup.

Preparing and Serving

Aromatic ripe melons are best eaten raw, on their own, in a fruit salad (use the melon shell as a container) or as an hors d'oeuvre with Parma ham or salami. Melons can be served in long slices, balls or cubes. They should always be chilled. A sprinkling of salt and pepper or ground ginger enhances the flavour. Small round varieties can be halved horizontally, seeded and served as they are or with a filling like raspberry coulis or ice cream. They can also be filled with port, although purists frown on this practice. For single-portion melons, cut off a lid and scoop out the seeds. Always scoop out melons into a sieve set over a bowl to catch all the juice. The seeds can be dried and roasted in the oven to make a delicious snack.

Melon goes well with sweet or savoury ingredients. It makes a refreshing salad if mixed with cucumber and tossed in lemon juice, a light cream cheese or

Above: Piel de Sapo – its name means "toad's skin".

Left: Galia melons are fragrant and juicy.

yogurt dressing, or a vinaigrette made with lemon juice. Add cubes of blue cheese, such as Cambozola or Dolcelatte. Melon cubes also enhance cold chicken, prawns and other seafood bound in a light mayonnaise.

For the simplest and prettiest of desserts, scoop out balls of different-coloured melon flesh (white, yellow, orange – perhaps even red watermelon), pile into a glass bowl and serve chilled, with a sprinkling of sugar if needed and a decoration of mint sprigs or nasturtium flowers. Melons make very refreshing sorbets, fools, mousses and ice creams. Spiced with pieces of preserved ginger, they also make excellent jams.

Chunks of melon can be made into a cool pickle that goes well with hot and cold meats or cold ham and poultry. The rind can also be pickled; remove the hard, outer, coloured layer of rind, leaving the white inner rind.

Preparing melons for serving

1 If the melons are small, either cut off the lids or cut the melons in half, then scoop out the seeds into a sieve set over a bowl. Pour any juice from the bowl back into the melons; serve them plain or with a filling of other fruit like strawberries and raspberries.

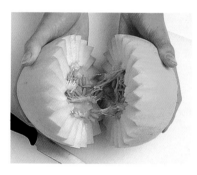

2 For a prettier effect, "vandyke" the melon. Make a 2.5cm/1in diagonal cut where you want the lid to be. Turn the knife and cut down on the opposite diagonal to make an inverted V. Continue to cut zig-zags all round the fruit in this way, then lift off the lid. Remove the seeds.

3 For melon slices, cut a large melon in half lengthways. Scoop out the seeds and cut the melon into long wedges.

4 To make melon "boats", slice the melon as in step 3. Run a flexible knife between the melon rind and flesh to release the flesh. Slice the flesh on the rind into 2cm/¾in chunks. Push alternate chunks in opposite directions to give a staggered effect.

*Above:
Honeydew melons*

WATERMELONS

Watermelons are huge round or oval fruits that weigh up to 12kg/26½lb – much larger than sweet melons. They have solid dark green or paler striped skins, and vibrant pink or red flesh studded with large, flat, black, edible seeds. The flesh is very watery, and can taste rather insipid, but a slice of chilled watermelon is one of the most refreshing experiences imaginable.

History

Watermelons are thought to have originated in India, but may have come from tropical Africa. They were enjoyed by the Ancient Egyptians, but were unknown in Europe until the thirteenth century. They became a symbol of the martyrdom of San Lorenzo in Italy; every year on August 10th in Florence, the patron saint of cooks is celebrated with an orgy of watermelon-eating.

Varieties

Smaller varieties of watermelon are now available, weighing from 2.5–4.5kg/ 5½–10lb. These include **Sugar Baby,** a particularly sweet, round variety with very dark green skin and red flesh. **Tiger** has a paler green skin, striped with yellow or green, as its name suggests. **Golden watermelons** have bright yellow flesh and a more delicate (or dull) flavour than the red-fleshed varieties. They do, however, look very pretty when mixed with red watermelons.

Nutrition

The high water content of watermelons means that they are low in calories; only 30 kilocalories per 100g/3¾oz. They contain some vitamins B and C.

Buying and Storing

Watermelons should be firm and evenly coloured and feel heavy. Tap them with your knuckles; they should not sound hollow. The side where the melon has rested should be yellowish, not white or green. Watermelons are usually sold cut into wedges. Do not buy those with faded flesh, or with white seeds; these are unripe. Whole and cut watermelons can be wrapped in clear film and kept in the fridge for at least a week.

Preparing and Serving

Watermelons are generally cut into wedges and eaten on their own as a thirst-quencher. Cubes or balls make an attractive addition to fruit salads and melon medleys, and they can be made into sorbets (add plenty of lemon for flavour). In some African countries, unripe watermelons are prepared like marrows as a vegetable dish. The rind can be pickled, and is sometimes candied. The seeds can be toasted and eaten (discard the outer shell).

Left: Tiger watermelons are – as the name suggests – striped.

GRAPES

These best known of all vine fruits grow in pendulous bunches on a stalk. The skins can be green, pale yellow, purple, bluish or red; green grapes are known as "white" and purple as "black". Some grapes have a bloom; others have almost waxy skins. Inside, the pulp is translucent and usually contains a few pips, although there are several varieties of seedless grapes.

Some varieties are grown as dessert or table grapes, others are cultivated exclusively for wine-making. Some varieties are also grown for drying into raisins, currants and sultanas. Generally speaking, table grapes are not used for wine-making and vice versa, but there are one or two dual-purpose varieties.

History

Grapes are among the oldest cultivated fruits and were known to man long before Noah planted his vineyard on Mount Ararat. Wild grapes were already established in the Caucasus in the Stone Age, and it was not long before man discovered

Right: Alphonse Lavalle grapes are firm and crisp to eat.

how to ferment them into wine. It is certain that the Ancient Egyptians made wine, although they used it for temple rituals rather than social drinking. The Ancient Greeks and Romans, however, were enthusiastic consumers of wine and grapes and planted a huge number of vineyards. They also learnt the technique of drying the fruit.

It was the Gauls who first put wine into wooden casks and later medieval monks became expert wine-makers. They also pressed grapes into *verjus,* a sour liquid resembling vinegar. In nineteenth-century England, the Victorians were hugely enthusiastic about grapes and cultivated magnificent specimens in hothouses. At the same time, in France, a *uvarium* or grape spa offered medicinal and slimming cures consisting entirely of grapes.

Varieties

A wide variety of table grapes is available, both seedless and seeded,

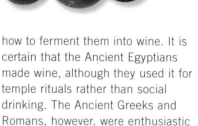

Left: Red and white grape juice is refreshing to drink on its own, or topped up with fizzy mineral water.

the finest by far being **Muscat.** Seedless grapes contain less tannin than the seeded fruit and are easier to eat. The main varieties are listed below.

WHITE GRAPES

Italia The nearest inexpensive alternative to Muscat grapes, Italia are very large, roundish, seeded fruit with greenish-yellow skins and a luscious musky flavour.

Perlette Small, seedless, thin-skinned grapes with a rather tart flavour.

Sultana These small, elongated grapes with thin, greenish-gold, bloomy skins and sweet, juicy pulp grow in compact conical bunches. The varieties Perlette and Thompson are both hybrids of Sultana.

Thompson Seedless Medium-sized elongated fruit with thin, bloomy skins and very sweet, juicy pulp.

BLACK GRAPES

Alphonse Lavalle These large, round, seeded grapes grow in a compact bunch. They have thick, purplish-black skin, with firm, crisp pulp.

Cardinal Large oval fruit with reddish-purple skin and firm, fleshy pulp, which can sometimes lack flavour. They grow in large, unevenly shaped bunches.

Flame Seedless A smallish grape with thin, wine-red skin and very sweet, juicy pulp. These are mostly grown in Chile.

Napoleon The thick, dark purple skin on these large grapes has a heavy white bloom. The flesh is particularly sweet, although not very juicy.

MUSCAT GRAPES

Without doubt, these are the king of grapes, with a wonderful perfumed flavour, almost like nectar. The very best are hothouse-grown and are displayed in shops cocooned in padded paper to preserve their beautiful bloom. All Muscats are large; the white varieties are pale green or golden, while black Muscats can be either red or black. The best Muscat grape of all is the white **Chasselas,** whose skin turns almost bronze when ripe.

Muscat grapes are used for making sweet Muscat dessert wines, which encapsulate the honeyed flavour of the grapes.

Nutrition

Grapes are highly nutritious, containing natural sugars, potassium, iron and dietary fibre. They provide about 80 kilocalories per 100g/3¾oz.

Buying and Storing

Now that grapes are available all year round, many are sold under-ripe. The best way to judge a bunch of grapes is to taste a stray fruit; there is nearly always one that has fallen off the bunch. A perfect bunch of grapes should be of equal size and shape, with the bloom still on. White grapes should have a golden or amber tinge; avoid any

Right: Black Muscat grapes can either be black (as here) or red.

Below: Wonderfully perfumed, White Muscat are the king of grapes.

Left: Italia grapes, which can be green (as here) or black, have a luscious musky flavour and are the nearest inexpensive alternative to Muscat grapes.

Peeling and de-seeding grapes

1 Put the grapes in a heatproof bowl and pour over enough boiling water to cover. Leave for about 20 seconds.

2 Drain off the hot water, rinse the grapes in cold water, then peel off the skins with your fingers.

3 Cut each grape in half and pick out the pips with the tip of a sharp knife.

Right: Grown mostly in Chile, rich-coloured Flame seedless grapes are sweet and juicy, with thin easy-to-eat skins.

Above: Immensely popular, Thompson seedless grapes are very sweet, with thin bloomy skins.

that are uniformly vivid green. Black varieties should not be tinged with green. It is easier to spot over-ripe grapes, as they will fall off the bunch and often show traces of browning or mould. Do not buy wrinkled grapes, or bunches with tiny specimens attached; these will be very sour.

Store grapes in a bowl in a cool, dry place; they will keep for at least a week. To store them for longer, place in a sealed polythene bag and keep in the salad drawer of the fridge for up to two weeks. Remove the grapes from the fridge and keep at room temperature for at least an hour before serving so that the flavour can develop fully.

Grape juice Naturally sweet, clear red and white grape juice, from crushed grapes, is delicious served chilled on its own or topped up with sparkling mineral water.

Grapeseed oil Grape pips are pressed into a very pale oil with a delicate, almost neutral flavour. This healthy oil is extremely rich in polyunsaturated fats. It can be used for cooking, but is best used in its natural state, in salad dressings, for example. It is the perfect oil to choose for making mayonnaise as it has such a mild flavour, and it never separates.

Above: Large, golden muscatel raisins from Muscat grapes are often dried and sold on their stems.

DRIED GRAPES

The best of these are sun-dried, without undergoing any chemical processes. Dried grapes – raisins, currants and sultanas – sometimes contain bits of stalk and the occasional pip, so pick them over carefully before using.

Artificially dried grapes are usually cleaner, but may need to be plumped up in boiling water for a few seconds before being added to cake mixtures.

Raisins The best raisins are made from Muscat grapes and come from California and Spain. These large, deep amber fruit are tender and sweet and can be eaten on their own, with cheese and nuts, or used in rice and couscous dishes. Smaller, black raisins are used for making cakes and puddings, muesli and mincemeat. All raisins benefit from being plumped up in brandy before cooking.

Currants These small dried fruits are made from Turkish and Greek seedless black grapes.

Sultanas These small golden dried fruit are made from seedless white grapes. They are deliciously moist, with a tender texture and delicate flavour.

Serving and Cooking

Grapes are best eaten on their own as a snack or dessert, or at the end of a meal with cheese or nuts. For an unusual sandwich, try Brie with halved grapes. They make a good addition to fruit salad and savoury salads, combined with crunchy vegetables and walnuts. White and black grapes make attractive garnishes, particularly in small clusters frosted with egg white and sugar. They can be used to make jams and jellies; a few small grapes look beautiful suspended in a clear jelly.

Their slight acidity makes grapes a good foil for rich meats like *foie gras* and calves' liver. They can also be used to stuff quail, chicken or guinea fowl, or to make a sauce for poultry or ham. A classic French dish is

Above: Clockwise from top left, sultanas, currants and raisins.

Caramelizing grapes

1 Combine 200g/7oz/scant 1 cup granulated sugar and 60ml/4 tbsp water in a small heavy-based saucepan. Stir over a low heat until the sugar has dissolved. Bring to the boil, add 5ml/1 tsp lemon juice and boil until the syrup turns a deep golden brown.

2 Carefully add 15ml/1 tbsp hot water (protecting your hand with an oven glove as the mixture will "spit") and shake the pan to mix. Spear a pair of grapes on a fork by the stem and dip them into the caramel to coat. Slide the caramelized grapes off the fork and leave on an oiled baking sheet for about 10 minutes until the caramel cools and hardens.

---

sole Véronique; rolled fillets of sole poached in white wine and garnished with white grapes. It is best to peel and deseed grapes before cooking and to poach them lightly in wine or syrup so that they keep their shape. For savoury dishes, they can be sautéed in butter.

FIGS

These oval or pear-shaped fruits are among the most luscious of all and can be eaten fresh or dried. They are not juicy in the conventional sense, nor do they have a particularly strong flavour, but they are succulent and sweet, conjuring up images of sunny Mediterranean gardens.

Figs come in three main varieties – white, black and red – and range in colour from palest green to dark gold, burnished brown or deep purple. The entire fig is edible (although some people prefer to peel them), from the soft thin skin to the sweet succulent red or purplish flesh and the myriad tiny seeds. Skin colour makes little difference to the taste of a fig. Their high natural sugar content makes them the sweetest of all fruits. The flavour varies, depending on where they were grown and how ripe they are.

History

Figs were said to grow in the Garden of Eden and their leaves, it is alleged, were used to cover the nakedness of Adam and Eve. Over the centuries, prudes have delighted in defacing works of art depicting naked bodies with carefully placed fig leaves.

Below: Although green in colour, these figs are classified as white.

Figs probably originated in Asia Minor and were one of the first fruits to be cultivated. They were certainly known to the Ancient Egyptians at the time of the Pharaohs and were brought to the Mediterranean long before the arrival of the Ancient Greeks and Romans, rapidly becoming an important part of the Mediterranean diet. The world's oldest known living fig tree is said to be growing in a Sicilian garden.

Figs are now widely cultivated and exported from France, Greece, Turkey and Brazil.

Above: Turkish purple figs

Varieties

You will seldom find figs in shops or markets labelled according to their variety; instead they are classified by colour – white, black and red. In reality, they range from palest green to dark gold, burnished brown or deep purple. In Italy, you are most likely to find the green **Kadota,** while in France you may come across **Buissone, Barbillone** and **Dauphine Violette.** Imported figs from Turkey are generally purple with deep red flesh.

Nutrition

Figs consist of 83% natural sugars. They are a good source of calcium and are high in fibre, and contain vitamins A, B and C. They are well known for their laxative and

digestive properties. A single fig provides about 30 kilocalories.

Buying and Storing

Ripe figs are very delicate and do not travel well, so it is often difficult to find imported fruit at a perfect stage of maturity. Look for unblemished fruit that is soft and yielding when gently squeezed but still holds its shape. Figs should have a faint, delicate aroma; if they smell sour, they are over-ripe and will taste sour too. If you are buying figs in their country of origin, you may find some with split skins. Provided you are going to eat them immediately, this does not matter. Be careful not to squash the figs on the way home, or you will end up with a squishy inedible pulp.

Ripe figs should ideally be eaten on the day they are bought, but can be stored in the salad drawer of the fridge for up to three days. Remove them well before serving, as chilling spoils the delicate flavour. Under-ripe fruit can be kept at room temperature for a day or two until the skin softens, but they will never develop the wonderful flavour of figs that have ripened in the sun naturally on the tree.

Right: Dried figs are sometimes sold strung together in a ring.

DRIED FIGS

Dried figs are made from very ripe autumn fruits, usually golden Smyrna figs or deep purple Mission figs from Turkey. They are spread out on hurdles to dry in the sun and must be turned several times before they are dried completely. This process flattens the figs into the familiar cushion shape. Dried figs contain large amounts of sugar and are highly nutritious. The best have a soft texture and are sold loosely packed so that they remain plump. Less high quality figs are commonly sold in blocks or strung together like a necklace. Store them in a cool, dry place.

Eat dried figs as they are, or stuff them

Left: Dried figs – the best, soft-textured fruits are sold loosely packed.

with marzipan, nuts or cream cheese. They are used in compotes, poached in wine or served with creamy custard puddings. They can be baked in cakes, steamed puddings and teabreads. They are extensively used in Middle Eastern cooking and go especially well with poultry and game. Dried figs can be substituted for prunes in chicken, pork and rabbit recipes, such as terrines, stews and casseroles. Soak them – preferably in red wine – for several hours before cooking.

Dried figs are also used to make syrup of figs, the intensely sweet laxative traditionally loathed by most children. They can also be combined with juniper berries to make a drink called *figuette*.

CANNED OR BOTTLED FIGS

These are usually green Kadota figs preserved in heavy syrup. Canned or bottled figs are very sweet and are best served in a fruit compote. A dollop of whipped cream or Greek yogurt will temper the sweetness.

Preparing and Cooking

The best way to enjoy a fig is to pick a perfectly sun-ripened fruit straight off the tree. Wash it briefly and pat it dry very gently. Serve it whole. Always serve figs at room temperature, never chilled. They look particularly attractive on a bed of fig leaves, especially if each fruit is slit into four and opened out to resemble a flower. The centres can be

*Above: Dried figs
– dusted with
cornflour to
keep the
fruits
separate.*

*Above: Almost too sweet
on their own, green
bottled figs are best
served with cream or
natural yogurt.*

or ice cream. They also go well with savoury dishes like duck and lamb. To poach figs, put them in a saucepan and cover with syrup, red or white wine or port. Add your chosen flavourings – honey, cinnamon, vanilla and lemon are all suitable. Bring to the boil, lower the heat, cover and simmer gently for about 15 minutes, until the figs are tender. Using a slotted spoon, transfer the figs to a serving dish, then boil the poaching liquid until it is thick and syrupy before pouring it over the fruit.

To cook figs in butter, cut them in half vertically, then arrange them cut-side up in a heatproof dish. Put a knob of butter on each fig half. Sprinkle with port or Marsala and a pinch of cinnamon or nutmeg, and grill until lightly browned. Serve with meat or poultry, or brush with honey before grilling and serve as a dessert.

To caramelize figs, dip the fruit in water, then roll in caster or vanilla sugar until completely coated. Place in a shallow baking dish and bake in a preheated oven at 220°C/425°F/Gas 7 for about 15 minutes, or until the sugar has caramelized. Leave to cool, then chill before serving.

stuffed, if you like. Cream cheese mixed with honey and chopped nuts, fresh rasperries or raspberry mousse make delicious fillings.

Fresh figs are usually eaten raw as a dessert fruit, or as an hors d'oeuvre with Parma ham or salami. They have an affinity with nuts such as walnuts, pistachios and almonds and make an excellent addition to a cheese platter with grapes and nuts.

They can be stuffed with sweet or savoury fillings like cream or blue cheese, celery and walnuts or marzipan, and are especially delicious filled with mascarpone and berries. Figs can also be successfully cooked in compotes, preserves and jams. For desserts, they can be poached in wine, honey or syrup, they can also be caramelized or made into tarts

Making fig flowers

Cut each fig downwards into quarters, starting from the stalk end and leaving the quarters attached at the base. Gently pull the sections apart to open them out like the petals of a flower. Serve the figs plain or pile in your chosen creamy filling.

RHUBARB

Strictly speaking, rhubarb is not a fruit, but a vegetable; it is the fleshy stalk of the rhubarb plant, a relative of sorrel and dock. The stems are succulent, but too sour to eat raw, and the leaves contain oxalic acid, which makes them highly poisonous. The normal growing season is late spring to late summer, but early forced rhubarb, grown under covered pots, is available throughout the spring months. Maincrop rhubarb stalks vary from green to purplish-pink; the forced variety has spindly, tender bright pink or red stems, crowned with yellow leaves, and tastes much nicer.

History

Rhubarb originated in Northern Asia and Siberia. It has been cultivated for centuries, but was originally used as a medicinal and ornamental plant. It was not until the eighteenth century that British gardeners began to grow rhubarb for cooking.

Preparing rhubarb

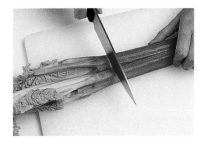

1 Using a large knife, cut off and discard the leaves and the root end of the stalk. Peel off any stringy fibres with a swivel-blade vegetable peeler.

2 Cut the rhubarb into pieces.

Nutrition

Rhubarb is one of the lowest calorie foods, providing only 7 kilocalories per 100g/3¾oz. It contains significant amounts of calcium, potassium and thiamine (vitamin B1) and has natural laxative properties.

Buying and Storing

Choose crisp, firm stalks that look bright and release sap when you snap them. Rhubarb can be stored for a few days in the bottom of the fridge, but wilts quite quickly. It freezes well: cut the stalks into short lengths, blanch briefly in boiling water, refresh in iced water and freeze in polythene bags.

Preparing and Cooking

All rhubarb needs to be sweetened when it is cooked, usually with sugar. This can be added at the outset, or when it has been cooked until tender. Use a stainless steel pan and only a spoonful or two of water. Poach gently until the fruit is tender. Rhubarb makes a wonderful pie or tart filling, and a delicious crumble, especially when mixed with banana.

Puréed rhubarb can be made into ice cream, sorbets, mousses and fools. Citrus fruits and spices, particularly ginger, vanilla and cinnamon, complement the flavour of rhubarb. Rhubarb can be combined with any of these to make excellent jams and chutneys. Because it is a vegetable, rhubarb goes well with savoury dishes like scrambled eggs, but you will still need to add sugar. It adds piquancy to rich casseroles, particularly pork, lamb and duck. Its sharp acidity makes it a good substitute for sorrel in sauces, especially to serve with oily fish, such as mackerel.

Above: Early forced rhubarb, grown under covered pots, is pink and tender.

Below: Tougher, maincrop rhubarb is grown in the open.

COOKING WITH FRUIT

Apple, Pear and Quince Recipes

Stone Fruit Recipes

Berry and Currant Recipes

Citrus Fruit Recipes

Exotic Fruit Recipes

Melon, Grape, Fig and

Rhubarb Recipes

APPLE, PEAR AND QUINCE RECIPES

Apples, pears and quinces are wonderfully versatile. Dutch Apple Cake and Chocolate Pear and Pecan Pie are just two of the tempting teatime treats in store, while Hot Quince Soufflés and Iced Pear Terrine make memorable desserts.

ICED PEAR TERRINE <u>WITH</u> CALVADOS <u>AND</u> CHOCOLATE SAUCE

THIS TERRINE, BASED ON A CLASSIC FRENCH DESSERT, MAKES A REFRESHING AND IMPRESSIVE END TO ANY MEAL. FOR FLAVOUR, BE SURE THE PEARS ARE RIPE AND JUICY.

SERVES EIGHT

INGREDIENTS

  1.5kg/3–3½lb ripe Williams pears
  juice of 1 lemon
  115g/4oz/½ cup caster sugar
  10 whole cloves
  90ml/6 tbsp water
  julienne strips of orange rind,
   to decorate
For the sauce
  200g/7oz plain chocolate
  60ml/4 tbsp hot strong black coffee
  200ml/7fl oz/1 cup double cream
  30ml/2 tbsp Calvados or brandy

1 Peel, core and slice the pears. Place them in a saucepan with the lemon juice, sugar, cloves and water. Cover and simmer for 10 minutes. Remove the cloves. Allow the pears to cool.

2 Process the pears with their juice, in a food processor or blender until smooth. Pour the purée into a freezerproof bowl, cover and freeze until firm.

3 Meanwhile, line a 900g/2lb loaf tin with clear film. Allow the film to overhang the sides of the tin. Remove the frozen pear purée from the freezer and spoon it into a food processor or blender. Process until smooth. Pour into the prepared tin, cover and freeze until firm.

4 Make the sauce. Break the chocolate into a large heatproof bowl. Place the bowl over a saucepan of hot water. When the chocolate has melted, stir in the coffee until smooth. Gradually stir in the cream and then the Calvados or brandy. Set the sauce aside.

5 About 20 minutes before serving, remove the tin from the freezer. Invert the terrine on to a plate, lift off the clear film and place the terrine in the fridge to soften slightly. Warm the sauce over hot water. Place a slice of terrine on each dessert plate and spoon over some of the sauce. Decorate with julienne strips of orange rind and serve at once.

QUINCE <u>AND</u> GINGER MOUSSE <u>WITH</u> ALMOND BISCUITS

QUINCES AND GINGER ARE PERFECTLY MATCHED FLAVOUR PARTNERS. AS WITH ANY QUINCE RECIPE, YOU CAN SUBSTITUTE PEARS OR APPLES WITH EQUALLY DELICIOUS RESULTS.

SERVES FOUR

INGREDIENTS

450g/1lb quinces
75g/3oz/⅓ cup caster sugar
grated rind of ½ lemon
90ml/6 tbsp water
2 pieces stem ginger in syrup, finely chopped, plus 15ml/1 tbsp syrup from the jar
15ml/1 tbsp powdered gelatine
150ml/¼ pint/⅔ cup double cream
2 egg whites
mint leaves and blackberries dusted with caster sugar, to decorate
For the biscuits
50g/2oz/¼ cup butter
30ml/2 tbsp caster sugar
50g/2oz/½ cup plain flour
50g/2oz/½ cup ground almonds
a few drops of almond essence

1 Grease four ramekins and line the bases with non-stick baking paper. Peel the quinces, core and put in a saucepan with the sugar, lemon rind and 60ml/4 tbsp of the water. Bring to the boil, lower the heat, cover and simmer for 10 minutes or until softened. Remove the lid; continue cooking until the liquid has almost evaporated.

2 Cool the quince mixture slightly, then purée in a food processor or blender. Press the purée through a sieve into a large bowl, then stir in the ginger and ginger syrup and set aside.

3 Pour the remaining 30ml/2 tbsp water into a small heatproof bowl and sprinkle the gelatine on top. Leave to soak for 5 minutes. Stand the bowl in a pan of hot water until the gelatine has dissolved, stirring occasionally.

4 Lightly whip the cream. Stir the gelatine into the quince purée, then fold in the whipped cream. In a grease-free bowl, whisk the egg whites to stiff peaks; fold into the quince mixture. Divide among the prepared ramekins, level the tops and chill until firm. Preheat the oven to 190°C/375°F/Gas 5.

5 Make the biscuits. Line a baking sheet with non-stick baking paper. Cream the butter and sugar until smooth. Add the flour, almonds and almond essence and mix to a dough with a knife. Roll out thinly on a lightly floured surface; cut into rounds with a 7.5cm/3in cutter. Transfer to the baking sheet. Chill for 10 minutes, then bake for 10–12 minutes.

6 Cool slightly on the paper, then lift on to a wire rack to cool. Run a knife around each mousse; turn out on to dessert plates. Discard the paper. Decorate and serve with biscuits.

SPICED APPLE CRUMBLE

ANY FRUIT CAN BE USED IN THIS POPULAR DESSERT, BUT YOU CAN'T BEAT THE FAVOURITES OF BLACKBERRY AND APPLE. HAZELNUTS AND CARDAMOM SEEDS GIVE THE TOPPING EXTRA FLAVOUR.

SERVES FOUR TO SIX

INGREDIENTS
    butter, for greasing
    450g/1lb Bramley apples
    115g/4oz/1 cup blackberries
    grated rind and juice of 1 orange
    50g/2oz/⅓ cup light muscovado sugar
    custard, to serve
For the topping
    175g/6oz/1½ cups plain flour
    75g/3oz/⅓ cup butter
    75g/3oz/⅓ cup caster sugar
    25g/1oz/¼ cup chopped hazelnuts
    2.5ml/½ tsp crushed cardamom seeds

VARIATIONS
This wonderfully good-natured pudding can be made with all sorts of fruit. Try plums, apricots, peaches or pears, alone or in combination with apples. Rhubarb makes a delectable crumble, especially when partnered with bananas.

1 Preheat the oven to 200°C/400°F/ Gas 6. Generously butter a 1.2 litre/ 2 pint/5 cup baking dish. Peel and core the apples, then slice them into the prepared baking dish. Level the surface, then scatter the blackberries over. Sprinkle the orange rind and light muscovado sugar evenly over the top, then pour over the orange juice. Set the fruit mixture aside while you make the crumble topping.

2 Make the topping. Sift the flour into a bowl and rub in the butter until the mixture resembles coarse breadcrumbs. Stir in the caster sugar, hazelnuts and cardamom seeds. Scatter the topping over the top of the fruit.

3 Press the topping around the edges of the dish to seal in the juices. Bake for 30–35 minutes or until the crumble is golden. Serve hot, with custard.

BAKED STUFFED APPLES

THIS TRADITIONAL APPLE DESSERT IS EXCEPTIONALLY SIMPLE AND SPEEDY. BAKE THE APPLES IN THE OVEN ON THE SHELF UNDER THE SUNDAY ROAST FOR A DELICIOUS END TO THE MEAL.

SERVES FOUR

INGREDIENTS
    4 large Bramley apples
    75g/3oz/½ cup light muscovado sugar
    75g/3oz/⅓ cup butter, softened
    grated rind and juice of ½ orange
    1.5ml/¼ tsp ground cinnamon
    30ml/2 tbsp crushed ratafia biscuits
    50g/2oz/½ cup pecan nuts, chopped
    50g/2oz/½ cup luxury mixed glacé
       fruit, chopped

COOK'S TIP
Use a little butter or oil to grease the baking dish, if you like, or pour a small amount of water around the stuffed apples to stop them from sticking to the dish during baking.

1 Preheat the oven to 180°C/350°F/ Gas 4. Wash and dry the apples. Remove the cores with an apple corer, then carefully enlarge each core cavity to twice its size, by shaving off more flesh with the corer. Score each apple around its equator, using a sharp knife. Stand the apples in a baking dish.

2 Mix the sugar, butter, orange rind and juice, cinnamon and ratafia crumbs. Beat well, then stir in the nuts and glacé fruit. Divide the filling among the apples, piling it high. Shield the filling in each apple with a small piece of foil. Bake for 45–60 minutes until each apple is tender.

APPLE CRÊPES WITH BUTTERSCOTCH SAUCE

THESE WONDERFUL DESSERT CRÊPES ARE FLAVOURED WITH SWEET CIDER, FILLED WITH CARAMELIZED
APPLES AND DRIZZLED WITH A RICH, SMOOTH BUTTERSCOTCH SAUCE.

3 Make the filling. Core the apples and cut them into thick slices. Heat 15g/ ½ oz/1 tbsp of the butter in a large frying pan. Add the apples to the pan. Cook until golden on both sides, then transfer the slices to a bowl with a slotted spoon and set them aside.

4 Add the rest of the butter to the pan. As soon as it has melted, add the muscovado sugar. When the sugar has dissolved and the mixture is bubbling, stir in the cream. Continue cooking until it forms a smooth sauce.

5 Fold each pancake in half, then fold in half again to form a cone; fill each with some of the fried apples. Place two filled pancakes on each dessert plate, drizzle over some of the butterscotch sauce and serve at once.

SERVES FOUR

INGREDIENTS
  115g/4oz/1 cup plain flour
  pinch of salt
  2 eggs
  175ml/6fl oz/¾ cup creamy milk
  120ml/4fl oz/½ cup sweet cider
  butter, for frying
For the filling and sauce
  4 Braeburn apples
  90g/3½ oz/scant ½ cup butter
  225g/8oz/1⅓ cups light
    muscovado sugar
  150ml/¼ pint/⅔ cup double cream

1 Make the crêpe batter. Sift the flour and salt into a large bowl. Add the eggs and milk and beat until smooth. Stir in the cider; set aside for 30 minutes.

2 Heat a small heavy-based non-stick frying pan. Add a knob of butter and ladle in enough batter to coat the pan thinly. Cook until the crêpe is golden underneath, then flip it over and cook the other side until golden. Slide the crêpe on to a plate. Repeat with the remaining mixture to make seven more.

VARIATIONS
You could just as easily use plums, pears, strawberries or bananas to fill the crêpes. If you like, add a touch of Grand Marnier to the apples towards the end of cooking.

PEAR AND CINNAMON FRITTERS

IF YOU DON'T LIKE DEEP FRYING AS A RULE, DO MAKE AN EXCEPTION FOR THIS DISH. FRITTERS ARE IRRESISTIBLE, AND A WONDERFUL WAY OF PERSUADING CHILDREN TO EAT MORE FRUIT.

SERVES FOUR

INGREDIENTS
    3 ripe, firm pears
    30ml/2 tbsp caster sugar
    30ml/2 tbsp Kirsch
    groundnut oil, for frying
    50g/2oz/1 cup amaretti biscuits,
        finely crushed
For the batter
    75g/3oz/¾ cup plain flour
    1.5ml/¼ tsp salt
    1.5ml/¼ tsp ground cinnamon
    60ml/4 tbsp milk
    2 eggs, separated
    45ml/3 tbsp water
To serve
    30ml/2 tbsp caster sugar
    1.5ml/¼ tsp ground cinnamon
    clotted cream

1 Peel the pears, cut them in quarters and remove the cores. Toss the wedges in the caster sugar and Kirsch. Set aside for 15 minutes.

2 Make the batter. Sift the flour, salt and cinnamon into a large bowl. Beat in the milk, egg yolks and water until smooth. Set aside for 10 minutes.

3 Whisk the egg whites in a grease-free bowl until they form stiff peaks; lightly fold them into the batter. Preheat the oven to 150°C/300°F/Gas 2.

4 Pour oil into a deep heavy-based saucepan to a depth of 7.5cm/3in. Heat to 185°C/360°F or until a bread cube, added to the oil, browns in 45 seconds.

5 Toss a pear wedge in the amaretti crumbs, then spear it on a fork and dip it into the batter until evenly coated. Lower it gently into the hot oil and use a knife to push it off the fork. Add more wedges in the same way but do not overcrowd the pan. Cook the fritters for 3–4 minutes or until golden. Drain on kitchen paper. Keep hot in the oven while cooking successive batches.

6 Mix the sugar and cinnamon and sprinkle some over the fritters. Sprinkle a little cinnamon sugar over the clotted cream; serve with the hot fritters.

VARIATIONS
Also try apples, apricots and bananas.

POACHED PEARS IN PORT SYRUP

THE PERFECT CHOICE FOR AUTUMN ENTERTAINING, THIS SIMPLE DESSERT HAS A BEAUTIFUL RICH COLOUR AND FANTASTIC FLAVOUR THANKS TO THE TASTES OF PORT AND LEMON.

SERVES FOUR

INGREDIENTS

2 ripe, firm pears, such as Williams
  or Comice
pared rind of 1 lemon
175ml/6fl oz/¾ cup ruby port
50g/2oz/¼ cup caster sugar
1 cinnamon stick
60ml/4 tbsp cold water
fresh cream, to serve

To decorate

30ml/2 tbsp sliced hazelnuts, toasted
fresh mint, pear or rose leaves

COOK'S TIP
Choose pears of similar size, with the stalks intact, for the most attractive effect when fanned on the plate.

1 Peel the pears, cut them in half and remove the cores. Place the lemon rind, port, sugar, cinnamon stick and water in a shallow pan. Bring to the boil over a low heat. Add the pears, lower the heat, cover and poach for 5 minutes. Let the pears cool in the syrup.

2 When the pears are cold, transfer them to a bowl with a slotted spoon. Return the syrup to the heat. Boil rapidly until it has reduced to form a syrup that will coat the back of a spoon lightly. Remove the cinnamon stick and lemon rind and leave the syrup to cool.

3 To serve, place each pear in turn on a board, cut side down. Keeping it intact at the stalk end, slice it lengthways, then using a palette knife, carefully lift it off and place on a dessert plate. Press gently so that the pear fans out. When all the pears have been fanned, spoon over the port syrup. Top each portion with a few hazelnuts and decorate with fresh mint, pear or rose leaves. Serve with cream.

APPLE CHARLOTTES

THESE TEMPTING LITTLE FRUIT CHARLOTTES ARE A WONDERFUL WAY TO USE WINDFALLS.

SERVES FOUR

INGREDIENTS

175g/6oz/¾ cup butter
450g/1lb Bramley apples
225g/8oz Braeburn apples
60ml/4 tbsp water
130g/4½oz/scant ⅔ cup caster sugar
2 egg yolks
pinch of grated nutmeg
9 thin slices white bread,
   crusts removed
extra-thick double cream or custard,
   to serve

COOK'S TIP
A mixture of cooking and eating apples gives the best flavour, but there's no reason why you can't use only cooking apples; just sweeten the pulp to taste.

1 Preheat the oven to 190°C/375°F/ Gas 5. Put a knob of the butter in a saucepan. Peel and core the apples, dice them finely and put them in the pan with the water. Cover and cook for 10 minutes or until the cooking apples have pulped down. Stir in 115g/4oz/ ½ cup of the caster sugar. Boil, uncovered, until any liquid has evaporated and what remains is a thick pulp. Remove from the heat, beat in the egg yolks and nutmeg and set aside.

2 Melt the remaining butter in a separate saucepan over a low heat until the white curds start to separate from the clear yellow liquid. Remove from the heat. Leave to stand for a few minutes, then strain the clear clarified butter through a muslin-lined sieve.

3 Brush four 150ml/¼ pint/⅔ cup individual charlotte moulds or pudding tins with a little of the clarified butter; sprinkle with the remaining caster sugar. Cut the bread slices into 2.5cm/1in strips. Dip the strips into the remaining clarified butter; use to line the moulds or tins. Overlap the strips on the base to give the effect of a swirl and let the excess bread overhang the tops of the moulds or tins.

4 Fill each bread case with apple pulp. Fold the excess bread over the top of each mould or tin to make a lid; press down lightly. Bake for 45–50 minutes or until golden. Run a knife between each charlotte and its mould or tin, then turn out on to dessert plates. Serve with extra-thick double cream or custard.

Hot Quince Soufflés

These delicious fruits are more often picked than purchased as they are seldom found in shops or markets. You can use pears instead, but the flavour will not be as intense.

SERVES SIX

INGREDIENTS
   2 quinces, peeled and cored
   60ml/4 tbsp water
   115g/4oz/½ cup caster sugar,
     plus extra for sprinkling
   5 egg whites
   melted butter, for greasing
   icing sugar, for dusting
For the pastry cream
   250ml/8fl oz/1 cup milk
   1 vanilla pod
   3 egg yolks
   75g/3oz/⅓ cup caster sugar
   25g/1oz/¼ cup plain flour
   15ml/1 tbsp Poire William liqueur

1 Cut the quinces into cubes. Place in a saucepan with the water. Stir in half the sugar. Bring to the boil, lower the heat, cover and simmer for 10 minutes or until tender. Remove the lid; boil until most of the liquid has evaporated.

2 Cool slightly, then purée the fruit in a blender or food processor. Press through a sieve into a bowl; set aside.

3 Make the pastry cream. Pour the milk into a small saucepan. Add the vanilla pod and bring to the boil over a low heat. Meanwhile, beat the egg yolks, caster sugar and flour in a bowl until smooth.

4 Gradually strain the hot milk on to the yolks, whisking frequently until the mixture is smooth.

5 Discard the vanilla pod. Return the mixture to the clean pan and heat gently, stirring until thickened. Cook, for a further 2 minutes, whisking constantly, to ensure that the sauce is smooth and the flour is cooked.

6 Remove the pan from the heat and stir in the quince purée and liqueur. Cover the surface of the pastry cream with clear film to prevent it from forming a skin. Allow to cool slightly, while you prepare the ramekins.

7 Preheat the oven to 220ºC/425ºF/ Gas 7. Place a baking sheet in the oven to heat up. Butter six 150ml/¼ pint/ ⅔ cup ramekins and sprinkle the inside of each with caster sugar. In a grease-free bowl, whisk the egg whites to stiff peaks. Gradually whisk in the remaining caster sugar, then fold the egg whites into the pastry cream.

8 Divide the mixture among the prepared ramekins and level the surface of each. Carefully run a sharp knife between the side of each ramekin and the mixture, then place the ramekins on the hot baking sheet and bake for 8–10 minutes until the tops of the soufflés are well risen and golden. Generously dust the tops with icing sugar and serve the soufflés at once.

COOK'S TIP
Poire William is a clear, colourless pear eau-de-vie, which sometimes is sold with a ripe pear in the bottle. Kirsch, made from cherries, also works well in this recipe to complement the flavour of the quinces.

TARTE TATIN

IF YOU USE READY-ROLLED PUFF PASTRY, THIS TASTY TART CAN BE MADE VERY EASILY.

SERVES SIX TO EIGHT

INGREDIENTS

  3 Braeburn or Cox's Orange
    Pippin apples
  juice of ½ lemon
  50g/2oz/¼ cup butter, softened
  75g/3oz/⅓ cup caster sugar
  250g/9oz ready-rolled puff pastry
  cream, to serve

1 Preheat the oven to 220°C/425°F/ Gas 7. Cut the apples in quarters and remove the cores. Toss the apple quarters in the lemon juice to prevent them discolouring.

2 Spread the butter over the base of a 20cm/8in heavy-based omelette pan that can safely be used in the oven. Sprinkle the caster sugar over the base of the pan and add the apple wedges, rounded side down.

3 Cook over a medium heat for 15–20 minutes or until the sugar and butter have melted and the apples are golden. Cut the pastry into a 25cm/10in round and place on top of the apples; tuck the edges in with a knife. Place the pan in the oven and bake for 15–20 minutes or until the pastry is golden. Carefully invert the tart on to a plate. Cool slightly before serving with cream.

COOK'S TIP
To turn out the Tarte Tatin, place the serving plate upside down on top of it, then, protecting your arms with oven gloves, hold both pan and plate firmly together and deftly turn them over. Lift off the pan.

FILO-TOPPED APPLE PIE

WITH ITS SCRUNCHY FILO TOPPING AND MINIMAL BUTTER, THIS MAKES A REALLY LIGHT DESSERT. A GOOD CHOICE FOR THE APPLE PIE ADDICT WATCHING HIS OR HER FAT INTAKE.

SERVES SIX

INGREDIENTS
  900g/2lb Bramley apples
  75g/3oz/⅓ cup caster sugar
  grated rind of 1 lemon
  15ml/1 tbsp lemon juice
  75g/3oz/½ cup sultanas
  2.5ml/½ tsp ground cinnamon
  4 large sheets filo pastry, thawed
    if frozen
  25g/1oz/2 tbsp butter, melted
  icing sugar, for dusting

VARIATION
To make filo crackers, cut the buttered filo into 20cm/8in wide strips. Spoon a little of the filling along one end of each strip, leaving the sides clear. Roll up and twist the ends to make a cracker. Brush with more butter; bake for 20 minutes.

1 Peel, core and dice the apples. Place them in a saucepan with the caster sugar and lemon rind. Drizzle the lemon juice over. Bring to the boil, stir well, then cook for 5 minutes or until the apples have softened. Stir in the sultanas and cinnamon. Spoon the mixture into a 1.2 litre/2 pint/5 cup pie dish and level the top. Allow to cool.

2 Preheat the oven to 180°C/350°F/ Gas 4. Place a pie funnel in the centre of the fruit. Brush each sheet of filo with melted butter. Scrunch up loosely and place on the fruit to cover it completely.

3 Bake for 20–30 minutes until the filo is golden. Dust the pie with icing sugar before serving with custard or cream.

CHOCOLATE, PEAR AND PECAN PIE

THE RICHNESS OF DEEP, DARK CHOCOLATE COUPLED WITH JUICY PEARS GIVES A CLASSIC PECAN PIE AN OUT-OF-THE-ORDINARY TWIST. THE RESULT IS UTTERLY DELICIOUS — AND UTTERLY IRRESISTIBLE.

SERVES EIGHT TO TEN

INGREDIENTS
300g/11oz shortcrust pastry, thawed
   if frozen
3 small pears
165g/5½oz/scant ¾ cup caster sugar
150ml/¼ pint/⅔ cup water
pared rind of 1 lemon
50g/2oz good quality plain chocolate
50g/2oz/¼ cup unsalted butter, diced
225g/8oz/¾ cup golden syrup
3 eggs, beaten
5ml/1 tsp pure vanilla essence
150g/5oz/1¼ cups pecan
   nuts, chopped
15ml/1 tbsp maple syrup (optional)
ice cream, to serve

1 Preheat the oven to 200°C/400°F/ Gas 6. Roll out the pastry on a lightly floured surface and line a deep 23cm/ 9in fluted flan tin. Chill the pastry case for 20 minutes, then line it with non-stick baking paper and baking beans. Bake for 10 minutes. Lift out the paper and beans and return the pastry case to the oven for 5 minutes. Allow to cool.

2 Peel the pears, cut them in half and remove the cores with a small spoon. Place 50g/2oz/¼ cup of the sugar in a pan with the water. Add the lemon rind and bring to the boil. Add the pears. Cover, lower the heat and simmer for 10 minutes. Remove the pears from the pan with a slotted spoon and set aside to cool. Discard the cooking liquid.

3 Break the chocolate into a large heatproof bowl. Melt over a pan of barely simmering water. Beat in the butter until combined. Set aside. In a saucepan, heat the remaining sugar and golden syrup together over a low heat until most of the sugar has dissolved. Bring to the boil, lower the heat and simmer for 2 minutes.

4 Whisk the eggs into the chocolate mixture until combined, then whisk in the syrup mixture. Stir in the vanilla essence and pecan nuts.

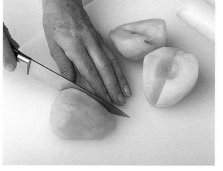

5 Place the pear halves flat side down on a board. Using a fine sharp knife, make lengthways cuts all along each pear, taking care not to cut all the way through. Using a palette knife, lift the pear halves and arrange in the pastry case. Pour the pecan mixture over the top, so that the pears are visible through the mixture.

6 Bake for 25–30 minutes or until the filling is set, then allow to cool on a wire rack. If you like, glaze the surface of the pie with maple syrup before serving with ice cream.

FRENCH APPLE TART

*THIS GLORIOUS TART MAKES A TRULY INDULGENT DESSERT. FOR AN EARLY MORNING TREAT, TRY A
SLICE FOR BREAKFAST WITH A CUP OF STRONG BLACK COFFEE.*

SERVES EIGHT

INGREDIENTS
    350g/12oz sweet shortcrust pastry,
      thawed if frozen
    whipped cream, to serve
For the filling
    115g/4oz/½ cup butter, softened
    115g/4oz/½ cup caster sugar
    2 large eggs, beaten
    115g/4oz/1 cup ground almonds
    25g/1oz/¼ cup plain flour
For the topping
    3 Braeburn apples
    60ml/4 tbsp apricot jam
    15ml/1 tbsp water

1 Preheat the oven to 190°C/375°F/
Gas 5. Place a baking sheet in the
oven to heat up. Roll out the shortcrust
pastry on a lightly floured surface and
line a 23cm/9in fluted flan tin.

4 Using a palette knife, carefully
transfer each row of apple slices to the
tart, arranging them on the filling so
that they resemble the spokes of a
wheel. You may need to overlap the
slices in the middle slightly to fit. Press
the slices down well into the filling.
Warm the apricot jam with the water,
then press the mixture through a sieve
into a small bowl.

5 Using a pastry brush, brush half this
jam glaze over the apples. Place the tin
on the hot baking sheet and bake the
tart for 45 minutes or until the pastry is
golden and the apples have started to
singe slightly.

6 Warm the remaining jam glaze and
brush it over the apples. Let the tart
cool slightly before serving with cream.

2 Beat all the ingredients for the filling
together until light and fluffy. Spoon into
the pastry case and level the surface.

3 Make the topping. Peel the apples,
remove the cores, and cut them in half.
Place each half, cut side down, on a
board. Using a sharp, fine knife, slice
the apples thinly, keeping the shape,
then press down lightly to fan each
apple half in a row.

VARIATION
A redcurrant glaze would also look good
on this tart. Warm redcurrant jelly with
a little lemon juice and brush it over the
apples. Sieving is not needed.

DUTCH APPLE CAKE

THE APPLE TOPPING MAKES THIS CAKE REALLY MOIST. IT IS JUST AS GOOD HOT AS IT IS COLD.

MAKES EIGHT TO TEN SLICES

INGREDIENTS
    250g/9oz/2¼ cups self-raising flour
    10ml/2 tsp baking powder
    5ml/1 tsp ground cinnamon
    130g/4½oz/generous ½ cup
      caster sugar
    50g/2oz/¼ cup butter, melted
    2 eggs, beaten
    150ml/¼ pint/⅔ cup milk
For the topping
    2 Cox's Orange Pippin apples
    15g/½oz/1 tbsp butter, melted
    60ml/4 tbsp demerara sugar
    1.5ml/¼ tsp ground cinnamon

VARIATION
Add a few sultanas or raisins to the apples if you like.

1 Preheat the oven to 200°C/400°F/ Gas 6. Grease and line a 20cm/8in round cake tin. Sift the flour, baking powder and cinnamon into a large mixing bowl. Stir in the caster sugar. In a separate bowl, whisk the melted butter, eggs and milk together, then stir the mixture into the dry ingredients.

2 Pour the cake mixture into the prepared tin, smooth the surface, then make a shallow hollow in a ring around the edge of the mixture.

3 Make the topping. Peel and core the apples, slice them into wedges and slice the wedges thinly. Arrange the slices around the hollow of the cake mixture. Brush with the melted butter, then scatter the demerara sugar and ground cinnamon over the top.

4 Bake for 45–50 minutes or until the cake has risen well, is golden and a skewer inserted into the centre comes out clean. Serve immediately as a dessert with cream, or remove from the tin, peel off the lining paper and cool on a wire rack before slicing.

PEAR AND POLENTA CAKE

POLENTA GIVES THE LIGHT SPONGE THAT TOPS SLICED PEARS A NUTTY CORN FLAVOUR THAT COMPLEMENTS THE FRUIT PERFECTLY. SERVE AS A DESSERT WITH CUSTARD OR CREAM.

MAKES TEN SLICES

INGREDIENTS
    175g/6oz/¾ cup golden caster sugar
    4 ripe pears
    juice of ½ lemon
    30ml/2 tbsp clear honey
    3 eggs
    seeds from 1 vanilla pod
    120ml/4fl oz/½ cup sunflower oil
    115g/4oz/1 cup self-raising flour
    50g/2oz/⅓ cup instant polenta

1 Preheat the oven to 180°C/350°F/ Gas 4. Generously grease and line a 21cm/8½in round cake tin. Scatter 30ml/2 tbsp of the golden caster sugar over the base of the prepared tin.

COOK'S TIP
Use the tip of a small, sharp knife to scrape out the vanilla pod seeds. If you do not have a vanilla pod, use 5ml/1 tsp pure vanilla essence instead.

2 Peel and core the pears. Cut them into chunky slices and toss in the lemon juice. Arrange them on the base of the prepared cake tin. Drizzle the honey over the pears and set aside.

3 Mix together the eggs, seeds from the vanilla pod and the remaining golden caster sugar in a bowl.

4 Beat the egg mixture until thick and creamy, then gradually beat in the oil. Sift together the flour and polenta and fold into the egg mixture.

5 Pour the mixture carefully into the tin over the pears. Bake for about 50 minutes or until a skewer inserted into the centre comes out clean. Cool in the tin for 10 minutes, then turn the cake out on to a plate, peel off the lining paper, invert and slice.

APPLE AND CIDER SAUCE

*THIS SAUCE COULDN'T BE SIMPLER TO MAKE. IT TASTES GREAT
WITH ROAST PORK, DUCK OR GOOSE.*

MAKES 450G/1LB

INGREDIENTS
    450g/1lb Bramley apples
    150ml/¼ pint/⅔ cup sweet cider
    2.5ml/½ tsp cider vinegar
    25g/1oz/2 tbsp butter
    2 whole cloves
    a few sprigs of fresh thyme
    15ml/1 tbsp clear honey
    2 tsp Dijon mustard

1 Peel, core and slice the apples.
Place them in a saucepan with the
cider, cider vinegar, butter, cloves and
thyme. Simmer over a low heat for
10 minutes or until the apples are soft
and pulpy, stirring occasionally, then
raise the heat and cook until most of
the liquid has evaporated.

2 Remove the cloves and thyme sprigs
and beat in the honey and mustard.
Taste and add more honey if necessary,
but the sauce is best when slightly tart.

COOK'S TIP
Press the sauce through a sieve if you
prefer it to be perfectly smooth.

APPLE AND RED ONION MARMALADE

*THIS MARMALADE CHUTNEY IS GOOD ENOUGH TO EAT ON ITS OWN.
SERVE IT WITH GOOD PORK SAUSAGES FOR THOROUGHLY MODERN
HOT DOGS OR IN A HAM SANDWICH INSTEAD OF MUSTARD.*

MAKES 450G/1LB

INGREDIENTS
    60ml/4 tbsp extra virgin olive oil
    900g/2lb red onions, thinly sliced
    75g/3oz/½ cup demerara sugar
    2 Cox's Orange Pippin apples
    90ml/6 tbsp cider vinegar

1 Heat the oil in a large, heavy-based
saucepan and add the onions.

2 Stir in the sugar and cook,
uncovered, over a medium heat for
about 40 minutes, stirring occasionally,
or until the onions have softened and
become a rich golden colour.

3 Peel, core and grate the apples. Add
them to the pan with the vinegar and
continue to cook for 20 minutes until
the chutney is thick and sticky. Spoon
into a sterilized jar and cover.

4 When cool, label and store in the
fridge for up to 1 month.

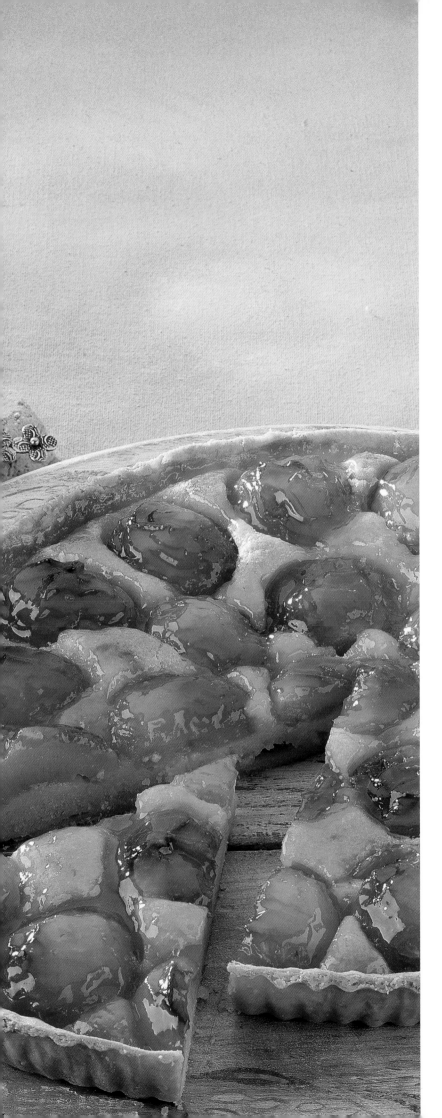

STONE FRUIT RECIPES

Juicy and full of flavour, peaches, plums, apricots, cherries and nectarines make perfect partners for crisp pastry. Try the irresistible Baked Lattice Peaches or Plum and Marzipan Pastries. For simpler, but equally delicious desserts, plump for Peach Melba Syllabub or Plum and Custard Creams.

Plum and Custard Creams

IF YOU WERE RELUCTANTLY RAISED ON STEWED PLUMS AND CUSTARD, THIS SOPHISTICATED VERSION, PRETTILY LAYERED IN A GLASS, WILL BRING A SMILE TO YOUR LIPS.

SERVES SIX

INGREDIENTS
675g/1½lb red plums, stoned
  and sliced
grated rind and juice of 1 orange
50g/2oz/¼ cup caster sugar
400g/14oz carton ready-made
  custard sauce
300ml/½ pint/1¼ cups double cream
30ml/2 tbsp water
15ml/1 tbsp powdered gelatine
1 egg white
plum slices and fresh mint sprigs,
  to decorate

COOK'S TIP
Use a long metal skewer or thin metal spoon handle to marble the custard and plum purée mixtures together.

1 Put the plums in a saucepan with the orange rind and juice. Add the caster sugar and heat, stirring constantly, until the sugar has dissolved. Cook the plums for 5 minutes until tender. Cool slightly, then purée in a food processor until smooth. Press through a sieve into a bowl and set aside to cool.

2 Put the custard in a saucepan, add half the cream and heat until boiling. Meanwhile, pour the water into a heatproof bowl and sprinkle the gelatine on top; set aside for 5 minutes until sponged. Whisk the soaked gelatine into the hot custard until it has dissolved. Allow the mixture to cool.

3 Whip the remaining cream to soft peaks, then fold it into the custard mixture. In a grease-free bowl, whisk the egg white to soft peaks; fold it into the custard too. Set aside, stirring occasionally, until just starting to set.

4 Quickly spoon alternate spoonfuls of the custard and plum purée into six tall dessert glasses. Marble the mixtures together. Chill for 2–3 hours or until the custard has set. Decorate each dessert with plum slices and fresh mint sprigs just before serving.

SPICED FRUITS JUBILEE

BASED ON THE CLASSIC CHERRIES JUBILEE, THIS IS A GREAT WAY TO USE A GLUT OF ANY PITTED FRUIT. THE SPICED SYRUP IS A DELICIOUS BONUS. SERVE WITH THE BEST DAIRY VANILLA ICE CREAM.

SERVES SIX

INGREDIENTS
   115g/4oz/½ cup caster sugar
   thinly pared rind of 1 unwaxed lemon
   1 cinnamon stick
   4 whole cloves
   300ml/½ pint/1¼ cups water
   225g/8oz tart red plums, stoned
     and sliced
   225g/8oz nectarines, stoned
     and chopped
   225g/8oz/1½ cups cherries, stoned
   5ml/1 tsp arrowroot
   75ml/5 tbsp brandy
   vanilla ice cream, to serve

1 Put the sugar, lemon rind, cinnamon stick, cloves and water in a pan. Bring to the boil, stirring. Lower the heat and simmer for 5 minutes, then lift out the spices with a slotted spoon and discard.

2 Add the fruit, cover the pan and simmer for 5 minutes. Drain the fruit and set it aside; return the syrup to the pan. Boil it, uncovered, for 2 minutes or until thick and syrupy.

3 Put the arrowroot in a small bowl and stir in 30ml/2 tbsp of the brandy. Stir the mixture into the syrup. Continue cooking and stirring, until the sauce thickens. Return the fruit to the pan.

4 Place scoops of ice cream in serving bowls and spoon the hot fruit over. Warm the remaining brandy in a small pan, then set it alight. Ladle it over the fruit at the table for maximum effect.

PEACH MELBA SYLLABUB

IF YOU ARE MAKING THESE SOPHISTICATED TEMPTATIONS FOR A DINNER PARTY, COOK THE PEACHES AND RASPBERRIES THE DAY BEFORE TO ALLOW THE FRUIT TO CHILL. WHIP UP THE SYLLABUB AT THE VERY LAST MINUTE TO MAKE A DELICIOUS, LIGHT~AS~A~CLOUD TOPPING.

SERVES SIX

INGREDIENTS
4 peaches, peeled, stoned and sliced
300ml/½ pint/1¼ cups blush or red grape juice
115g/4oz/⅔ cup raspberries
raspberry or mint leaves, to decorate
ratafias or other dessert biscuits, to serve

For the syllabub
60ml/4 tbsp peach schnapps
30ml/2 tbsp blush or red grape juice
300ml/½ pint/1¼ cups double cream

VARIATIONS
Use dessert pears and sliced kiwi fruit instead of peaches and raspberries. Instead of the syllabub, top the fruit with whipped cream flavoured with Advocaat and finely chopped preserved ginger.

1 Place the peach slices in a large saucepan. Add the grape juice. Bring to the boil, then cover, lower the heat and simmer for 5–7 minutes or until tender.

2 Add the raspberries and remove from the heat. Set aside in the fridge until cold. Divide the peach and raspberry mixture among six dessert glasses.

3 For the syllabub, place the peach schnapps and grape juice in a large bowl and whisk in the cream until it forms soft peaks.

4 Spoon the syllabub on top of the fruit and decorate each portion with a fresh raspberry or mint leaf. Serve with ratafias or other dessert biscuits.

NECTARINE AND HAZELNUT MERINGUES

IF IT'S INDULGENCE YOU'RE SEEKING, LOOK NO FURTHER. SWEET NECTARINES AND CREAM SYLLABUB PAIRED WITH CRISP HAZELNUT MERINGUES MAKE A SUPERB SWEET.

SERVES FIVE

INGREDIENTS
3 egg whites
175g/6oz/¾ cup caster sugar
50g/2oz/½ cup chopped hazelnuts, toasted
300ml/½ pint/1¼ cups double cream
60ml/4 tbsp sweet dessert wine
2 nectarines, stoned and sliced
fresh mint sprigs, to decorate

VARIATIONS
Use apricots instead of nectarines if you prefer, or try this with a raspberry filling.

1 Preheat the oven to 140°C/275°F/ Gas 1. Line two large baking sheets with non-stick baking paper. Whisk or beat the egg whites in a grease-free bowl until they form stiff peaks when the whisk or beaters are lifted. Gradually whisk in the caster sugar a spoonful at a time until the mixture forms a stiff, glossy meringue.

2 Fold in two thirds of the chopped toasted hazelnuts, then spoon five large ovals on to each lined baking sheet. Scatter the remaining hazelnuts over five of the meringue ovals. Flatten the tops of the remaining five ovals.

3 Bake the meringues for 1–1¼ hours until crisp and dry, then carefully lift them off the baking paper and cool completely on a wire rack.

4 Whip the cream with the dessert wine until the mixture forms soft peaks. Spoon some of the cream syllabub on to each of the plain meringues. Arrange a few nectarine slices on each. Put each meringue on a dessert plate with a hazelnut-topped meringue. Decorate each portion with mint sprigs and serve the meringues immediately.

BLACK CHERRY CLAFOUTIS

THIS FAVOURITE RECIPE HAS BEEN REPRODUCED WITH ALL MANNER OF FRUIT, BUT YOU SIMPLY CAN'T BEAT THE CLASSIC VERSION USING SLIGHTLY TART BLACK CHERRIES.

SERVES SIX

INGREDIENTS
    25g/1oz/2 tbsp butter, for greasing
    450g/1lb/2 cups black
      cherries, stoned
    25g/1oz/¼ cup plain flour
    50g/2oz/½ cup icing sugar, plus extra
      for dusting
    4 eggs, beaten
    250ml/8fl oz/1 cup creamy milk
    30ml/2 tbsp Kirsch

1 Preheat the oven to 180°C/350°F/
Gas 4. Use the butter to thickly grease
a 1.2 litre/2 pint/5 cup gratin dish.
Scatter the cherries over the base.

2 Sift the flour and icing sugar together
into a large mixing bowl and gradually
whisk in the eggs until the mixture is
smooth. Whisk in the milk until
blended, then stir in the Kirsch.

3 Pour the batter carefully over the
cherries, then bake for 35–45 minutes
or until just set and lightly golden.

4 Allow the pudding to cool for about
15 minutes. Dust liberally with icing
sugar just before serving.

VARIATIONS
Try other liqueurs in this dessert.
Almond-flavoured liqueur is delicious
teamed with cherries. Hazelnut,
raspberry or orange liqueur would also
work nicely.

ICED GIN AND DAMSON SOUFFLÉS

FOR AN UNFORGETTABLE TASTE SENSATION, USE SLOE GIN FOR THESE DELICIOUS INDIVIDUAL FROZEN
SOUFFLÉS. THEY ARE PERFECT FOR A PARTY AND CAN BE MADE AHEAD.

MAKES SIX

INGREDIENTS
    500g/1¼lb damsons
    250ml/8fl oz/1 cup water
    275g/10oz/1¼ cups caster sugar
    30ml/2 tbsp gin or sloe gin
    4 large egg whites
    300ml/½ pint/1¼ cups double
      cream, whipped
    fresh mint leaves, to decorate

1 You will need six 150ml/¼ pint/⅔ cup ramekins. Give each a collar of greased non-stick baking paper that extends about 5cm/2in above the rim.

2 Slice two damsons and set aside for the decoration. Put the rest of the damsons in a pan with half the water and 50g/2oz/¼ cup of the caster sugar. Cover and simmer the mixture for about 7 minutes, or until the damsons are tender. Press the pulp through a sieve placed over a bowl to remove all the stones and skin, then stir in the gin and set aside.

3 Combine the remaining sugar and water in the clean pan and heat gently until the sugar has dissolved. Bring to the boil and cook the syrup until it registers 119°C/238°F on a sugar thermometer, or until a small amount of the mixture dropped into a cup of cold water can be moulded to a soft ball.

4 Meanwhile, whisk the egg whites in a grease-free bowl until they form stiff peaks. Still whisking, slowly pour in the hot syrup until the meringue mixture is stiff and glossy. Fold in the whipped cream and fruit purée until combined.

5 Spoon into the dishes to come 2.5cm/1in above the rim of each. Freeze until firm. Remove from the freezer 10 minutes before serving. Remove the collars, then decorate each with damson slices and mint leaves.

CARAMELIZED APRICOTS <u>WITH</u> PAIN PERDU

PAIN PERDU IS A FRENCH INVENTION THAT LITERALLY TRANSLATES AS "LOST BREAD". AMERICANS CALL IT FRENCH TOAST, WHILE A BRITISH VERSION IS KNOWN AS POOR KNIGHTS.

SERVES FOUR

INGREDIENTS
    75g/3oz/6 tbsp unsalted
      butter, clarified
    450g/1lb apricots, stoned and
      thickly sliced
    115g/4oz/½ cup caster sugar
    150ml/¼ pint/⅔ cup double cream
    30ml/2 tbsp apricot brandy or brandy
For the pain perdu
    600ml/1 pint/2½ cups milk
    1 vanilla pod
    50g/2oz/¼ cup caster sugar
    4 large eggs, beaten
    115g/4oz/½ cup unsalted
      butter, clarified
    6 brioche slices, diagonally halved
    2.5ml/½ tsp ground cinnamon

1 Heat a heavy-based frying pan, then melt a quarter of the butter. Add the apricot slices and cook for 2–3 minutes until golden. Using a slotted spoon, transfer them to a bowl. Add the rest of the butter to the pan with the sugar and heat gently, stirring, until golden.

2 Pour in the cream and brandy and cook gently until the mixture forms a smooth sauce. Boil for 2–3 minutes until thickened, then pour the sauce over the apricots and set aside.

3 To make the pain perdu, pour the milk into a saucepan and add the vanilla pod and half the sugar. Heat gently until almost boiling, then set aside to cool.

4 Remove the vanilla pod and pour the flavoured milk into a shallow dish. Whisk in the eggs. Heat a sixth of the butter in the clean frying pan. Dip each slice of brioche in turn into the milk mixture, add it to the pan and fry until golden brown on both sides. Add the remaining butter as needed. As the pain perdu is cooked, remove the slices; keep hot.

5 Warm the apricot sauce and spoon it on to the pain perdu. Mix the remaining sugar with the cinnamon and sprinkle a little of the mixture over each portion.

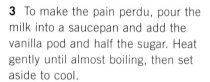

COOK'S TIP
To clarify the butter, melt it in a small saucepan, then leave it to stand for a few minutes. Carefully pour the clear butter on the surface (the clarified butter) into a small bowl, leaving the milky solids behind in the pan.

FRESH CHERRY AND HAZELNUT STRUDEL

SERVE THIS WONDERFUL OLD-WORLD TREAT AS A WARM DESSERT WITH CUSTARD, OR ALLOW IT TO COOL AND OFFER IT AS A SCRUMPTIOUS CAKE WITH AFTERNOON TEA OR COFFEE.

SERVES SIX TO EIGHT

INGREDIENTS
  75g/3oz/6 tbsp butter
  90ml/6 tbsp light muscovado sugar
  3 egg yolks
  grated rind of 1 lemon
  1.5ml/¼ tsp grated nutmeg
  250g/9oz/generous 1 cup ricotta
    cheese
  8 large sheets filo pastry, thawed
    if frozen
  75g/3oz ratafias, crushed
  450g/1lb/2½ cups cherries, stoned
  30ml/2 tbsp chopped hazelnuts
  icing sugar, for dusting
  crème fraîche, to serve

1 Preheat the oven to 190°C/375°F/ Gas 5. Soften 15g/½oz/1 tbsp of the butter. Place it in a bowl and beat in the sugar and egg yolks until light and fluffy. Beat in the lemon rind, nutmeg and ricotta, then set aside.

2 Melt the remaining butter in a small pan. Working quickly, place a sheet of filo on a clean tea towel and brush it generously with melted butter. Place a second sheet on top and repeat the process. Continue until all the filo has been layered and buttered, reserving some of the melted butter.

3 Scatter the crushed ratafias over the top, leaving a 5cm/2in border around the outside. Spoon the ricotta mixture over the biscuits, spread it lightly to cover, then scatter over the cherries.

4 Fold in the filo pastry border and use the dish towel to carefully roll up the strudel, Swiss-roll style, beginning from one of the long sides of the pastry. Grease a baking sheet with the remaining melted butter.

5 Place the strudel on the baking sheet and scatter the hazelnuts over the surface. Bake for 35–40 minutes or until the strudel is golden and crisp. Dust with icing sugar and serve with a dollop of crème fraîche.

BAKED LATTICE PEACHES

IF YOU WOULD RATHER USE NECTARINES FOR THE RECIPE, THERE'S NO NEED TO PEEL THEM FIRST.

MAKES SIX

INGREDIENTS
    3 peaches
    juice of ½ lemon
    75g/3oz/scant ½ cup white marzipan
    375g/13oz ready-rolled puff pastry,
      thawed if frozen
    a large pinch of ground cinnamon
    beaten egg, to glaze
    caster sugar, for sprinkling
For the caramel sauce
    50g/2oz/¼ cup caster sugar
    30ml/2 tbsp cold water
    150ml/¼ pint/⅔ cup double cream

1 Preheat the oven to 190°C/375°F/ Gas 5. Place the peaches in a large bowl and pour over boiling water to cover. Leave for 60 seconds, then drain the peaches and peel off the skins. Toss the skinned fruit in the lemon juice to stop them going brown.

2 Divide the marzipan into six pieces and shape each to form a small round. Cut the peaches in half and remove their stones. Fill the stone cavity in each with a marzipan round.

3 Unroll the puff pastry and cut it in half. Set one half aside, then cut out six rounds from the rest, making each round slightly larger than a peach half. Sprinkle a little cinnamon on each pastry round, then place a peach half, marzipan side down, on the pastry.

4 Cut the remaining pastry into lattice pastry, using a special cutter if you have one. If not, simply cut small slits in rows all over the pastry, starting each row slightly lower than the last. Cut the lattice pastry into six equal squares.

COOK'S TIP
Take care when adding the cream to the hot caramel as the mixture is liable to spit. Pour it from a jug, protecting your hand with an oven glove, and use a long-handled wooden spoon for stirring.

5 Dampen the edges of the pastry rounds with a little water, then drape a lattice pastry square over each peach half. Press around the edge to seal, then trim off the excess pastry and decorate with small peach leaves made from the trimmings. Transfer the peach pastries to a baking sheet. Brush with the beaten egg and sprinkle with the caster sugar. Bake for 20 minutes or until the pastries are golden.

6 Meanwhile, make the caramel sauce. Heat the sugar with the water in a small pan until it dissolves. Bring to the boil and continue to boil until the syrup turns a dark golden brown. Stand back and add the cream. Heat gently, stirring until smooth. Serve the peach pastries with the sauce.

PEACH AND REDCURRANT TARTLETS

TART REDCURRANTS AND SWEET PEACHES MAKE A WINNING COMBINATION IN THESE SIMPLE TARTLETS.

MAKES FOUR

INGREDIENTS
    25g/1oz/2 tbsp butter, melted
    16 × 15cm/6in squares of filo pastry,
      thawed if frozen
    icing sugar, for dusting
    redcurrant sprigs, to decorate
For the filling
    150ml/¼ pint/⅔ cup double cream
    125g/4¼oz carton peach and mango
      fromage frais
    a few drops of pure vanilla essence
    15ml/1 tbsp icing sugar, sifted
For the topping
    2 peaches
    50g/2oz/½ cup redcurrants

COOK'S TIP
To strip redcurrants from their stalks,
pull the stalks through the tines of a fork.

1 Preheat the oven to 190ºC/375ºF/
Gas 5. Use a little of the butter to grease
four large bun tins or individual tartlet
tins. Brush the pastry squares with
butter, stack them in fours, then place in
the tins to make four pastry cases.

2 Bake for 12–15 minutes until golden.
Cool the filo cases on a wire rack.

3 Make the filling. Whip the cream to
soft peaks, then lightly fold in the
fromage frais, vanilla essence and icing
sugar. Divide among the pastry cases.

4 Slice the peaches and fan them out
on top of the filling, interspersing with
a few redcurrants. Decorate with redcurrant sprigs and dust with icing sugar.

PLUM AND MARZIPAN PASTRIES

THESE DANISH PASTRIES CAN BE MADE WITH ANY PITTED FRUIT. TRY APRICOTS, CHERRIES, DAMSONS OR GREENGAGES, ADDING A GLAZE MADE FROM CLEAR HONEY OR A COMPLEMENTARY JAM.

MAKES SIX

INGREDIENTS
   375g/13oz ready-rolled puff pastry
   90ml/6 tbsp plum jam
   115g/4oz/½ cup white
     marzipan, coarsely grated
   3 red plums, halved and stoned
   1 egg, beaten
   50g/2oz/½ cup flaked almonds
For the glaze
   30ml/2 tbsp plum jam
   15ml/1 tbsp water

1 Preheat the oven to 220°C/425°F/ Gas 7. Unroll the pastry, cut it into six equal squares and place on one or two dampened baking sheets

2 Spoon 15ml/1 tbsp jam into the centre of each pastry square. Divide the marzipan among them. Place half a plum, hollow-side down, on top of each marzipan mound.

3 Brush the edges of the pastry with beaten egg. Bring up the corners and press them together lightly, then open out the pastry corners at the top. Glaze the pastries with a little beaten egg, then press a sixth of the flaked almonds on each.

4 Bake the pastries for 20–25 minutes or until lightly golden.

5 Meanwhile, make the glaze by heating the jam and water in a small pan, stirring until smooth. Press the mixture through a sieve into a small bowl, then brush it over the tops of the pastries while they are still warm. Leave to cool on a wire rack.

YELLOW PLUM TART

In this tart, glazed yellow plums sit atop a delectable almond filling in a crisp pastry shell. When they are in season, greengages make an excellent alternative to the plums.

SERVES EIGHT

INGREDIENTS
  175g/6oz/1½ cups plain flour
  pinch of salt
  75g/3oz/scant ½ cup butter, chilled
  30ml/2 tbsp caster sugar
  a few drops of pure vanilla essence
  45ml/3 tbsp iced water
  cream or custard, to serve
For the filling
  75g/3oz/⅓ cup caster sugar
  75g/3oz/scant ½ cup butter, softened
  75g/3oz/¾ cup ground almonds
  1 egg, beaten
  30ml/2 tbsp plain flour
  450g/1lb yellow plums or greengages,
    halved and stoned
For the glaze
  45ml/3 tbsp apricot jam, sieved
  15ml/1 tbsp water

1 Sift the flour and salt into a bowl, then rub in the chilled butter until the mixture resembles fine breadcrumbs. Stir in the caster sugar, vanilla essence and enough of the iced water to make a soft dough.

COOK'S TIP
Ceramic baking beans are ideal for baking blind, but any dried beans will do. You can use them over and over again, but make sure you keep them in a special jar, separate from the rest of your dried beans, as you cannot use them for conventional cooking.

2 Knead the dough gently on a lightly floured surface until smooth, then wrap in clear film and chill for 10 minutes.

3 Preheat the oven to 200°C/400°F/ Gas 6. Roll out the pastry and line a 23cm/9in fluted flan tin, allowing excess pastry to overhang the top. Prick the base with a fork and line with non-stick baking paper and baking beans.

4 Bake blind for 10 minutes, remove the paper and beans, then return the pastry case to the oven for 10 minutes. Remove and allow to cool. Trim off any excess pastry with a sharp knife.

5 To make the filling, whisk or beat together all the ingredients except the plums or greengages. Spread on the base of the pastry case. Arrange the plums or greengages on top, placing them cut side down. Make a glaze by heating the jam with the water. Stir well, then brush a little of the jam glaze over the top of the fruit.

6 Bake the tart for 50–60 minutes, until the almond filling is cooked and the plums or greengages are tender. Warm any remaining jam glaze and brush it over the top. Cut into slices and serve with cream or custard.

APRICOT PARCELS

THESE LITTLE FILO PARCELS CONTAIN A SPECIAL APRICOT AND MINCEMEAT FILLING. A GOOD WAY TO USE UP ANY MINCEMEAT AND MARZIPAN THAT HAVE BEEN IN YOUR CUPBOARD SINCE CHRISTMAS!

MAKES EIGHT

INGREDIENTS
  350g/12oz filo pastry, thawed
    if frozen
  50g/2oz/¼ cup butter, melted
  8 apricots, halved and stoned
  60ml/4 tbsp luxury mincemeat
  12 ratafias, crushed
  30ml/2 tbsp grated marzipan
  icing sugar, for dusting

COOK'S TIP
Filo pastry dries out quickly, so keep any squares not currently being used covered under a clean damp dish towel. Also, work as quickly as possible. If the filo should turn dry and brittle, simply brush it with melted butter to moisten.

1 Preheat the oven to 200°C/400°F/ Gas 6. Cut the filo pastry into 32 × 18cm/7in squares. Brush four of the squares with a little melted butter and stack them, giving each layer a quarter turn so that the stack acquires a star shape. Repeat to make eight stars.

2 Place an apricot half, hollow up, in the centre of each pastry star. Mix together the mincemeat, crushed ratafias and marzipan and spoon a little of the mixture into the hollow in each apricot.

3 Top with another apricot half, then bring the corners of each pastry together and squeeze to make a gathered purse.

4 Place the purses on a baking sheet and brush each with a little melted butter. Bake for 15–20 minutes or until the pastry is golden and crisp. Lightly dust with icing sugar to serve. Whipped cream, flavoured with a little brandy, makes an ideal accompaniment.

CRUNCHY-TOPPED FRESH APRICOT CAKE

ALMONDS ARE PERFECT PARTNERS FOR FRESH APRICOTS, AND THIS IS A GREAT WAY TO USE UP FIRM FRUITS. SERVE COLD AS A CAKE OR WARM WITH CUSTARD FOR A DESSERT.

MAKES EIGHT SLICES

INGREDIENTS
  175g/6oz/1½ cups self-raising flour
  175g/6oz/¾ cup butter, softened
  175g/6oz/¾ cup caster sugar
  115g/4oz/1 cup ground almonds
  3 eggs
  5ml/1 tsp almond essence
  2.5ml/½ tsp baking powder
  8 firm apricots, stoned and chopped
For the topping
  30ml/2 tbsp demerara sugar
  50g/2oz/½ cup slivered almonds

1 Preheat the oven to 160°C/325°F/ Gas 3. Grease an 18cm/7in round cake tin and line with non-stick baking paper. Put all the cake ingredients, except the apricots, in a large mixing bowl and whisk until creamy.

2 Fold the apricots into the cake mixture, then spoon into the prepared cake tin. Make a hollow in the centre with the back of a large spoon, then scatter 15ml/1 tbsp of the demerara sugar over for the topping, with the slivered almonds.

3 Bake for 1½ hours or until a skewer inserted into the middle comes out clean. Scatter the remaining demerara sugar over the top of the cake and leave to cool for 10 minutes in the tin. Remove from the tin, peel off the paper and finish cooling on a wire rack.

PICKLED PEACH AND CHILLI CHUTNEY

THIS IS A REALLY SPICY, RICH CHUTNEY THAT IS GREAT SERVED WITH COLD ROAST MEATS SUCH AS HAM, PORK OR TURKEY. IT IS ALSO GOOD WITH A STRONG FARMHOUSE CHEDDAR CHEESE.

MAKES 450G/1LB

INGREDIENTS
475ml/16fl oz/2 cups cider vinegar
275g/10oz/1⅔ cups light
  muscovado sugar
225g/8oz/1 cup dried dates, pitted
  and finely chopped
5ml/1 tsp ground allspice
5ml/1 tsp ground mace
450g/1lb ripe peaches, stoned and
  cut into small chunks
3 onions, thinly sliced
4 fresh red chillies, seeded and
  finely chopped
4 garlic cloves, crushed
5cm/2in piece of fresh root ginger,
  finely grated
5ml/1 tsp salt

1 Place the vinegar, sugar, dates and spices in a large saucepan and bring to the boil, stirring occasionally.

2 Add all the remaining ingredients and return to the boil. Lower the heat and simmer for 40–50 minutes or until thick. Stir often to prevent the mixture from burning on the base of the pan.

3 Spoon into clean sterilized jars and seal. When cold, store the jars in the fridge and use within 2 months.

COOK'S TIP
To test the consistency of the finished chutney before bottling, spoon a little of the mixture on to a plate: the chutney is ready once it holds its shape.

NECTARINE RELISH

THIS SWEET AND TANGY FRUIT RELISH GOES VERY WELL WITH HOT ROAST MEATS AND GAME BIRDS, SUCH AS GUINEA FOWL, PHEASANT AND PORK. MAKE WHILE NECTARINES ARE PLENTIFUL AND KEEP TIGHTLY COVERED IN THE FRIDGE TO SERVE AT CHRISTMAS FOR A REALLY SPECIAL TREAT.

MAKES 450G/1LB

INGREDIENTS
45ml/3 tbsp olive oil
2 Spanish onions, thinly sliced
1 fresh green chilli, seeded and
  finely chopped
5ml/1 tsp finely chopped
  fresh rosemary
2 bay leaves
450g/1lb nectarines, stoned and cut
  into chunks
150g/5oz/1 cup raisins
10ml/2 tsp crushed coriander seeds
350g/12oz/2 cups demerara sugar
200ml/7fl oz/scant 1 cup red
  wine vinegar

1 Heat the oil in a large pan. Add the onions, chilli, rosemary and bay leaves. Cook, stirring often, for 15–20 minutes or until the onions are soft.

COOK'S TIP
Jars of this relish make a welcome gift. Add a colourful tag reminding the recipient to keep it in the fridge.

2 Add all the remaining ingredients and bring to the boil slowly, stirring often. Lower the heat and simmer for 1 hour or until the relish is thick and sticky, stirring occasionally.

3 Spoon into sterilized jars and seal. Cool, then chill. The relish will keep in the fridge for up to 5 months.

BERRY AND CURRANT RECIPES

For sheer beauty, berries take a lot of beating. Make the most of their tantalizing colours and flavours by serving them simply, as a topping for shortcakes or in a summer pudding. Fresh Blueberry Muffins, Berry Brûlée Tarts, Bramble Jelly — these are berries at their best.

SUMMER PUDDING

NO FRUIT BOOK WOULD BE COMPLETE WITHOUT THIS WELL-LOVED CLASSIC RECIPE. DON'T RESERVE IT SOLELY FOR SUMMER: IT FREEZES WELL AND PROVIDES A DELICIOUS DESSERT FOR CHRISTMAS DAY, AS A LIGHT AND REFRESHING ALTERNATIVE TO THE TRADITIONAL PUDDING.

SERVES FOUR TO SIX

INGREDIENTS
8 × 1cm/½in thick slices of day-old white bread, crusts removed
800g/1¾lb/6–7 cups mixed berry fruit, such as strawberries, raspberries, blackcurrants, redcurrants and blueberries
50g/2oz/¼ cup golden caster sugar
lightly whipped double cream or crème fraîche, to serve

1 Trim a slice of bread to fit in the base of a 1.2 litre/2 pint/5 cup pudding basin, then trim another 5–6 slices to line the sides of the basin.

2 Place all the fruit in a saucepan with the sugar. Cook gently for 4–5 minutes until the juices begin to run – it will not be necessary to add any water. Allow the mixture to cool slightly, then spoon the berries and enough of their juices to moisten into the bread-lined pudding basin. Save any leftover juice to serve with the pudding.

3 Fold over the excess bread, then cover the fruit with the remaining bread slices, trimming them to fit. Place a small plate or saucer directly on top of the pudding, fitting it inside the basin. Weight it with a 900g/2lb weight if you have one, or use a couple of full cans.

4 Leave the pudding in the fridge for at least 8 hours or overnight. To serve, run a knife between the pudding and the basin and turn it out on to a plate. Spoon any reserved juices over the top and serve with whipped cream or crème fraîche.

HOT BLACKBERRY AND APPLE SOUFFLÉS

AS THE BLACKBERRY SEASON IS SO SHORT AND THE APPLE SEASON SO LONG, IT'S ALWAYS WORTH FREEZING A BAG OF BLACKBERRIES TO HAVE ON HAND FOR TREATS LIKE THIS ONE.

2 Cook the blackberries and diced apple with the orange rind and juice in a pan for 10 minutes or until the apple has pulped down well. Press through a sieve into a bowl. Stir in 50g/2oz/¼ cup of the caster sugar. Set aside to cool.

3 Put a spoonful of the fruit purée into each prepared dish and smooth the surface. Set the dishes aside.

4 Whisk the egg whites in a large grease-free bowl until they form stiff peaks. Very gradually whisk in the remaining caster sugar to make a stiff, glossy meringue mixture.

5 Fold in the remaining fruit purée and spoon the flavoured meringue into the prepared dishes. Level the tops with a palette knife, and run a table knife around the edge of each dish.

6 Place the dishes on the hot baking sheet and bake for 10–15 minutes until the soufflés have risen well and are lightly browned. Dust the tops with icing sugar and serve immediately.

MAKES SIX

INGREDIENTS
butter, for greasing
150g/5oz/⅔ cup caster sugar, plus
    extra for dusting
350g/12oz/3 cups blackberries
1 large cooking apple, peeled, cored
    and finely diced
grated rind and juice of 1 orange
3 egg whites
icing sugar, for dusting

COOK'S TIP
Running a table knife around the edge of the soufflés before baking helps them to rise evenly without any part sticking to the rim of the dishes.

1 Preheat the oven to 200°C/400°F/ Gas 6. Generously grease six 150ml/ ¼ pint/⅔ cup individual soufflé dishes with butter and dust with caster sugar, shaking out the excess sugar. Put a baking sheet in the oven to heat.

SUMMER BERRY CRÊPES

THE DELICATE FLAVOUR OF THESE FLUFFY CRÊPES CONTRASTS BEAUTIFULLY WITH TANGY BERRY FRUITS.

SERVES FOUR

INGREDIENTS
  115g/4oz/1 cup self-raising flour
  1 large egg
  300ml/½ pint/1¼ cups milk
  a few drops of pure vanilla essence
  15g/½oz/1 tbsp butter
  15ml/1 tbsp sunflower oil
  icing sugar, for dusting
For the fruit
  25g/1oz/2 tbsp butter
  50g/2oz/¼ cup caster sugar
  juice of 2 oranges
  thinly pared rind of ½ orange
  350g/12oz/3 cups mixed summer
    berries, such as sliced strawberries,
    yellow raspberries, blueberries
    and redcurrants
  45ml/3 tbsp Grand Marnier or other
    orange liqueur

1 Preheat the oven to 150°C/300°F/ Gas 2. To make the crêpes, sift the flour into a large bowl and make a well in the centre. Break in the egg and gradually whisk in the milk to make a smooth batter. Stir in the vanilla essence. Set the batter aside in a cool place for up to half an hour.

2 Heat the butter and oil together in an 18cm/7in non-stick frying pan. Swirl to grease the pan, then pour off the excess fat into a small bowl.

3 If the batter has been allowed to stand, whisk it thoroughly until smooth. Pour a little of the batter into the hot pan, swirling to cover the base of the pan evenly. Cook until the mixture comes away from the sides and the crêpe is golden underneath.

4 Flip over the crêpe with a large palette knife and cook the other side briefly until golden.

5 Slide the crêpe onto a heatproof plate. Make seven more crêpes in the same way, greasing the pan with more butter and oil mixture as needed. Cover the crêpes with foil or another plate and keep them hot in the oven.

COOK'S TIP
For safety, when igniting a mixture for flambéing, use a long taper or long wooden match. Stand back as you set the mixture alight.

6 To prepare the fruit, melt the butter in a heavy-based frying pan, stir in the sugar and cook gently until the mixture is golden brown. Add the orange juice and rind and cook until syrupy.

7 Add the fruits and warm through, then add the liqueur and set it alight. Shake the pan to incorporate the liqueur until the flame dies down.

8 Fold the pancakes into quarters and arrange two on each plate. Spoon over some of the fruit mixture and dust liberally with the icing sugar. Serve any remaining fruit mixture separately.

FRESH BERRY PAVLOVA

PAVLOVA IS THE SIMPLEST OF DESSERTS, BUT IT CAN ALSO BE THE MOST STUNNING. FILL WITH A MIX OF BERRY FRUITS IF YOU LIKE — RASPBERRIES AND BLUEBERRIES MAKE A MARVELLOUS COMBINATION.

SERVES SIX TO EIGHT

INGREDIENTS

4 egg whites, at room temperature
225g/8oz/1 cup caster sugar
5ml/1 tsp cornflour
5ml/1 tsp cider vinegar
2.5ml/½ tsp pure vanilla essence
300ml/½ pint/1¼ cups double cream
150ml/¼ pint/⅔ cup crème fraîche
175g/6oz/1 cup raspberries
175g/6oz/1½ cups blueberries
fresh mint sprigs, to decorate
icing sugar, for dusting

COOK'S TIP

To begin, invert a plate on the baking paper and draw round it with a pencil. Turn the paper over and use the circle as a guide for the meringue.

1 Preheat the oven to 140ºC/275ºF/ Gas 1. Line a baking sheet with non-stick baking paper. Whisk the egg whites in a large grease-free bowl until they form stiff peaks. Gradually whisk in the sugar to make a stiff, glossy meringue. Sift the cornflour over and fold it in with the vinegar and vanilla.

2 Spoon the meringue mixture on to the paper-lined sheet, using the circle drawn on the paper as a guide (see Cook's Tip). Spread into a round, swirling the top, and bake for 1¼ hours or until the meringue is crisp and very lightly golden. Switch off the oven, keeping the door closed, and allow the meringue to cool for 1–2 hours.

3 Carefully peel the paper from the meringue and transfer it to a serving plate. Whip the cream in a large mixing bowl until it forms soft peaks, fold in the crème fraîche, then spoon the mixture into the centre of the meringue case. Top with the raspberries and blueberries and decorate with the mint sprigs. Sift icing sugar over the top and serve at once.

GOOSEBERRY AND ELDERFLOWER FOOL

GOOSEBERRIES AND ELDERFLOWERS ARE A MATCH MADE IN HEAVEN, EACH BRINGING OUT THE FLAVOUR OF THE OTHER. SERVE WITH AMARETTI OR OTHER DESSERT BISCUITS FOR DIPPING.

SERVES SIX

INGREDIENTS
    450g/1lb/4 cups gooseberries, topped
        and tailed
    30ml/2 tbsp water
    50–75g/2–3oz/¼–⅓ cup caster sugar
    30ml/2 tbsp elderflower cordial
    400g/14oz carton ready-made
        custard sauce
    green food colouring (optional)
    300ml/½ pint/1¼ cups double cream
    crushed amaretti biscuits, to decorate
    amaretti biscuits, to serve

1 Put the gooseberries and water in
a pan. Cover and cook for 5–6 minutes
or until the berries pop open.

2 Add the sugar and elderflower cordial
to the gooseberries, then stir vigorously
or mash until the fruit forms a pulp.
Remove the pan from the heat, spoon
the gooseberry pulp into a bowl and set
aside to cool.

3 Stir the custard into the fruit. Add a
few drops of food colouring, if using.
Whip the cream to soft peaks, then fold
it into the mixture and chill. Serve in
dessert glasses, decorated with crushed
amaretti, and accompanied by amaretti.

FRUITS OF THE FOREST WITH WHITE CHOCOLATE CREAMS

COLOURFUL FRUITS MACERATED IN A MIXTURE OF WHITE COCONUT RUM AND SUGAR MAKE A FANTASTIC ACCOMPANIMENT TO A DELIGHTFULLY CREAMY WHITE CHOCOLATE MOUSSE.

SERVES FOUR

INGREDIENTS
  75g/3oz white cooking chocolate,
    in squares
  150ml/¼ pint/⅔ cup double cream
  30ml/2 tbsp crème fraîche
  1 egg, separated
  5ml/1 tsp powdered gelatine
  30ml/2 tbsp cold water
  a few drops of pure vanilla essence
  115g/4oz/1 cup small
    strawberries, sliced
  75g/3oz/½ cup raspberries
  75g/3oz/¾ cup blueberries
  45ml/3 tbsp caster sugar
  75ml/5 tbsp white coconut rum
  strawberry leaves, to decorate
    (optional)

1 Melt the chocolate in a heatproof bowl set over a pan of hot water. Heat the cream in a separate pan until almost boiling, then stir into the chocolate with the crème fraîche. Cool slightly, then beat in the egg yolk.

2 Sprinkle the gelatine over the cold water in another heatproof bowl and set aside for a few minutes to swell.

COOK'S TIP
For a dramatic effect, decorate each white chocolate cream with dark chocolate leaves, made by coating the veined side of unsprayed rose leaves with melted chocolate. Let them dry before gently pulling off the leaves.

3 Set the bowl in a pan of hot water until the gelatine has dissolved completely. Stir the dissolved gelatine into the chocolate mixture and add the vanilla essence. Set aside until starting to thicken and set.

4 Brush four dariole moulds or individual soufflé dishes with oil; line the base of each with non-stick baking paper.

5 In a grease-free bowl, whisk the egg white to soft peaks, then fold into the chocolate mixture.

6 Spoon the mixture into the prepared moulds or soufflé dishes, then level the surface of each and chill for 2–3 hours or until firm.

7 Meanwhile, place the fruits in a bowl. Add the caster sugar and coconut rum and stir gently to mix. Cover and chill until required.

8 Ease the chocolate cream away from the rims of the moulds or dishes and turn out on to dessert plates. Spoon the fruits around the outside. Decorate with the strawberry leaves, if you like, then serve at once.

FRESH STRAWBERRY ICE CREAM

YOU CAN MAKE THE ICE CREAM BY HAND IF YOU FREEZE IT OVER A PERIOD OF SEVERAL HOURS, WHISKING IT EVERY HOUR OR SO, BUT THE TEXTURE WON'T BE AS GOOD.

SERVES SIX

INGREDIENTS
300ml/½ pint/1¼ cups creamy milk
1 vanilla pod
3 large egg yolks
225g/8oz/1½–2 cups strawberries
juice of ½ lemon
75g/3oz/¾ cup icing sugar
300ml/½ pint/1¼ cups double cream
sliced strawberries, to serve

1 Put the milk into a pan, add the vanilla pod and bring to the boil over a low heat. Remove from the heat. Leave for 20 minutes, then remove the vanilla pod. Strain the warm milk into a bowl containing the egg yolks; whisk well.

2 Return the mixture to the clean pan and heat, stirring, until the custard just coats the back of the spoon. Pour the custard into a bowl, cover the surface with clear film and set aside to cool.

COOK'S TIP
Use free-range eggs if possible, bought from a reputable supplier.

3 Meanwhile, purée the strawberries with the lemon juice in a food processor or blender. Press the strawberry purée through a sieve into a bowl. Stir in the icing sugar and set aside.

4 Whip the cream to soft peaks, then gently but thoroughly fold it into the custard with the strawberry purée. Pour the mixture into an ice cream maker. Churn for 20–30 minutes or until the mixture holds its shape. Transfer the ice cream to a freezerproof container, cover and freeze until firm. Soften briefly before serving with the strawberries.

BLACKCURRANT SORBET

THIS LUSCIOUS SORBET IS EASILY MADE BY HAND, BUT IT IS IMPORTANT TO ALTERNATELY FREEZE AND BLEND OR PROCESS THE MIXTURE FIVE OR SIX TIMES TO GET THE BEST RESULT. IF YOU MAKE LOTS OF ICE CREAM AND SORBETS, IT IS WORTH INVESTING IN AN ICE CREAM MAKER.

SERVES SIX

INGREDIENTS
    300ml/½ pint/1¼ cups water, plus
      30ml/2 tbsp
    115g/4oz/½ cup caster sugar
    225g/8oz/2 cups blackcurrants
    30ml/2 tbsp crème de cassis or other
      blackcurrant liqueur
    5ml/1 tsp lemon juice
    2 egg whites

1 Pour 300ml/½ pint/1¼ cups of the water into a saucepan and add the sugar. Place over a low heat until the sugar has dissolved. Bring to the boil and boil rapidly for 10 minutes, then set the syrup aside to cool.

2 Meanwhile, cook the blackcurrants with the remaining 30ml/2 tbsp water over a low heat for 5–7 minutes. Press the blackcurrants and juice through a sieve placed over a jug, then stir the blackcurrant purée into the syrup with the liqueur and lemon juice. Allow to cool completely, then chill for 1 hour.

3 Pour the chilled blackcurrant syrup into a freezerproof bowl; freeze until slushy, whisking occasionally. Whisk the egg whites in a grease-free bowl until they form soft peaks, then fold into the semi-frozen blackcurrant mixture.

4 Freeze the mixture again until firm, then spoon into a food processor or blender and process. Alternately freeze and process or blend until completely smooth. Serve the sorbet straight from the freezer.

RASPBERRY AND ROSE PETAL SHORTCAKES

ROSEWATER-SCENTED CREAM AND FRESH RASPBERRIES FORM THE FILLING FOR THIS DELECTABLE DESSERT. THOUGH THEY LOOK IMPRESSIVE, THESE SHORTCAKES ARE EASY TO MAKE.

MAKES SIX

INGREDIENTS
   115g/4oz/½ cup unsalted
      butter, softened
   50g/2oz/¼ cup caster sugar
   ½ vanilla pod, split, seeds reserved
   115g/4oz/1 cup plain flour, plus
      extra for dusting
   50g/2oz/⅓ cup semolina
   icing sugar, for dusting
For the filling
   300ml/½ pint/1¼ cups double cream
   15ml/1 tbsp icing sugar
   2.5ml/½ tsp rosewater
   450g/1lb/4 cups raspberries
For the decoration
   12 miniature roses, unsprayed
   6 mint sprigs
   1 egg white, beaten
   caster sugar, for dusting

1 Cream the butter, caster sugar and vanilla seeds in a bowl until pale and fluffy. Sift the flour and semolina together, then gradually work the dry ingredients into the creamed mixture to make a biscuit dough.

VARIATIONS
Other soft red summer berries, such as mulberries, loganberries and tayberries, would be equally good in this dessert.

COOK'S TIP
For best results, serve the shortcakes as soon as possible after assembling them. Otherwise, they are likely to turn soggy from the berries' liquid.

2 Gently knead the dough on a lightly floured surface until smooth. Roll out quite thinly and prick all over with a fork. Using a 7.5cm/3in fluted cutter, cut out 12 rounds. Place these on a baking sheet and chill for 30 minutes.

3 Meanwhile, make the filling. Whisk the cream with the icing sugar until soft peaks form. Fold in the rosewater and chill until required.

4 Preheat the oven to 180°C/350°F/ Gas 4. To make the decoration, paint the roses and leaves with the egg white. Dust with sugar; dry on a wire rack.

5 Bake the shortcakes for 15 minutes or until lightly golden. Lift them off the baking sheet with a metal fish slice and cool on a wire rack.

6 To assemble the shortcakes, spoon the rosewater cream on to half the biscuits. Add a layer of raspberries, then top with a second shortcake. Dust with icing sugar. Decorate with the frosted roses and mint sprigs.

FRESH CURRANT BREAD AND BUTTER PUDDING

FRESH MIXED CURRANTS ADD A TART TOUCH TO THIS SCRUMPTIOUS HOT PUDDING.

SERVES SIX

INGREDIENTS
    8 medium-thick slices day old bread,
      crusts removed
    50g/2oz/¼ cup butter, softened
    115g/4oz/1 cup redcurrants
    115g/4oz/1 cup blackcurrants
    4 eggs, beaten
    75g/3oz/6 tbsp caster sugar
    475ml/16fl oz/2 cups creamy milk
    5ml/1 tsp pure vanilla essence
    freshly grated nutmeg
    30ml/2 tbsp demerara sugar
    single cream, to serve

1 Preheat the oven to 160°C/325°F/
Gas 3. Generously butter a 1.2 litre/
2 pint/5 cup oval baking dish.

VARIATION
A mixture of blueberries and raspberries
would work just as well as the currants.

2 Spread the slices of bread generously
with the butter, then cut them in half
diagonally. Layer the slices in the dish,
buttered side up, scattering the currants
between the layers.

3 Beat the eggs and caster sugar
lightly together in a large mixing bowl,
then gradually whisk in the milk, vanilla
essence and a large pinch of freshly
grated nutmeg.

4 Pour the milk mixture over the bread,
pushing the slices down. Scatter the
demerara sugar and a little nutmeg over
the top. Place the dish in a baking tin
and fill with hot water to come halfway
up the sides of the dish. Bake for
40 minutes, then increase the oven
temperature to 180°C/350°F/Gas 4 and
bake for 20–25 minutes more or until
the top is golden. Cool slightly, then
serve with single cream.

CRANBERRY AND BLUEBERRY STREUSEL CAKE

CRANBERRIES ARE SELDOM USED IN SWEET DISHES BUT ONCE THEY ARE SWEETENED, THEY HAVE A GREAT FLAVOUR AND ARE PERFECT WHEN PARTNERED WITH BLUEBERRIES.

MAKES TEN SLICES

INGREDIENTS

175g/6oz/¾ cup butter, softened
115g/4oz/½ cup caster sugar
350g/12oz/3 cups plain flour
2 large eggs, beaten
5ml/1 tsp baking powder
5ml/1 tsp pure vanilla essence
115g/4oz/1 cup cranberries
115g/4oz/1 cup blueberries
50g/2oz/⅓ cup light muscovado sugar
2.5ml/½ tsp crushed cardamom seeds
icing sugar, for dusting

1 Preheat the oven to 190ºC/375ºF/ Gas 5. Grease and base-line a 21cm/ 8½in round springform cake tin.

2 Cream the butter and caster sugar together until smooth, then rub in the flour with your fingers until the mixture resembles fine breadcrumbs. Take out 200g/7oz/generous 1 cup of the mixture and set this aside.

3 Beat the eggs, baking powder and vanilla essence into the remaining mixture until soft and creamy. Spoon on to the base of the prepared tin and spread evenly. Arrange the cranberries and blueberries on top, then sprinkle the muscovado sugar over.

4 Stir the cardamom seeds into the reserved flour mixture, then scatter evenly over the top of the fruit. Bake for 50–60 minutes or until the topping is golden. Cool the cake in the tin for 10 minutes, then remove the sides of the tin. Slide it on to a wire rack, lifting it off its base at the same time. Cool the cake completely, then dust with icing sugar and serve with whipped cream.

FRESH BLUEBERRY MUFFINS

MAKE THESE POPULAR AMERICAN TREATS IN PAPER CASES FOR MOISTER MUFFINS — IF YOU CAN'T FIND THEM, JUST GREASE THE TIN WELL BEFORE FILLING. THESE ARE BEST SERVED SLIGHTLY WARM.

MAKES TWELVE

INGREDIENTS
    275g/10oz/2½ cups plain flour
    15ml/1 tbsp baking powder
    75g/3oz/6 tbsp caster sugar
    250ml/8fl oz/1 cup milk
    3 eggs, beaten
    115g/4oz/½ cup butter, melted
    a few drops of pure vanilla essence
    225g/8oz/2 cups blueberries
For the topping
    50g/2oz/½ cup pecan nuts,
        coarsely chopped
    30ml/2 tbsp demerara sugar

COOK'S TIP
Don't be tempted to beat the muffin
mixture; it should be fairly wet and
needs to be quite lumpy. Overmixing will
create tough muffins.

1 Preheat the oven to 200°C/400°F/
Gas 6. Stand 12 paper muffin cases in
a muffin tin, or simply grease the tin
thoroughly. Sift the flour and baking
powder into a large bowl. Stir in the
caster sugar. Mix the milk, eggs, melted
butter and vanilla essence in a jug and
whisk lightly. Add to the flour mixture
and fold together lightly.

2 Fold in the blueberries, then divide
the mixture among the muffin cases.
Scatter a few nuts and a little demerara
sugar over the top of each. Bake for
20–25 minutes, or until the muffins are
well risen and golden.

3 Remove the warm muffins from the
tin; cool slightly on a wire rack.

BLUEBERRY PIE

AMERICAN BLUEBERRIES OR EUROPEAN BILBERRIES CAN BE USED FOR THIS PIE. YOU MAY NEED TO ADD A LITTLE MORE SUGAR IF YOU ARE LUCKY ENOUGH TO FIND NATIVE BILBERRIES.

SERVES SIX

INGREDIENTS
  2 × 225g/8oz ready-rolled shortcrust
    pastry sheets, thawed if frozen
  800g/1¾lb/7 cups blueberries
  75g/3oz/6 tbsp caster sugar, plus
    extra for sprinkling
  45ml/3 tbsp cornflour
  grated rind and juice of ½ orange
  grated rind of ½ lemon
  2.5ml/½ tsp ground cinnamon
  15g/½oz/1 tbsp unsalted
    butter, diced
  beaten egg, to glaze
  whipped cream, to serve

1 Preheat the oven to 200°C/400°F/ Gas 6. Use one sheet of pastry to line a 23cm/9in pie tin, leaving the excess pastry hanging over the edges.

2 Mix the blueberries, caster sugar, cornflour, orange rind and juice, lemon rind and cinnamon in a large bowl. Spoon into the pastry case and dot with the butter. Dampen the rim of the pastry case with a little water and top with the remaining pastry sheet.

VARIATION
Substitute a crumble topping for the pastry lid. The contrast with the juicy blueberry filling is sensational.

3 Cut the pastry edge at 2.5cm/1in intervals, then fold each section over on itself to form a triangle and create a sunflower edge. Trim off the excess pastry and cut out decorations from the trimmings. Attach them to the pastry lid with a little of the beaten egg.

4 Glaze the pastry with the egg and sprinkle with caster sugar. Bake for 30–35 minutes or until golden. Serve warm or cold with whipped cream.

BERRY BRÛLÉE TARTS

*THIS QUANTITY OF PASTRY IS ENOUGH FOR EIGHT TARTLETS, SO FREEZE HALF FOR ANOTHER DAY.
THE BRÛLÉE TOPPING IS BEST ADDED NO MORE THAN TWO HOURS BEFORE SERVING THE TARTS.*

MAKES FOUR

INGREDIENTS
  250g/9oz/2¼ cups plain flour
  pinch of salt
  25g/1oz/¼ cup ground almonds
  15ml/1 tbsp icing sugar
  150g/5oz/⅔ cup unsalted butter,
    chilled and diced
  1 egg yolk
  about 45ml/3 tbsp cold water
For the filling
  4 egg yolks
  15ml/1 tbsp cornflour
  50g/2oz/¼ cup caster sugar
  a few drops of pure vanilla essence
  300ml/½ pint/1¼ cups creamy milk
  225g/8oz/2 cups mixed berry fruits,
    such as small strawberries,
    raspberries, blackcurrants
    and redcurrants
  50g/2oz/½ cup icing sugar

1 Mix the flour, salt, ground almonds and icing sugar in a bowl. Rub in the butter by hand or in a food processor until the mixture resembles fine breadcrumbs. Add the egg yolk and enough cold water to form a dough. Knead the dough gently, then cut it in half and freeze half for use later.

2 Cut the remaining pastry into four equal pieces and roll out thinly.

COOK'S TIP
If you possess a culinary blow torch – and are confident about operating it safely – use it to easily melt and caramelize the brûlée topping.

3 Use the pastry rounds to line four individual tartlet tins, letting the excess pastry hang over the edges. Chill for 30 minutes.

4 Preheat the oven to 200°C/400°F/ Gas 6. Line the pastry with non-stick baking paper and baking beans. Bake blind for 10 minutes. Remove the paper and beans and return the tartlet cases to the oven for 5 minutes until golden. Allow the pastry to cool, then carefully trim off the excess pastry.

5 Beat the egg yolks, cornflour, caster sugar and vanilla essence in a bowl.

6 Warm the milk in a heavy-based pan, pour it on to the egg yolks, whisking constantly, then return the mixture to the clean pan.

7 Heat, stirring, until the custard thickens, but do not let it boil. Remove from the heat, press a piece of clear film directly on the surface of the custard and allow to cool.

8 Scatter the berries in the tartlet cases and spoon over the custard. Chill the tarts for 2 hours.

9 To serve, sift icing sugar generously over the tops of the tartlets. Preheat the grill to the highest setting. Place the tartlets under the hot grill until the sugar melts and caramelizes. Allow the topping to cool and harden for about 10 minutes before serving the tarts.

BRAMBLE JELLY

THIS JELLY IS ONE OF THE BEST. IT HAS TO BE MADE WITH HAND-PICKED WILD BLACKBERRIES FOR THE BEST FLAVOUR. MAKE SURE YOU INCLUDE A FEW RED UNRIPE BERRIES FOR A GOOD SET.

MAKES 900G/2LB

INGREDIENTS
    900g/2lb/8 cups blackberries
    300ml/½ pint/1¼ cups water
    juice of 1 lemon
    about 900g/2lb/4 cups caster sugar
    hot buttered toast or English muffins,
      to serve

VARIATION
Redcurrant jelly is made in the same way, but with less sugar. Reduce the quantity to 350g/12oz/1½ cups for every 600ml/1 pint/2½ cups juice.

1 Put the fruit, water and lemon juice into a large saucepan. Cover the pan and cook for 15–30 minutes or until the blackberries are very soft.

2 Ladle into a jelly bag or a large sieve lined with muslin and set over a large bowl. Leave to drip overnight to obtain the maximum amount of juice.

3 Discard the fruit pulp. Measure the exuded juice and allow 450g/1lb/2 cups sugar to every 600ml/1 pint/2½ cups juice. Place both in a large heavy-based pan and bring the mixture slowly to a boil, stirring all the time until the sugar has dissolved.

4 Boil rapidly until the jelly registers 105°C/220°F on a sugar thermometer or test for setting by spooning a small amount on to a chilled saucer. Chill for 3 minutes, then push the mixture with your finger; if wrinkles form on the surface, it is ready. Cool for 10 minutes.

5 Skim off any scum and pour the jelly into warm sterilized jars. Cover and seal while the jelly is still hot and label when the jars are cold. Serve the jelly with hot buttered toast or English muffins.

STRAWBERRY JAM

CAPTURE THE ESSENCE OF SUMMER IN A JAR OF HOME-MADE STRAWBERRY JAM.

MAKES ABOUT 1.4KG/3LB

INGREDIENTS
    1kg/2¼lb/8 cups small strawberries
    900g/2lb/4 cups granulated sugar
    juice of 2 lemons
    scones and clotted cream, to serve

1 Layer the strawberries and sugar in a large bowl. Cover and leave overnight.

2 The next day, scrape the strawberries and their juice into a large heavy-based pan. Add the lemon juice. Gradually bring to the boil over a low heat, stirring until the sugar has dissolved.

COOK'S TIPS
For best results when making jam, don't wash the strawberries unless absolutely necessary. Instead, brush off any dirt, or wipe the strawberries with a damp cloth. If you have to wash any, pat them dry and then spread them out on a clean dish towel to dry further.

To sterilize jam jars, wash in hot soapy water, then rinse thoroughly and drain. Place the jars on a baking sheet and dry in a warm oven for 15–20 minutes.

3 Boil steadily for 10–15 minutes or until the jam registers 105ºC/220ºF on a sugar thermometer. Alternatively, test for setting by spooning a small amount on to a chilled saucer. Chill for 3 minutes, then push the jam with your finger; if wrinkles form on the surface, it is ready. Cool for 10 minutes.

4 Pour the strawberry jam into warm sterilized jars, filling them right to the top. Cover and seal while the jam is still hot and label when the jars are cold. Serve with scones and clotted cream, if you like. This jam can be stored in a cool dark place and should keep for up to 1 year.

CITRUS FRUIT RECIPES

Put the squeeze on citrus for some of the finest puddings and preserves in the good cook's repertoire. Lemon Surprise Pudding, Moist Orange and Almond Cake, Key Lime Pie and Lemon Meringue Pie are perennially popular, while new delights include Lemon Coeur à la Crème with Cointreau Oranges.

LEMON COEUR À LA CRÈME
WITH COINTREAU ORANGES

THIS ZESTY DESSERT IS THE IDEAL CHOICE TO FOLLOW A RICH MAIN COURSE SUCH AS ROAST PORK.

SERVES FOUR

INGREDIENTS
  225g/8oz/1 cup cottage cheese
  250g/9oz/generous 1 cup mascarpone
    cheese
  50g/2oz/¼ cup caster sugar
  grated rind and juice of 1 lemon
  spirals of orange rind, to decorate
For the Cointreau oranges
  4 oranges
  10ml/2 tsp cornflour
  15ml/1 tbsp icing sugar
  60ml/4 tbsp Cointreau

1 Put the cottage cheese in a food processor or blender and whizz until smooth. Add the mascarpone, caster sugar, lemon rind and juice and process briefly to mix the ingredients.

2 Line four coeur à la crème moulds with muslin, then divide the mixture among them. Level the surface of each, then place the moulds on a plate to catch any liquid that drains from the cheese. Cover and chill overnight.

3 Make the Cointreau oranges. Squeeze the juice from two oranges and pour into a measuring jug. Make the juice up to 250ml/8fl oz/1 cup with water, then pour into a small saucepan. Blend a little of the juice mixture with the cornflour and add to the pan with the icing sugar. Heat the sauce, stirring until thickened.

4 Using a sharp knife, peel and segment the remaining oranges. Add the segments to the pan, stir to coat, then set aside. When cool, stir in the Cointreau. Cover and chill overnight.

5 Turn the moulds out on to plates and surround with the oranges. Decorate with spirals of orange rind and serve at once.

CLEMENTINE JELLY

JELLY ISN'T ONLY FOR CHILDREN: THIS ADULT VERSION HAS A CLEAR FRUITY TASTE AND CAN BE MADE EXTRA SPECIAL BY ADDING A LITTLE WHITE RUM OR COINTREAU.

SERVES FOUR

INGREDIENTS
    12 clementines
    clear grape juice (see method
      for amount)
    15ml/1 tbsp powdered gelatine
    30ml/2 tbsp caster sugar
    whipped cream, to decorate

VARIATION
Use four ruby grapefruit instead of clementines, if you prefer. Squeeze the juice from half of them and segment the rest, discarding any bitter white pith.

1 Squeeze the juice from eight of the clementines and pour it into a jug. Make up to 600ml/1 pint/2½ cups with the grape juice, then strain the juice mixture through a fine sieve.

2 Pour half the juice mixture into a pan. Sprinkle the gelatine on top, leave for 5 minutes, then heat gently until the gelatine has dissolved. Stir in the sugar, then the remaining juice; set aside.

3 Pare the rind very thinly from the remaining fruit and set it aside. Using a small sharp knife, cut between the membrane and fruit to separate the citrus segments. Discard the membrane and white pith.

4 Place half the segments in four dessert glasses and cover with some of the liquid fruit jelly. Place in the fridge and allow to set.

5 When the jellies are set, arrange the remaining segments on top. Carefully pour over the remaining liquid jelly and chill until set. Cut the pared clementine rind into fine shreds. Serve the jellies topped with a generous spoonful of whipped cream scattered with clementine rind shreds.

RUBY ORANGE SHERBET IN GINGER BASKETS

THIS SUPERB FROZEN DESSERT IS PERFECT FOR PEOPLE WITHOUT ICE CREAM MAKERS WHO CAN'T BE BOTHERED WITH THE FREEZING AND STIRRING THAT HOME-MADE ICES NORMALLY REQUIRE. IT IS ALSO IDEAL FOR SERVING AT A SPECIAL DINNER PARTY AS BOTH THE SHERBET AND GINGER BASKETS CAN BE MADE IN ADVANCE AND THE DESSERT SIMPLY ASSEMBLED BETWEEN COURSES.

SERVES SIX

INGREDIENTS

grated rind and juice of
  2 blood oranges
175g/6oz/1½ cups icing sugar
300ml/½ pint/1¼ cups double cream
200g/7oz/scant 1 cup Greek-style
  natural yogurt
blood orange segments, to
  decorate (optional)
For the ginger baskets
  25g/1oz/2 tbsp unsalted butter
  15ml/1 tbsp golden syrup
  30ml/2 tbsp caster sugar
  1.5ml/¼ tsp ground ginger
  15ml/1 tbsp finely chopped mixed
    citrus peel
  15ml/1 tbsp plain flour

2 Whisk the double cream in a large bowl until the mixture forms soft peaks, then fold in the yogurt.

3 Gently stir in the orange juice mixture, then pour into a freezerproof container. Cover and freeze until firm.

6 Lightly grease two baking sheets. Using about 10ml/2 tsp of the mixture at a time, drop three portions of the ginger dough on to each baking sheet, spacing them well apart. Spread each one to a 5cm/2in circle, then bake for 12–14 minutes or until the biscuits are dark golden in colour.

1 Place the orange rind and juice in a bowl. Sift the icing sugar over the top and set aside for 30 minutes, then stir until smooth.

COOK'S TIP
When making the ginger baskets it is essential to work quickly. Have the greased tins or cups ready before you start. If the biscuits cool and firm up before you have time to drape them all, return them to the oven for a few seconds to soften them again.

4 Make the baskets. Preheat the oven to 180°C/350°F/Gas 4. Place the butter, syrup and sugar in a heavy-based saucepan and heat gently until melted.

5 Add the ground ginger, mixed citrus peel and flour and stir until the mixture is smooth.

7 Remove the biscuits from the oven and allow to stand on the baking sheets for 1 minute to firm slightly. Lift off with a fish slice and drape over six greased mini pudding tins or upturned cups; flatten the top (which will become the base) and flute the edges to form a basket shape.

8 When cool, lift the baskets off the tins or cups and place on individual dessert plates. Arrange small scoops of the frozen orange sherbet in each basket. Decorate each portion with a few orange segments, if you like.

CHOCOLATE AND MANDARIN TRUFFLE SLICE

CHOCOHOLICS WILL LOVE THIS WICKEDLY RICH DESSERT. THE MANDARINS GIVE IT A DELICIOUS TANG.

SERVES EIGHT

INGREDIENTS
  400g/14oz plain chocolate
  4 egg yolks
  3 mandarin oranges
  200ml/7fl oz/scant 1 cup crème
    fraîche
  30ml/2 tbsp raisins
  chocolate curls, to decorate
For the sauce
  30ml/2 tbsp Cointreau
  120ml/4fl oz/½ cup crème fraîche

1 Grease a 450g/1lb loaf tin and line it with clear film. Break the chocolate in to a large heatproof bowl. Place over a pan of hot water until melted.

2 Remove the bowl of chocolate from the heat and whisk in the egg yolks.

COOK'S TIP
Chocolate-tipped mandarin slices would also make a superb decoration. Use small segments; pat dry on kitchen paper, then half dip them in melted chocolate. Leave on non-stick baking paper until the chocolate has set.

3 Pare the rind from the mandarins, taking care to leave the pith behind. Cut the rind into slivers.

4 Stir the slivers of mandarin rind into the chocolate with the crème fraîche and raisins. Beat until smooth, then spoon the mixture into the prepared loaf tin and chill for 4 hours.

5 Cut the pith and any remaining rind from the mandarins, then slice thinly.

6 For the sauce, stir the Cointreau into the crème fraîche. Remove the truffle loaf from the tin, peel off the clear film and slice. Serve each slice on a dessert plate with some sauce and mandarin slices, and decorate.

LEMON <u>AND</u> LIME CHEESECAKE

TANGY LEMON CHEESECAKES ARE ALWAYS A HIT. THE LIME SYRUP MAKES THIS A CITRUS SENSATION.

2 Make the topping. Place the lemon rind and juice in a small saucepan and sprinkle over the gelatine. Leave to sponge for 5 minutes. Heat gently until the gelatine has melted, then set the mixture aside to cool slightly. Beat the ricotta cheese and sugar in a bowl. Stir in the cream and egg yolks, then whisk in the cooled gelatine mixture.

3 Whisk the egg whites in a grease-free bowl until they form soft peaks. Fold them into the cheese mixture. Spoon on to the biscuit base, level the surface and chill for 2–3 hours.

MAKES EIGHT SLICES

INGREDIENTS
- 150g/5oz/1½ cups digestive biscuits
- 40g/1½oz/3 tbsp butter

For the topping
- grated rind and juice of 2 lemons
- 10ml/2 tsp powdered gelatine
- 250g/9oz/generous 1 cup ricotta cheese
- 75g/3oz/⅓ cup caster sugar
- 150ml/¼ pint/⅔ cup double cream
- 2 eggs, separated

For the lime syrup
- finely pared rind and juice of 3 limes
- 75g/3oz/⅓ cup caster sugar
- 5ml/1 tsp arrowroot mixed with 30ml/2 tbsp water
- a little green food colouring (optional)

1 Lightly grease a 20cm/8in round springform cake tin. Place the biscuits in a food processor or blender and process until they form fine crumbs. Melt the butter in a large saucepan, then stir in the crumbs until well coated. Spoon into the prepared cake tin, press the crumbs down well in an even layer, then chill.

4 Meanwhile, make the lime syrup. Place the lime rind, juice and caster sugar in a small saucepan. Bring to the boil, stirring, then boil the syrup for 5 minutes. Stir in the arrowroot mixture and continue to stir until the syrup boils again and thickens slightly. Tint pale green with a little food colouring, if you like. Cool, then chill until required.

5 Spoon the lime syrup over the set cheesecake. Remove from the tin and cut into slices to serve.

LEMON SURPRISE PUDDING

THIS IS A MUCH-LOVED DESSERT MANY OF US REMEMBER FROM CHILDHOOD. THE SURPRISE IS THE UNEXPECTED SAUCE CONCEALED BENEATH THE DELECTABLE SPONGE.

SERVES FOUR

INGREDIENTS
50g/2oz/¼ cup butter, plus extra
   for greasing
grated rind and juice of 2 lemons
115g/4oz/½ cup caster sugar
2 eggs, separated
50g/2oz/½ cup self-raising flour
300ml/½ pint/1¼ cups milk

1 Preheat the oven to 190°C/375°F/ Gas 5. Use a little butter to grease a 1.2 litre/2 pint/5 cup baking dish.

2 Beat the lemon rind, remaining butter and caster sugar in a bowl until pale and fluffy. Add the egg yolks and flour and beat together well. Gradually whisk in the lemon juice and milk (don't be alarmed if the mixture curdles horribly!). In a grease-free bowl whisk the egg whites until they form stiff peaks.

3 Fold the egg whites lightly into the lemon mixture, then pour into the prepared baking dish.

4 Place the dish in a roasting tin and pour in hot water to come halfway up the side of the dish. Bake for about 45 minutes until golden. Serve at once.

CRÊPES SUZETTE

SIMPLY SUPERB — THAT'S THE VERDICT ON THIS PERENNIALLY POPULAR DESSERT. THESE CRÊPES DESERVE NOTHING LESS THAN THE BEST QUALITY VANILLA ICE CREAM YOU CAN FIND.

SERVES FOUR

INGREDIENTS
8 crêpes (see Summer Berry Crêpes
   for method)
25g/1oz/2 tbsp unsalted butter
50g/2oz/¼ cup caster sugar
juice of 2 oranges
juice of ½ lemon
60ml/4 tbsp Cointreau or other
   orange liqueur
best quality vanilla ice cream,
   to serve

COOK'S TIP
Crêpes freeze well and can be reheated by the method described in step 1, or simultaneously thawed and reheated in the microwave. A stack of eight crêpes, interleaved with greaseproof paper, will take 2–3 minutes on High (100% power). Be sure to cover the top crêpe with paper as well.

1 Warm the cooked crêpes between two plates placed over a saucepan of simmering water.

2 Melt the butter in a heavy-based frying pan. Stir in the caster sugar and cook over a medium heat, tilting the pan occasionally, until the mixture is golden brown. Add the orange and lemon juices and stir until the caramel has completely dissolved.

3 Add a crêpe to the pan. Using kitchen tongs, fold it in half, then in half again. Slide to the side of the pan. Repeat with the remaining crêpes.

4 When all the crêpes have been folded in the sauce, pour over the Cointreau and set it alight. Shake the pan until the flames die down. Divide the crêpes and sauce among dessert plates and serve at once with vanilla ice cream.

CITRUS FRUIT FLAMBÉ
WITH PISTACHIO PRALINE

A FRUIT FLAMBÉ MAKES A DRAMATIC FINALE FOR A DINNER PARTY. TOPPING THIS REFRESHING CITRUS FRUIT DESSERT WITH CRUNCHY PISTACHIO PRALINE MAKES IT EXTRA SPECIAL.

SERVES FOUR

INGREDIENTS
    4 oranges
    2 ruby grapefruit
    2 limes
    50g/2oz/¼ cup butter
    50g/2oz/⅓ cup light muscovado sugar
    45ml/3 tbsp Cointreau
    fresh mint sprigs, to decorate
For the praline
    oil, for greasing
    115g/4oz/½ cup caster sugar
    50g/2oz/½ cup pistachio nuts

1 First, make the pistachio praline. Brush a baking sheet lightly with oil. Place the caster sugar and nuts in a small heavy-based saucepan and cook gently, swirling the pan occasionally until the sugar has melted.

2 Continue to cook over a fairly low heat until the nuts start to pop and the sugar has turned a dark golden colour. Pour on to the oiled baking sheet and set aside to cool. Using a sharp knife, chop the praline into rough chunks.

3 Cut off all the rind and pith from the citrus fruit. Holding each fruit in turn over a large bowl, cut between the membranes so that the segments fall into the bowl, with any juice.

COOK'S TIP
If desired, use a rolling pin or toffee hammer to break up the praline.

4 Heat the butter and muscovado sugar together in a heavy-based frying pan until the sugar has melted and the mixture is golden. Strain the citrus juices into the pan and continue to cook, stirring occasionally, until the juice has reduced and is syrupy.

5 Add the fruit segments and warm through without stirring. Pour over the Cointreau and set it alight. As soon as the flames die down, spoon the fruit flambé into serving dishes. Scatter some praline over each portion and decorate with mint. Serve at once.

COLD LEMON SOUFFLÉ WITH CARAMELIZED ALMOND TOPPING

THIS TERRIFIC-TO-LOOK-AT, REFRESHING DESSERT SOUFFLÉ IS LIGHT AND LUSCIOUS.

SERVES SIX

INGREDIENTS
   oil, for greasing
   grated rind and juice of
     3 large lemons
   5 large eggs, separated
   115g/4oz/½ cup caster sugar
   25ml/1½ tbsp powdered gelatine
   450ml/¾ pint/scant 2 cups double
     cream
For the decoration
   75g/3oz/¾ cup flaked almonds
   75g/3oz/¾ cup icing sugar
   3 physalis

COOK'S TIP
When peeling off the soufflé collar,
hold the blade of a knife against the
set soufflé so that it keeps its shape.

1 Make the soufflé collar. Cut a strip of non-stick baking paper long enough to fit around a 900ml/1½ pint/3¾ cup soufflé dish and wide enough to extend 7.5cm/3in above the rim. Fit the strip around the dish, tape, then tie it around the top of the dish with string. Brush the inside of the paper lightly with oil.

2 Put the lemon rind and egg yolks in a bowl. Add 75g/3oz/6 tbsp of the caster sugar and whisk until light and creamy.

3 Place the lemon juice in a small heatproof bowl and sprinkle over the gelatine. Set aside for 5 minutes, then place the bowl in a pan of simmering water. Heat, stirring occasionally, until the gelatine has dissolved. Cool slightly, then stir the gelatine mixture into the egg yolk mixture.

4 In a separate bowl, lightly whip the cream to soft peaks. Fold into the egg yolk mixture and set aside.

5 Whisk the egg whites in a grease-free bowl until stiff peaks form. Gradually whisk in the remaining caster sugar until the mixture is stiff and glossy. Quickly and lightly fold the whites into the yolk mixture. Pour into the prepared dish, smooth the surface and chill for 4–5 hours or until set.

6 Make the decoration. Brush a baking sheet lightly with oil. Preheat the grill. Scatter the almonds over the sheet and sift the icing sugar over. Grill until the nuts are golden and the sugar has caramelized. Allow to cool, then remove the mixture from the tray with a palette knife and break it into pieces.

7 When the soufflé has set, carefully peel off the paper. Pile the caramelized almonds on top of the soufflé and decorate with the physalis.

LEMON ROULADE <u>WITH</u> LEMON CURD CREAM

THIS FEATHERLIGHT ROULADE FILLED WITH A RICH LEMON CURD CREAM MAKES A MARVELLOUS DESSERT OR TEA-TIME TREAT. THE LEMON CURD CAN BE MADE AHEAD AND KEPT IN THE FRIDGE.

MAKES EIGHT SLICES

INGREDIENTS
   4 eggs, separated
   115g/4oz/½ cup caster sugar
   finely grated rind of 2 lemons
   5ml/1 tsp pure vanilla essence
   25g/1oz/¼ cup ground almonds
   40g/1½oz/⅓ cup plain flour, sifted
   45ml/3 tbsp icing sugar, for dusting
For the lemon curd cream
   300ml/½ pint/1¼ cups double cream
   60ml/4 tbsp fresh lemon curd
   (recipe below right)

1 Preheat the oven to 190°C/375°F/ Gas 5. Grease a 33 × 23cm/13 × 9in Swiss roll tin and line with non-stick baking paper.

2 In a large bowl, beat the egg yolks with half the caster sugar until light and foamy. Beat in the lemon rind and vanilla essence, then lightly fold in the ground almonds and flour using a large metal spoon or spatula.

COOK'S TIP
Having filled and rolled the roulade, keep it wrapped in the non-stick baking paper and hold it together for about a minute to allow the shape to set before removing the paper and transferring the roulade to a plate.

3 Whisk the egg whites in a grease-free bowl until they form stiff, glossy peaks. Gradually whisk in the remaining caster sugar to form a stiff meringue. Stir half the meringue mixture into the egg yolk mixture and fold in the rest.

4 Pour into the prepared tin, level the surface with a palette knife and bake for 10 minutes or until risen and spongy to the touch. Cover loosely with a sheet of non-stick baking paper and a damp dish towel. Leave to cool in the tin.

5 Make the lemon cream. Whip the cream; then lightly fold in the lemon curd.

6 Sift the icing sugar liberally over a piece of non-stick baking paper. Turn the sponge out on to it. Peel off the lining paper and spread the lemon curd cream over the surface of the sponge, leaving a border around the edge.

7 Using the paper underneath as a guide, roll up the sponge from one of the long sides. Place on a serving platter, with the seam underneath. Cut the roulade into slices to serve.

FRESH LEMON CURD
Put the grated rind and juice of 3 lemons into a pan with 115g/4oz/ ½ cup caster sugar. Bring to the boil, stirring until the sugar has dissolved. Stir in 15ml/1 tbsp cornflour mixed to a paste with 15ml/1 tbsp cold water. Off the heat, whisk in 2 egg yolks. Return to a low heat, whisk for about 2 minutes; remove from the heat. Gradually whisk in 50g/2oz/¼ cup butter, at room temperature. Pour into a sterilized jar, cover and seal at once. Leave to cool, then chill. Use within 2–3 weeks. Makes 450g/1lb.

LEMON MERINGUE PIE

CRISP SHORTCRUST IS FILLED WITH A MOUTHWATERING LEMON CREAM FILLING AND HEAPED WITH SOFT GOLDEN-TOPPED MERINGUE. THIS CLASSIC OPEN TART NEVER FAILS TO PLEASE. POPULAR WITH ADULTS AND CHILDREN, IT IS THE ESSENTIAL SUNDAY LUNCH DESSERT.

2 Meanwhile make the filling. Place all the ingredients in a bowl, mix lightly and leave to soak for 1 hour.

3 Preheat the oven to 200°C/400°F/ Gas 6. Beat the filling until smooth and pour into the chilled pastry case. Bake for 20 minutes or until the filling has just set and the pastry is golden. Remove from the oven and cool on a wire rack for 30 minutes or until a skin has formed on the surface. Lower the oven temperature to 180°C/350°F/Gas 4.

4 Make the topping. Whisk the egg whites in a grease-free bowl until they form stiff peaks. Whisk in the caster sugar to form a glossy meringue. Spoon on top of the set lemon filling and spread over, making sure you spread the meringue right to the rim of the pie shell. Swirl the meringue slightly.

5 Bake the pie for 20–25 minutes or until the meringue is crisp and golden brown. Allow to cool on a wire rack for 10 minutes before serving.

SERVES SIX

INGREDIENTS
    115g/4oz/1 cup plain flour
    pinch of salt
    50g/2oz/¼ cup butter
    50g/2oz/¼ cup lard
    15ml/1 tbsp caster sugar
    about 15ml/1 tbsp iced water
For the filling
    3 large egg yolks
    30ml/2 tbsp caster sugar
    grated rind and juice of 1 lemon
    25g/1oz/½ cup fresh
        white breadcrumbs
    250ml/8fl oz/1 cup milk
For the topping
    3 large egg whites
    115g/4oz/½ cup caster sugar

1 Sift the flour and salt into a bowl. Rub in the butter and lard until the mixture resembles fine breadcrumbs. Stir in the sugar and add enough iced water to make a soft dough. Roll out the pastry on a lightly floured surface and line a 21cm/8½in pie plate or tin. Chill until required.

FRESH LEMON TART

MADE FAMOUS BY ITS FRENCH TITLE – TARTE AUX CITRON – THIS TART SHOULD BE SERVED AT ROOM TEMPERATURE IF THE ZESTY LEMON FLAVOUR IS TO BE ENJOYED TO THE FULL.

SERVES SIX TO EIGHT

INGREDIENTS
 350g/12oz packet ready-made rich
  sweet shortcrust pastry, thawed
  if frozen
For the filling
 3 eggs
 115g/4oz/½ cup caster sugar
 115g/4oz/1 cup ground almonds
 105ml/7 tbsp double cream
 grated rind and juice of 2 lemons
For the topping
 2 thin-skinned unwaxed lemons,
  thinly sliced
 200g/7oz/scant 1 cup caster sugar
 105ml/7 tbsp water

COOK'S TIP
If you prefer not to candy the lemons, simply dust the tart with icing sugar.

1 Roll out the pastry and line a deep 23cm/9in fluted flan tin. Prick the base and chill for 30 minutes.

2 Preheat the oven to 200°C/400°F/ Gas 6. Line the pastry with non-stick baking paper and baking beans and bake blind for 10 minutes. Remove the paper and beans and return the pastry case to the oven for 5 minutes more.

3 Meanwhile, make the filling. Beat the eggs, caster sugar, almonds and cream in a bowl until smooth. Beat in the lemon rind and juice. Pour the filling into the pastry case. Lower the oven temperature to 190°C/375°F/Gas 5 and bake for 20 minutes or until the filling has set and the pastry is golden.

4 Make the topping. Place the lemon slices in a pan and pour over water to cover. Simmer for 15–20 minutes or until the skins are tender, then drain.

5 Place the sugar in a saucepan and stir in the measured water. Heat gently until the sugar has dissolved, stirring constantly, then boil for 2 minutes. Add the lemon slices and cook for 10–15 minutes until the skins become shiny and candied.

6 Lift out the candied lemon slices and arrange them over the top of the tart. Return the syrup to the heat and boil until reduced to a thick glaze. Brush this over the tart and allow to cool completely before serving.

KEY LIME PIE

THIS IS ONE OF AMERICA'S FAVOURITES. AS THE NAME SUGGESTS, IT ORIGINATED IN THE FLORIDA KEYS.

MAKES TEN SLICES

INGREDIENTS
   225g/8oz/2 cups plain flour
   115g/4oz/½ cup chilled
      butter, diced
   30ml/2 tbsp caster sugar
   2 egg yolks
   pinch of salt
   30ml/2 tbsp cold water
   thinly pared lime rind and mint
      leaves, to decorate
For the filling
   4 eggs, separated
   400g/14oz can condensed milk
   grated rind and juice of 3 limes
   a few drops of green food
      colouring (optional)
   30ml/2 tbsp caster sugar
For the topping
   300ml/½ pint/1¼ cups double cream
   2–3 limes, thinly sliced

1 Sift the flour into a mixing bowl and rub in the butter using your fingertips until the mixture resembles fresh breadcrumbs. Add the sugar, egg yolks, salt and water. Mix to a soft dough.

2 Roll out the pastry on a lightly floured surface and use to line a deep 21cm/8½in fluted flan tin, allowing the excess pastry to hang over the edge. Prick the pastry base and chill for at least 30 minutes.

3 Preheat the oven to 200°C/400°F/ Gas 6. Trim off the excess pastry from around the edge of the pastry case using a large sharp knife and line the pastry case with non-stick baking paper and baking beans.

4 Bake the pastry case blind for 10 minutes. Remove the paper and beans and return the pastry case to the oven for 10 minutes.

5 Meanwhile, make the filling. Beat the egg yolks in a large bowl until light and creamy, then beat in the condensed milk, with the lime rind and juice until well combined. Add the food colouring, if using, and continue to beat until the mixture is thick.

COOK'S TIP
You can make the pastry in a food processor, but take care not to overprocess the dough. Use the pulse button and process for a few seconds at a time; switch off the motor the moment the dough clumps together.

6 In a grease-free bowl, whisk the egg whites to stiff peaks. Whisk in the caster sugar, then fold into the lime mixture.

7 Lower the oven temperature to 160°C/325°F/Gas 3. Pour the lime filling into the pastry case. Bake for 20–25 minutes or until it has set and is starting to brown. Cool, then chill.

8 Just before serving, whip the double cream for the topping and spoon it around the edge of the pie. Cut the lime slices once from the centre to the edge, then twist each slice and arrange between the spoonfuls of cream. Decorate with lime rind and mint leaves.

MOIST ORANGE AND ALMOND CAKE

THE KEY TO THIS RECIPE IS TO COOK THE ORANGE SLOWLY FIRST, SO IT IS FULLY TENDER BEFORE BEING BLENDED. DON'T USE A MICROWAVE TO SPEED THINGS UP — THIS MAKES ORANGE SKIN TOUGH.

SERVES EIGHT

INGREDIENTS
    1 large orange
    3 eggs
    225g/8oz/1 cup caster sugar
    5ml/1 tsp baking powder
    225g/8oz/2 cups ground almonds
    25g/1oz/¼ cup plain flour
    icing sugar, for dusting
    whipped cream and orange slices
        (optional), to serve

1 Wash the orange and pierce it with a skewer. Put it in a deep saucepan and pour over water to cover completely. Bring to the boil then lower the heat, cover and simmer for 1 hour or until the skin is very soft. Drain, then cool.

COOK'S TIP
For a treat, serve this with spiced poached kumquats.

2 Preheat the oven to 180°C/350°F/ Gas 4. Grease a 20cm/8in round cake tin and line it with non-stick baking paper. Cut the cooled orange in half and discard the pips. Place the orange, skin and all, in a blender or food processor and purée until smooth and pulpy.

3 In a bowl, whisk the eggs and sugar until thick. Fold in the baking powder, almonds and flour. Fold in the purée.

4 Pour into the prepared tin, level the surface and bake for 1 hour or until a skewer inserted into the middle comes out clean. Cool the cake in the tin for 10 minutes, then turn out on to a wire rack, peel off the lining paper and cool completely. Dust the top liberally with icing sugar and serve as a dessert with whipped cream. For added colour, tuck thick orange slices under the cake just before serving.

LEMON <u>AND</u> LIME SYRUP CAKE

THIS CAKE IS PERFECT FOR BUSY COOKS AS IT CAN BE MIXED IN MOMENTS AND NEEDS NO ICING.
THE SIMPLE TANGY LIME TOPPING TRANSFORMS IT INTO A FABULOUSLY MOIST CAKE.

SERVES EIGHT

INGREDIENTS
225g/8oz/2 cups self-raising flour
5ml/1 tsp baking powder
225g/8oz/1 cup caster sugar
225g/8oz/1 cup butter, softened
4 eggs, beaten
grated rind of 2 lemons
30ml/2 tbsp lemon juice
For the topping
finely pared rind of 1 lime
juice of 2 limes
150g/5oz/⅔ cup caster sugar

1 Make the cake. Preheat the oven to 160°C/325°F/Gas 3. Grease and line a 20cm/8in round cake tin. Sift the flour and baking powder into a large bowl. Add the caster sugar, butter and eggs and beat together well until the mixture is smooth, creamy and fluffy.

2 Beat in the lemon rind and juice. Spoon the mixture into the prepared tin, then smooth the surface and make a shallow indentation in the top with the back of a spoon.

3 Bake for 1¼–1½ hours or until the cake is golden on top and spongy when lightly pressed, and a skewer inserted in the centre comes out clean.

4 Meanwhile, mix the topping ingredients together. As soon as the cake is cooked, remove it from the oven and pour the topping over the surface. Allow the cake to cool in the tin.

VARIATION
Use lemon rind and juice instead of lime for the topping if you prefer. You will need only one large lemon.

SPICED POACHED KUMQUATS

KUMQUATS ARE NOT AVAILABLE THROUGHOUT THE YEAR, BUT THEY ARE UNDOUBTEDLY AT THEIR BEST JUST BEFORE THE CHRISTMAS SEASON. THESE FRUITS CAN BE BOTTLED AND GIVEN AS PRESENTS. THEIR MARVELLOUS SPICY-SWEET CITRUS FLAVOUR COMPLEMENTS BOTH SWEET AND SAVOURY DISHES.

SERVES SIX

INGREDIENTS
450g/1lb/4 cups kumquats
115g/4oz/½ cup caster sugar
150ml/¼ pint/⅔ cup water
1 small cinnamon stick
1 star anise
a citrus leaf, to decorate

1 Cut the kumquats in half and discard the pips. Place the kumquats in a saucepan with the sugar, water and spices. Cook over a gentle heat, stirring until the sugar has dissolved.

2 Increase the heat, cover the pan and boil the mixture for 8–10 minutes until the kumquats are tender. To bottle the kumquats, spoon them into warm, sterilized jars, seal and label.

3 If you want to serve the spiced kumquats soon after making them, let the mixture cool, then chill it. Decorate with a citrus leaf, if you like.

COOK'S TIP
Try these delectable treats with baked ham, roast pork or slices of a raised pork pie. They would also make a perfect accompaniment for moist almond or chocolate cake.

THREE-FRUIT MARMALADE

SEVILLE ORANGES HAVE A FINE FLAVOUR AND ARE THE BEST VARIETY FOR MARMALADE. SWEET ORANGES CAN BE USED AT A PINCH, BUT THEY TEND TO MAKE THE MARMALADE CLOUDY.

MAKES 2.25KG/5–5¼LB

INGREDIENTS
2 Seville oranges
2 lemons
1 grapefruit
1.75 litres/3 pints/7½ cups water
1.5kg/3lb 6oz/6¾ cups granulated
sugar
croissants, to serve (optional)

1 Wash the fruit, halve and squeeze their juice. Pour into a large heavy-based saucepan or preserving pan. Tip the pips and pulp in a square of muslin, gather the sides into a bag and tie the neck tightly with string. Tie the bag to the handle of the pan so that it dangles in the citrus juice.

2 Cut the citrus skins into thin wedges; scrape off and discard the membranes and pith. Cut the rinds into slivers and add to the pan with the measured water. Bring to the simmer and cook gently for 2 hours until the rinds are very tender and the water has reduced by half. Test the rinds for softness by pressing a cooled piece with a finger.

3 Lift out the muslin bag, squeezing out the juice into the pan. Discard the bag. Stir the sugar into the pan and heat very gently, stirring occasionally, until all the sugar has dissolved.

4 Bring the mixture to the boil and boil for 10–15 minutes or until the marmalade registers 105°C/220°C.

5 Alternatively, test the marmalade for setting by pouring a small amount on to a chilled saucer. Chill for 2 minutes, then push the marmalade with your finger; if wrinkles form on the surface, it is ready. Cool for 15 minutes.

6 Stir the marmalade and pour it into warm, sterilized jars. Cover with waxed paper discs. Seal and label when cold. Store in a cool dark cupboard. Serve with warm croissants, if you like.

COOK'S TIP
Leaving the marmalade to cool slightly before potting lets it set enough to prevent the fruit from sinking. Stir before pouring it into the jars. Cover the surface with paper discs and seal while hot.

EXOTIC FRUIT RECIPES

Who can resist the colours, textures and flavours of exotic fruits? Now that many varieties are widely available all year, there's every excuse for taking the taste trip and trying such delights as Lychee and Elderflower Sorbet, Passion Fruit Crème Caramels with Dipped Physalis or Exotic Fruit Sushi.

COLD MANGO SOUFFLÉS TOPPED WITH TOASTED COCONUT

FRAGRANT, FRESH MANGO IS ONE OF THE MOST DELICIOUS EXOTIC FRUITS AROUND, WHETHER IT IS SIMPLY SERVED IN SLICES OR USED AS THE BASIS FOR AN ICE CREAM OR SOUFFLÉ.

MAKES FOUR

INGREDIENTS

4 small mangoes, peeled, stoned and chopped
30ml/2 tbsp water
15ml/1 tbsp powdered gelatine
2 egg yolks
115g/4oz/½ cup caster sugar
120ml/4fl oz/½ cup milk
grated rind of 1 orange
300ml/½ pint/1¼ cups double cream
toasted flaked or coarsely shredded coconut, to decorate

COOK'S TIP
Cool and creamy, these go down a treat after a curry. Add some juicy pieces of fresh mango on the side if you like.

1 Place a few pieces of mango in the base of each of four 150ml/¼ pint/ ⅔ cup ramekins. Wrap a greased collar of non-stick baking paper around the outside of each dish, extending well above the rim. Secure with adhesive tape, then tie tightly with string.

2 Pour the water into a small heatproof bowl and sprinkle the gelatine over the surface. Leave for 5 minutes or until spongy. Place the bowl in a pan of hot water, stirring occasionally, until the gelatine has dissolved.

3 Meanwhile, whisk the egg yolks with the caster sugar and milk in another heatproof bowl. Place the bowl over a saucepan of simmering water and continue to whisk until the mixture is thick and frothy. Remove from the heat and continue whisking until the mixture cools. Whisk in the liquid gelatine.

4 Purée the remaining mango pieces in a food processor or blender, then fold the purée into the egg yolk mixture with the orange rind. Set the mixture aside until starting to thicken.

5 Whip the double cream to soft peaks. Reserve 60ml/4 tbsp and fold the rest into the mango mixture. Spoon into the ramekins until the mixture is 2.5cm/1in above the rim of each dish. Chill for 3–4 hours or until set.

6 Carefully remove the paper collars from the soufflés. Spoon a little of the reserved cream on top of each soufflé and decorate with some toasted flaked or coarsely shredded coconut.

PASSION FRUIT CRÈME CARAMELS WITH DIPPED PHYSALIS

PASSION FRUIT HAS AN AROMATIC FLAVOUR THAT REALLY PERMEATES THESE CRÈME CARAMELS.
USE SOME OF THE CARAMEL TO DIP PHYSALIS TO CREATE A UNIQUE DECORATION.

MAKES FOUR

INGREDIENTS
    185g/6½oz/generous ¾ cup caster
      sugar
    75ml/5 tbsp water
    4 passion fruit
    4 physalis
    3 eggs plus 1 egg yolk
    150ml/¼ pint/⅔ cup double cream
    150ml/¼ pint/⅔ cup creamy milk

1 Place 150g/5oz/⅔ cup of the caster sugar in a heavy-based saucepan. Add the water and heat the mixture gently until the sugar has dissolved. Increase the heat and boil until the syrup turns a dark golden colour.

2 Meanwhile, cut each passion fruit in half. Scoop out the seeds from the passion fruit into a sieve set over a bowl. Press the seeds against the sieve to extract all their juice. Spoon a few of the seeds into each of four 150ml/¼ pint/⅔ cup ramekins. Set the juice aside.

3 Peel back the papery casing from each physalis and dip the orange berries into the caramel. Place on a sheet of non-stick baking paper and set aside. Pour the remaining caramel carefully into the ramekins.

4 Preheat the oven to 150°C/300°F/ Gas 2. Whisk the eggs, egg yolk and remaining sugar in a bowl. Whisk in the cream and milk, then the passion fruit juice. Strain through a sieve into each ramekin, then place the ramekins in a baking tin. Pour in hot water to come halfway up the sides of the dishes; bake for 40–45 minutes or until just set.

5 Remove the custards from the tin and leave to cool, then cover and chill them for 4 hours before serving. Run a knife between the edge of each ramekin and the custard and invert each in turn on to a dessert plate. Shake the ramekins firmly to release the custards. Decorate each with a dipped physalis.

LYCHEE AND ELDERFLOWER SORBET

THE FLAVOUR OF ELDERFLOWERS IS FAMOUS FOR BRINGING OUT THE ESSENCE OF GOOSEBERRIES, BUT WHAT IS LESS WELL KNOWN IS HOW WONDERFULLY IT COMPLEMENTS LYCHEES.

SERVES FOUR

INGREDIENTS

175g/6oz/¾ cup caster sugar
400ml/14fl oz/1⅔ cups water
500g/1¼lb fresh lychees, peeled
 and stoned
15ml/1 tbsp elderflower cordial
dessert biscuits, to serve

COOK'S TIP
Switch the freezer to the coldest setting before making the sorbet – the faster the mixture freezes, the smaller the ice crystals that form and the better the final texture will be. To ensure rapid freezing, use a metal freezerproof container and place it directly on the freezer shelf.

1 Place the sugar and water in a saucepan and heat gently until the sugar has dissolved. Increase the heat and boil for 5 minutes, then add the lychees. Lower the heat and simmer for 7 minutes. Remove from the heat and allow to cool.

2 Purée the fruit and syrup in a blender or food processor. Place a sieve over a bowl and pour the purée into it. Press through as much of the purée as possible with a spoon.

3 Stir the elderflower cordial into the strained purée, then pour the mixture into a freezerproof container. Freeze for 2 hours, until ice crystals start to form around the edges.

4 Remove the sorbet from the freezer and process briefly in a food processor or blender to break up the crystals. Repeat this process twice more, then freeze until firm. Transfer to the fridge for 10 minutes to soften slightly before serving in scoops, with biscuits.

EXOTIC FRUIT SUSHI

This idea can be adapted to incorporate a wide variety of fruits, but to keep to the exotic theme take your inspiration from the tropics. The sushi needs to chill overnight to ensure the rice mixture firms properly, so be sure you start this in good time.

SERVES FOUR

INGREDIENTS
150g/5oz/⅔ cup short grain
   pudding rice
350ml/12fl oz/1½ cups water
400ml/14fl oz/1⅔ cups coconut milk
75g/3oz/⅓ cup caster sugar
a selection of exotic fruit, such as
   1 mango, 1 kiwi fruit, 2 figs and
   1 star fruit, thinly sliced
30ml/2 tbsp apricot jam, sieved
For the raspberry sauce
   225g/8oz/2 cups raspberries
   25g/1oz/¼ cup icing sugar

COOK'S TIP
To cut the rice mixture into bars, turn
out of the tin, cut in half lengthways,
then make 7 crossways cuts for 16 bars.
Shape into ovals with damp hands.

1 Rinse the rice well under cold
running water, drain and place in a
saucepan with 300ml/½ pint/1¼ cups of
the water. Pour in 175ml/6fl oz/¾ cup
of the coconut milk. Cook over a very
low heat for 25 minutes, stirring often
and gradually adding the remaining
coconut milk, until the rice has
absorbed all the liquid and is tender.

2 Grease a shallow 18cm/7in square
tin and line it with clear film. Stir
30ml/2 tbsp of the caster sugar into
the rice mixture and pour it into the
prepared tin. Cool, then chill overnight.

3 Cut the rice mixture into 16 small
bars, shape into ovals and flatten the
tops. Place on a baking sheet lined with
non-stick baking paper. Arrange the
sliced fruit on top, using one type of
fruit only for each sushi.

4 Place the remaining sugar in a small
pan with the remaining 50ml/4 tbsp
water. Bring to the boil, then lower the
heat and simmer until thick and syrupy.
Stir in the jam and cool slightly.

5 To make the sauce, purée the
raspberries with the icing sugar in a
food processor or blender. Press
through a sieve, then divide among four
small bowls. Arrange a few different
fruit sushi on each plate and spoon over
a little of the cool apricot syrup. Serve
with the sauce.

LEMON GRASS SKEWERS <u>WITH</u> LIME CHEESE

GRILLED FRUITS MAKE A FINE FINALE TO A BARBECUE, WHETHER THEY ARE COOKED OVER THE COALS OR UNDER A HOT GRILL. THE LEMON GRASS SKEWERS GIVE THE FRUIT A SUBTLE LEMON TANG. THE FRUITS USED HERE MAKE AN IDEAL EXOTIC MIX, BUT ALMOST ANY SOFT FRUIT CAN BE SUBSTITUTED.

SERVES FOUR

INGREDIENTS
    4 long fresh lemon grass stalks
    1 mango, peeled, stoned and cut
        into chunks
    1 papaya, peeled, seeded and cut
        into chunks
    1 star fruit, cut into thick slices
        and halved
    8 fresh bay leaves
    a nutmeg
    60ml/4 tbsp maple syrup
    50g/2oz/⅓ cup demerara sugar
For the lime cheese
    150g/5oz/⅔ cup curd cheese or low
        fat soft cheese
    120ml/4fl oz/½ cup double cream
    grated rind and juice of ½ lime
    30ml/2 tbsp icing sugar

1 Prepare the barbecue or preheat the grill. Cut the top of each lemon grass stalk into a point with a sharp knife. Discard the outer leaves, then use the back of the knife to bruise the length of each stalk to release the aromatic oils. Thread each stalk, skewer-style, with the fruit pieces and bay leaves.

2 Support a piece of foil on a baking sheet and roll up the edges to make a rim. Grease the foil, lay the kebabs on top and grate a little nutmeg over each. Drizzle the maple syrup over and dust liberally with the demerara sugar. Grill for 5 minutes, until lightly charred.

3 Meanwhile, make the lime cheese. Mix together the cheese, cream, grated lime rind and juice and icing sugar in a bowl. Serve at once with the lightly charred fruit kebabs.

COOK'S TIP
Only fresh lemon grass will work as skewers for this recipe. It is now possible to buy lemon grass stalks in jars. These are handy for curries and similar dishes, but are too soft to use as skewers.

COCONUT JELLY <u>WITH</u> STAR ANISE FRUITS

SERVE THIS DESSERT AFTER ANY ORIENTAL-STYLE MEAL WITH PLENTY OF REFRESHING EXOTIC FRUIT.

SERVES FOUR

INGREDIENTS
    250ml/8fl oz/1 cup cold water
    75g/3oz/⅓ cup caster sugar
    15ml/1 tbsp powdered gelatine
    400ml/14fl oz/1⅔ cups coconut milk
For the syrup and fruit
    250ml/8fl oz/1 cup water
    3 star anise
    50g/2oz/¼ cup caster sugar
    1 star fruit, sliced
    12 lychees, peeled and stoned
    115g/4oz/1 cup blackberries

1 Pour the water into a saucepan and add the caster sugar. Heat gently until the sugar has dissolved. Sprinkle over the gelatine and continue to heat the mixture gently until the gelatine has dissolved, stirring occasionally. Stir in the coconut milk, remove from the heat and set aside to cool.

2 Grease an 18cm/7in square cake tin. Line with clear film. Pour in the coconut milk mixture and chill until set.

3 To make the syrup, combine the water, star anise and sugar in a pan. Bring to the boil, stirring, then lower the heat and simmer for 10–12 minutes until syrupy. Place the fruit in a heatproof bowl and pour over the hot syrup. Cool, then chill.

4 To serve, cut the coconut jelly into diamonds and remove from the tin. Arrange the coconut jelly on individual plates, adding a few of the fruits and their syrup to each portion.

COOK'S TIP
Coconut milk is available in cans or as a powder. If using the powder, reconstitute it with cold water according to the packet instructions.

PAPAYA BAKED <u>WITH</u> GINGER

GINGER ENHANCES THE FLAVOUR OF PAPAYA IN THIS RECIPE, WHICH TAKES NO MORE THAN TEN MINUTES TO PREPARE! DON'T OVERCOOK PAPAYA OR THE FLESH WILL BECOME VERY WATERY.

SERVES FOUR

INGREDIENTS

2 ripe papayas
2 pieces stem ginger in syrup, drained, plus 15ml/1 tbsp syrup from the jar
8 amaretti or other dessert biscuits, coarsely crushed
45ml/3 tbsp raisins
shredded, finely pared rind and juice of 1 lime
25g/1oz/¼ cup pistachio nuts, chopped
15ml/1 tbsp light muscovado sugar
60ml/4 tbsp crème fraîche, plus extra to serve

VARIATION

Use Greek yogurt and almonds instead of crème fraîche and pistachios.

1 Preheat the oven to 200°C/400°F/ Gas 6. Cut the papayas in half and scoop out their seeds. Place the halves in a baking dish and set aside. Cut the stem ginger into fine matchsticks.

2 Make the filling. Combine the crushed amaretti biscuits, stem ginger matchsticks and raisins in a bowl.

3 Stir in the lime rind and juice, two thirds of the nuts, then add the sugar and the crème fraîche. Mix well.

4 Fill the papaya halves and drizzle with the ginger syrup. Sprinkle with the remaining nuts. Bake for about 25 minutes or until tender. Serve with extra crème fraîche.

EXOTIC FRUIT SALAD <u>WITH</u> PASSION FRUIT DRESSING

PASSION FRUIT MAKES A SUPERB DRESSING FOR ANY FRUIT, BUT REALLY BRINGS OUT THE FLAVOUR OF EXOTIC VARIETIES. YOU CAN EASILY DOUBLE THE RECIPE, THEN SERVE THE REST FOR BREAKFAST.

SERVES SIX

INGREDIENTS
   1 mango
   1 papaya
   2 kiwi fruit
   coconut or vanilla ice cream, to serve
For the dressing
   3 passion fruit
   thinly pared rind and juice of 1 lime
   5ml/1 tsp hazelnut or walnut oil
   15ml/1 tbsp clear honey

COOK'S TIP
A clear golden honey scented with orange blossom or acacia blossom would be perfect for the dressing.

1 Peel the mango, cut it into three slices, then cut the flesh into chunks and place it in a large bowl. Peel the papaya and cut it in half. Scoop out the seeds, then chop the flesh.

2 Cut both ends off each kiwi fruit, then stand them on a board. Using a small sharp knife, cut off the skin from top to bottom. Cut each kiwi fruit in half lengthways, then cut into thick slices. Combine all the fruit in a large bowl.

3 Make the dressing. Cut each passion fruit in half and scoop the seeds out into a sieve set over a small bowl. Press the seeds well to extract all their juices. Lightly whisk the remaining dressing ingredients into the passion fruit juice, then pour the dressing over the fruit. Mix gently to combine. Leave to chill for 1 hour before serving with scoops of coconut or vanilla ice cream.

TROPICAL FRUIT GRATIN

THIS OUT-OF-THE-ORDINARY GRATIN IS STRICTLY FOR GROWN-UPS. A COLOURFUL COMBINATION OF FRUIT IS TOPPED WITH A SIMPLE SABAYON BEFORE BEING FLASHED UNDER THE GRILL.

SERVES FOUR

INGREDIENTS
2 tamarillos
½ sweet pineapple
1 ripe mango
175g/6oz/1½ cups blackberries
120ml/4fl oz/½ cup sparkling
  white wine
115g/4oz/½ cup caster sugar
6 egg yolks

VARIATION
Although boiling drives off the alcohol in the wine, children do not always appreciate the flavour, so substitute orange juice if making the gratin for them. White grape juice or pineapple juice would also work well.

1 Cut each tamarillo in half lengthways and then into thick slices. Cut the rind and core from the pineapple and take spiral slices off the outside to remove the eyes. Cut the flesh into chunks. Peel the mango, cut it in half and cut the flesh from the stone in slices.

2 Divide all the fruit, including the blackberries, among four 14cm/5½in gratin dishes set on a baking sheet and set aside. Heat the wine and sugar in a saucepan until the sugar has dissolved. Bring to the boil and cook for 5 minutes.

3 Put the egg yolks in a large heatproof bowl. Place the bowl over a pan of simmering water and whisk until pale. Slowly pour on the hot sugar syrup, whisking all the time, until the mixture thickens. Preheat the grill.

4 Spoon the mixture over the fruit. Place the baking sheet holding the dishes on a low shelf under the hot grill until the topping is golden. Serve hot.

GRILLED PINEAPPLE WITH PAPAYA SAUCE

PINEAPPLE COOKED THIS WAY TAKES ON A SUPERB FLAVOUR AND IS SENSATIONAL WHEN SERVED WITH THE PAPAYA SAUCE.

SERVES SIX

INGREDIENTS
1 sweet pineapple
melted butter, for greasing
  and brushing
2 pieces drained stem ginger in
  syrup, cut into fine matchsticks,
  plus 30ml/2 tbsp of the syrup
  from the jar
30ml/2 tbsp demerara sugar
pinch of ground cinnamon
fresh mint sprigs, to decorate
For the sauce
1 ripe papaya, peeled and seeded
175ml/6fl oz/¾ cup apple juice

1 Peel the pineapple and take spiral slices off the outside to remove the eyes. Cut it crossways into six slices, each 2.5cm/1in thick. Line a baking sheet with a sheet of foil, rolling up the sides to make a rim. Grease the foil with melted butter. Preheat the grill.

2 Arrange the pineapple slices on the lined baking sheet. Brush with butter, then top with the ginger matchsticks, sugar and cinnamon. Drizzle over the stem ginger syrup. Grill for 5–7 minutes or until the slices are golden and lightly charred on top.

3 Meanwhile, make the sauce. Cut a few slices from the papaya and set aside, then purée the rest with the apple juice in a blender or food processor.

4 Press the purée through a sieve placed over a bowl, then stir in any juices from cooking the pineapple. Serve the pineapple slices with a little sauce drizzled around each plate. Decorate with the reserved papaya slices and the mint sprigs.

COOK'S TIP
Try the papaya sauce with savoury dishes, too. It tastes great with grilled chicken and game birds as well as pork and lamb.

JAMAICAN FRUIT TRIFLE

THIS TRIFLE IS ACTUALLY BASED ON A CARIBBEAN FOOL THAT CONSISTS OF FRUIT STIRRED INTO THICK VANILLA-FLAVOURED CREAM. THIS VERSION IS MUCH LESS RICH, REDRESSING THE BALANCE WITH PLENTY OF FRUIT, AND WITH CRÈME FRAÎCHE REPLACING SOME OF THE CREAM.

2 Whip the double cream to very soft peaks, then lightly but thoroughly fold in the crème fraîche, sifted icing sugar, vanilla essence and rum.

3 Fold the drained chopped pineapple into the cream mixture. Place the chopped papayas and mangoes in a large bowl and pour over the lime juice. Gently stir the fruit mixture to combine. Shred the pared lime rind.

4 Divide the fruit mixture and the pineapple cream among eight dessert plates. Decorate with the lime shreds, toasted coconut and a few small pineapple leaves, if you like, and serve at once.

SERVES EIGHT

INGREDIENTS

  1 large sweet pineapple, peeled and
    cored, about 350g/12oz
  300ml/½ pint/1¼ cups double cream
  200ml/7fl oz/scant 1 cup crème
    fraîche
  60ml/4 tbsp icing sugar, sifted
  10ml/2 tsp pure vanilla essence
  30ml/2 tbsp white or coconut rum
  3 papayas, peeled, seeded
    and chopped
  3 mangoes, peeled, stoned
    and chopped
  thinly pared rind and juice of 1 lime
  25g/1oz/⅓ cup coarsely shredded or
    flaked coconut, toasted

1 Cut the pineapple into large chunks, place in a food processor or blender and process briefly until chopped. Tip into a sieve placed over a bowl and leave for 5 minutes so that most of the juice drains from the fruit.

COOK'S TIP

It is important to let the pineapple purée drain thoroughly, otherwise, the pineapple cream will be watery. Don't throw away the drained pineapple juice – mix it with fizzy mineral water for a refreshing drink.

POMEGRANATE JEWELLED CHEESECAKE

THIS LIGHT CHEESECAKE IS FLAVOURED WITH COCONUT AND HAS A STUNNING POMEGRANATE GLAZE.

SERVES EIGHT

INGREDIENTS
   225g/8oz oat biscuits
   75g/3oz/⅓ cup unsalted
      butter, melted
For the filling
   45ml/3 tbsp orange juice
   15ml/1 tbsp powdered gelatine
   250g/9oz/generous 1 cup mascarpone
      cheese
   200g/7oz/scant 1 cup full fat
      soft cheese
   75g/3oz/¾ cup icing sugar, sifted
   200ml/7fl oz/scant 1 cup coconut
      cream
   2 egg whites
For the topping
   2 pomegranates, peeled and
      seeds separated
   grated rind and juice of 1 orange
   30ml/2 tbsp caster sugar
   15ml/1 tbsp arrowroot, mixed to a
      paste with 30ml/2 tbsp Kirsch
   a few drops of red food colouring
      (optional)

2 For the filling, pour the orange juice into a heatproof bowl, sprinkle the gelatine on top and set aside for 5 minutes until sponged. Place the bowl in a pan of hot water and stir until the gelatine has dissolved.

3 In a bowl, beat together both cheeses and the icing sugar, then gradually beat in the coconut cream. Whisk the egg whites in a grease-free bowl to soft peaks. Quickly stir the melted gelatine into the coconut mixture and fold in the egg whites. Pour over the biscuit base, level and chill until set.

4 Make the cheesecake topping. Place the pomegranate seeds in a saucepan and add the orange rind and juice and caster sugar. Bring to the boil, then lower the heat, cover and simmer for 5 minutes. Add the arrowroot paste and heat, stirring constantly, until thickened. Stir in the food colouring, if using. Allow to cool, stirring occasionally.

5 Pour the glaze over the top of the set cheesecake, then chill. To serve, run a knife between the edge of the tin and the cheesecake, then remove the side of the tin.

1 Grease a 23cm/9in springform cake tin. Crumb the biscuits in a food processor or blender. Add the melted butter and process briefly to combine. Spoon into the prepared tin, press the mixture in well, then chill.

COOK'S TIP
If you do not have a blender or food processor, crumb the biscuits by placing them in a large, strong plastic bag and crushing them with a rolling pin. For the best results, crush the crumbs as finely as possible.

BANANA AND MASCARPONE CREAMS

IF YOU ARE A FAN OF COLD BANANA CUSTARD, YOU'LL LOVE THIS RECIPE. IT IS A GROWN-UP VERSION OF AN OLD FAVOURITE. NO ONE WILL GUESS THAT THE SECRET IS READY-MADE CUSTARD SAUCE.

SERVES FOUR TO SIX

INGREDIENTS
  250g/9oz/generous 1 cup mascarpone
    cheese
  300ml/½ pint/1¼ cups fresh ready-
    made custard sauce
  150ml/¼ pint/⅔ cup Greek yogurt
  4 bananas
  juice of 1 lime
  50g/2oz/½ cup pecan nuts,
    coarsely chopped
  120ml/4fl oz/½ cup maple syrup

VARIATION
Use clear honey instead of maple syrup
and walnuts instead of pecans, if you
like. Also, try layering in some crumbled
biscuits, such as amaretti or ratafia,
shortbread crumbs or crushed meringues.
Or add a handful of finely grated dark or
white chocolate.

1 Combine the mascarpone, custard
sauce and yogurt in a large bowl and
beat together until smooth. Make this
mixture up to several hours ahead, if you
like. Cover and chill, then stir before using.

2 Slice the bananas diagonally and
place in a separate bowl. Pour over the
lime juice and toss together until the
bananas are coated in the juice.

3 Divide half the custard mixture
among four or six dessert glasses and
top each portion with a generous
spoonful of the banana mixture.

4 Spoon the remaining custard mixture
into the glasses and top with the rest of
the bananas. Scatter the nuts over the
top. Drizzle maple syrup over each dessert
and chill for 30 minutes before serving.

BANANAS WITH LIME AND CARDAMOM SAUCE

SERVE THESE BANANAS SOLO, WITH VANILLA ICE CREAM, OR SPOON THEM OVER FOLDED CRÊPES.

SERVES FOUR

INGREDIENTS
  6 small bananas
  50g/2oz/¼ cup butter
  seeds from 4 cardamom
    pods, crushed
  50g/2oz/½ cup flaked almonds
  thinly pared rind and juice
    of 2 limes
  50g/2oz/⅓ cup light
    muscovado sugar
  30ml/2 tbsp dark rum
  vanilla ice cream, to serve

VARIATION
If you prefer not to use alcohol in your
cooking, replace the rum with orange
juice or even pineapple juice.

1 Peel the bananas and cut them in
half lengthways. Heat half the butter in
a large frying pan. Add half the
bananas, and cook until the undersides
are golden. Turn carefully, using a fish
slice. Cook until golden.

2 As they cook, transfer the bananas to
a heatproof serving dish. Cook the
remaining bananas in the same way.

3 Melt the remaining butter, then add
the cardamom seeds and almonds.
Cook, stirring until golden.

4 Stir in the lime rind and juice,
then the sugar. Cook, stirring, until the
mixture is smooth, bubbling and slightly
reduced. Stir in the rum. Pour the
sauce over the bananas and serve
immediately, with vanilla ice cream.

TOFFEE BANANAS

ALTHOUGH THE METHOD FOR THIS RECIPE SOUNDS SIMPLE, IT CAN BE A BIT TRICKY TO MASTER. YOU NEED TO WORK FAST, ESPECIALLY WHEN DIPPING THE FRUIT IN THE CARAMEL, AS IT WILL COOL AND SET QUITE QUICKLY. THE LUSCIOUS RESULTS, HOWEVER, ARE WORTH THE EFFORT.

2 Heat the groundnut, sunflower or corn oil in a deep pan until it registers 180°C/350°F or until a cube of bread, added to the oil, turns pale brown in 45 seconds.

3 Using a fork, remove a piece of banana from the batter, allowing the excess batter to drain back into the bowl. Gently lower the piece of banana into the hot oil. Add more pieces of battered banana in the same way; do not overcrowd the pan. Fry for about 2 minutes or until the coating is golden.

4 As they are cooked, remove the banana fritters from the oil with a slotted spoon and place on kitchen paper to drain. Cook the rest of the battered bananas in the same way.

SERVES FOUR

INGREDIENTS
  4 firm bananas
  75g/3oz/¾ cup plain flour
  50g/2oz/½ cup cornflour
  10ml/2 tsp baking powder
  175ml/6fl oz/¾ cup water
  5ml/1 tsp sesame oil
  groundnut, sunflower or corn oil, for
    deep frying
For the caramel
  225g/8oz/1 cup granulated sugar
  30ml/2 tbsp sesame seeds
  60ml/4 tbsp water

1 Peel the bananas, then cut them diagonally into thick slices. Sift the flours and baking powder into a large bowl. Quickly beat in the water and sesame oil, taking care not to overmix. Stir in the bananas until coated.

5 When all the banana pieces have been fried, make the caramel. Mix the sugar, sesame seeds and water in a pan. Heat gently, stirring occasionally, until the sugar has dissolved. Raise the heat slightly and continue cooking, without stirring, until the syrup becomes a light caramel. Remove from the heat.

6 Have ready a bowl of iced water. Working quickly, drop one fritter at a time into the hot caramel. Flip over with a fork, remove immediately and plunge the piece into the iced water. Remove from the water quickly (using your fingers for speed, but taking care) and drain on a wire rack while coating the rest. Serve immediately.

HOT DATE PUDDINGS <u>WITH</u> TOFFEE SAUCE

FRESH DATES MAKE THIS PUDDING LESS RICH THAN THE CONVENTIONAL DRIED DATE VERSION, BUT IT IS STILL A BIT OF AN INDULGENCE! IT IS PREFERABLE TO PEEL THE DATES AS THEY CAN BE RATHER TOUGH: SIMPLY SQUEEZE THEM BETWEEN YOUR THUMB AND FOREFINGER AND THE SKINS WILL POP OFF.

SERVES SIX

INGREDIENTS
  50g/2oz/¼ cup butter, softened
  75g/3oz/½ cup light muscovado sugar
  2 eggs, beaten
  115g/4oz/1 cup self-raising flour
  2.5ml/½ tsp bicarbonate of soda
  175g/6oz/1 cup fresh dates, peeled,
    stoned and chopped
  75ml/5 tbsp boiling water
  10ml/2 tsp coffee and chicory
    essence
For the toffee sauce
  75g/3oz/½ cup light muscovado sugar
  50g/2oz/¼ cup butter
  60ml/4 tbsp double cream
  30ml/2 tbsp brandy

1 Preheat the oven to 180°C/350°F/ Gas 4. Place a baking sheet in the oven to heat up. Grease six individual pudding moulds or tins. Cream the butter and sugar in a mixing bowl until pale and fluffy. Gradually add the eggs, beating well after each addition.

2 Sift the flour and bicarbonate of soda together and fold into the creamed mixture. Put the dates in a heatproof bowl, pour over the boiling water and mash with a potato masher. Add the coffee and chicory essence, then stir the paste into the creamed mixture.

3 Spoon the mixture into the prepared moulds or tins. Place on the hot baking sheet and bake for 20 minutes.

4 Meanwhile, make the toffee sauce. Put all the ingredients in a pan and heat very gently, stirring occasionally, until the mixture is smooth. Increase the heat and boil for 1 minute.

5 Turn the warm puddings out on to individual dessert plates. Spoon a generous amount of sauce over each portion and serve at once.

COOK'S TIP
The sauce is a great standby. Try it on poached apple or pear slices, over ice cream or with a steamed pudding.

RUM AND BANANA WAFFLES

TO SAVE TIME, THESE SCRUMPTIOUS DESSERT WAFFLES CAN BE MADE IN ADVANCE, WRAPPED TIGHTLY, FROZEN, AND THEN WARMED THROUGH IN THE OVEN JUST BEFORE SERVING.

SERVES FOUR

INGREDIENTS
225g/8oz/2 cups plain flour
10ml/2 tsp baking powder
5ml/1 tsp bicarbonate of soda
15ml/1 tbsp caster sugar
2 eggs
50g/2oz/¼ cup butter, melted
175ml/6fl oz/¾ cup milk, plus
  additional if needed
300ml/½ pint/1¼ cups buttermilk
5ml/1 tsp pure vanilla essence
single cream, to serve
For the bananas
6 bananas, thickly sliced
115g/4oz/1 cup pecan nuts, broken
  into pieces
50g/2oz/⅓ cup demerara sugar
75ml/5 tbsp maple syrup
45ml/3 tbsp dark rum

2 Add the buttermilk and vanilla to the batter and whisk well. Cover and leave to stand for 30 minutes. Preheat the oven to 150°C/300°F/Gas 2.

5 When the batter stops steaming, open the iron and lift out the waffle with a fork. Put it on a heatproof plate and keep it hot in the oven. Repeat with the remaining batter to make eight waffles in all. Preheat the grill.

3 Heat a hand-held waffle iron over the heat. Stir the batter and add more milk if required (the consistency should be quite thick). Open the waffle iron and pour some batter over two thirds of the surface. Close it and wipe off any excess batter.

4 Cook for 3–4 minutes, carefully turning the waffle iron over once during cooking. If using an electric waffle maker, follow the manufacturer's instructions for cooking.

6 Cook the bananas: spread them out on a large shallow baking tin and top with the nuts. Scatter over the demerara sugar. Mix the maple syrup and rum together and spoon over.

1 Sift the dry ingredients into a large mixing bowl. Make a well in the centre. Add the eggs, melted butter and milk. Whisk together, gradually incorporating the flour mixture, until smooth.

COOK'S TIP
If you don't own a waffle iron, prepare the batter as directed, but make small pancakes in a heavy-based frying pan. Alternatively, use ready-made waffles, which are available from large supermarkets, and reheat as directed on the packet before serving with the hot banana topping.

VARIATIONS
Use other fruits for the waffle topping, if you like. Small chunks of fresh or drained, canned pineapple, thin wedges of peaches or nectarines or even orange slices would be delicious alternatives to the banana.

7 Grill for 3–4 minutes or until the sugar begins to bubble. Serve on top of the waffles with single cream.

MANGO AND TAMARILLO PASTRIES

THESE FRUIT-TOPPED LITTLE PASTRIES GO DOWN A TREAT WITH A CUP OF AFTERNOON TEA.

MAKES EIGHT

INGREDIENTS

    225g/8oz ready-rolled puff pastry
      (30 × 25cm/12 × 10in rectangle)
    1 egg yolk, lightly beaten
    115g/4oz/½ cup white marzipan
    40ml/8 tsp ginger or apricot conserve
    1 mango, peeled and thinly sliced off
      the stone
    2 tamarillos, halved and sliced
    caster sugar, for sprinkling

1 Preheat the oven to 200°C/400°F/
Gas 6. Unroll the pastry and cut it into
8 rectangles. Place on baking sheets.

VARIATION
Use apricot slices instead of tamarillos,
or a mix of plums and peaches.

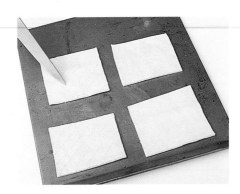

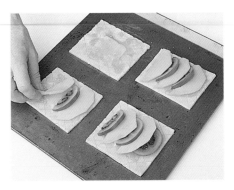

2 Using a sharp knife, score the
surface of each piece of pastry into a
diamond pattern, then brush with the
egg yolk to glaze. Cut eight thin slices
of marzipan and lay one slice on each
pastry rectangle. Top each with a
teaspoon of the ginger or apricot
conserve and spread over evenly.

3 Top the pastry rectangles with
alternate slices of mango and tamarillo.
Sprinkle with some of the caster sugar,
then bake for 15–20 minutes until the
pastry is well puffed up and golden.
Remove the pastries to a wire rack to
cool. Sprinkle with more caster sugar
before serving.

EXOTIC FRUIT TRANCHE

THIS IS A GOOD WAY TO MAKE THE MOST OF A SMALL SELECTION OF EXOTIC FRUIT.

SERVES EIGHT

INGREDIENTS
175g/6oz/1½ cups plain flour
50g/2oz/¼ cup unsalted butter
25g/1oz/2 tbsp white vegetable fat
50g/2oz/¼ cup caster sugar
2 egg yolks
about 15ml/1 tbsp cold water
115g/4oz/scant ½ cup apricot
  conserve, sieved and warmed
For the filling
150ml/¼ pint/⅔ cup double cream,
  plus extra to serve
250g/9oz/generous 1 cup mascarpone
  cheese
25g/1oz/¼ cup icing sugar, sifted
  grated rind of 1 orange
450g/1lb/3 cups mixed prepared
  fruits, such as mango, papaya, star
  fruit, kiwi fruit and blackberries
90ml/6 tbsp apricot conserve, sieved
15ml/1 tbsp white or coconut rum

1 Sift the flour into a bowl and rub in the butter and white vegetable fat until the mixture resembles fine breadcrumbs. Stir in the caster sugar. Add the egg yolks and enough cold water to make a soft dough. Thinly roll out the pastry between two sheets of clear film and use the pastry to line a 35 × 12cm/14 × 4½in fluted tranche tin. Allow the excess pastry to hang over the edge of the tin and chill for 30 minutes.

2 Preheat the oven to 200°C/400°F/ Gas 6. Prick the base of the pastry case and line with non-stick baking paper and baking beans. Bake for 10–12 minutes. Lift out the paper and beans and return the pastry case to the oven for 5 minutes. Trim off the excess pastry and brush the inside of the case with the warmed apricot conserve to form a seal. Leave to cool on a wire rack.

3 Make the filling. Whip the cream to soft peaks, then stir it into the mascarpone with the icing sugar and orange rind. Spread in the cooled pastry case and top with the prepared fruits. Warm the apricot conserve with the rum and drizzle or brush over the fruits to make a glaze. Serve with extra cream.

COOK'S TIP
If you don't have a tranche tin, line a 23cm/9in flan tin with the pastry.

MANGO PIE

THIS RECIPE COMES STRAIGHT FROM THE CARIBBEAN AND CAPTURES ALL THE SUNSHINE FLAVOURS OF THAT EXOTIC SETTING. FOR THE TASTIEST PIE, BE SURE THE MANGOES ARE GOOD AND RIPE.

SERVES SIX

INGREDIENTS

175g/6oz/1½ cups plain flour
pinch of salt
75g/3oz/⅓ cup unsalted butter,
   chilled and diced
25g/1oz/2 tbsp white vegetable fat,
   chilled and diced
15ml/1 tbsp caster sugar, plus extra
   for sprinkling
about 45ml/3 tbsp cold water
beaten egg, to glaze
vanilla ice cream, to serve
For the filling
2 ripe mangoes
45ml/3 tbsp fresh lime juice
115g/4oz/½ cup caster sugar
15ml/1 tbsp arrowroot mixed to a
   paste with 15ml/1 tbsp water

1 Sift the flour and salt into a large mixing bowl. Rub in the butter and white vegetable fat with your fingertips until the mixture resembles fine breadcrumbs, then stir in the caster sugar. Add just enough of the cold water to make a dough.

VARIATIONS
Make the pie using one mango and one papaya, peeled, seeded and sliced. Add a little ground cinnamon and some freshly grated nutmeg to the filling for a sweet spice flavour.

COOK'S TIP
If the top of the pie begins to brown too much during baking, simply cover it loosely with a piece of foil.

2 Knead lightly, then roll out two thirds of the pastry and line a 18cm/7in pie dish. Wrap the remaining pastry in clear film and chill both the pastry and the pastry case for 30 minutes.

3 Meanwhile, make the filling. Peel the mangoes and slice the flesh off the stone. Reserve half the sliced mango, and coarsely chop the rest.

4 Place the chopped mango in a saucepan with the lime juice and caster sugar. Cover and cook for 10 minutes or until soft. Pour in the arrowroot paste and cook, stirring all the time until thickened. Set the filling aside to cool.

5 Preheat the oven to 190°C/375°F/ Gas 5. Pour the cooled mango sauce into the chilled pastry case and top with the reserved mango slices. Roll out the remaining pastry to make a pie lid.

6 Dampen the rim of the pastry case and add the pastry lid. Crimp the edges to seal, then cut a cross in the centre to allow the steam to escape.

7 Glaze the pastry with the beaten egg and sprinkle lightly with caster sugar. Bake for 35–40 minutes until the pastry is golden brown. Cool slightly on a wire rack. Serve warm with vanilla ice cream.

BANANA AND PECAN BREAD

BANANAS AND PECANS JUST SEEM TO BELONG TOGETHER. THIS IS A REALLY MOIST AND DELICIOUS TEA BREAD. SPREAD IT WITH CREAM CHEESE OR JAM, OR SERVE AS A DESSERT WITH WHIPPED CREAM.

MAKES A 900G/2LB LOAF

INGREDIENTS
 115g/4oz/½ cup butter, softened
 175g/6oz/1 cup light muscovado
  sugar
 2 large eggs, beaten
 3 ripe bananas
 75g/3oz/¾ cup pecan nuts,
  coarsely chopped
 225g/8oz/2 cups self-raising flour
 2.5ml/½ tsp ground mixed spice

1 Preheat the oven to 180°C/350°F/ Gas 4. Generously grease a 900g/2lb loaf tin and line it with non-stick baking paper. Cream the butter and muscovado sugar in a large mixing bowl until the mixture is light and fluffy. Gradually add the eggs, beating after each addition, until well combined.

2 Peel and then mash the bananas with a fork. Add them to the creamed mixture with the chopped pecan nuts. Beat until well combined.

COOK'S TIP
If the mixture shows signs of curdling when you add the eggs, stir in a little of the flour to stabilize it.

3 Sift the flour and mixed spice together and fold into the banana mixture. Spoon into the tin, level the surface and bake for 1–1¼ hours or until a skewer inserted into the middle of the loaf comes out clean. Cool for 10 minutes in the tin, then invert the tin on a wire rack. Lift off the tin, peel off the lining paper and cool completely.

DATE AND WALNUT BROWNIES

THESE RICH BROWNIES ARE GREAT FOR AFTERNOON TEA, BUT THEY ALSO MAKE A FANTASTIC DESSERT. REHEAT SLICES BRIEFLY IN THE MICROWAVE OVEN AND SERVE WITH CRÈME FRAÎCHE.

MAKES TWELVE

INGREDIENTS
 350g/12oz plain chocolate, broken
  into squares
 225g/8oz/1 cup butter, diced
 3 large eggs
 115g/4oz/½ cup caster sugar
 5ml/1 tsp pure vanilla essence
 75g/3oz/¾ cup plain flour, sifted
 225g/8oz/1½ cups fresh dates,
  peeled, stoned and chopped
 200g/7oz/1¾ cups walnut pieces
 icing sugar, for dusting

COOK'S TIP
When melting the chocolate and butter, keep the water in the pan beneath hot, but do not let it approach boiling point. Chocolate is notoriously sensitive to heat; it is vital not to let it get too hot or it may stiffen into an unmanageable mass.

1 Preheat the oven to 190°C/375°F/ Gas 5. Generously grease a 30 × 20cm/ 12 × 8in baking tin and line with non-stick baking paper.

2 Put the chocolate and butter in a large heatproof bowl. Place the bowl over a pan of hot water and leave until both have melted. Stir until smooth, then lift the bowl out and cool slightly.

3 In a separate bowl, beat the eggs, sugar and vanilla. Beat into the chocolate mixture, then fold in the flour, dates and nuts. Pour into the tin.

4 Bake for 30–40 minutes, until firm and the mixture comes away from the sides of the tin. Cool in the tin, then turn out, remove the paper and dust with icing sugar.

MANGO CHUTNEY

THIS CLASSIC CHUTNEY IS CONVENTIONALLY SERVED WITH CURRIES AND INDIAN POPPADOMS, BUT IT IS ALSO DELICIOUS WITH BAKED HAM OR A TRADITIONAL CHEESE PLOUGHMAN'S LUNCH.

2 Place these in a large saucepan, add the vinegar and cover. Cook over a low heat for 10 minutes.

3 Stir in the muscovado sugar, chilli, ginger, garlic, bruised cardamoms and coriander. Add the bay leaf and salt. Bring to the boil slowly, stirring often.

4 Lower the heat and simmer, uncovered, for 30 minutes or until the mixture is thick and syrupy.

MAKES 450G/1LB

INGREDIENTS
  3 firm green mangoes
  150ml/¼ pint/⅔ cup cider vinegar
  130g/4½oz/⅔ cup light
    muscovado sugar
  1 small red finger chilli or jalapeño
    chilli, split
  2.5cm/1in piece of fresh root ginger,
    peeled and finely chopped
  1 garlic clove, finely chopped
  5 cardamom pods, bruised
  2.5ml/½ tsp coriander
    seeds, crushed
  1 bay leaf
  2.5ml/½ tsp salt

1 Peel the mangoes and cut the flesh off the stone. Slice the mangoes lengthways, then cut across into small chunks or thin wedges.

5 Ladle into hot sterilized jars, seal and label. Store for 1 week before eating. Keep chilled after opening.

PAPAYA <u>AND</u> LEMON RELISH

THIS CHUNKY RELISH IS BEST MADE WITH A FIRM, UNRIPE PAPAYA. IT SHOULD BE LEFT FOR A WEEK BEFORE EATING TO ALLOW ALL THE FLAVOURS TO MELLOW. STORE THE UNOPENED JARS IN A COOL PLACE, AWAY FROM SUNLIGHT. SERVE WITH ROAST MEATS OR WITH A ROBUST CHEESE AND CRACKERS.

MAKES 450G/1LB

INGREDIENTS

   1 large unripe papaya
   1 onion, thinly sliced
   40g/1½oz/⅓ cup raisins
   250ml/8fl oz/1 cup red wine vinegar
   juice of 2 lemons
   150ml/¼ pint/⅔ cup elderflower
     cordial
   165g/5½oz/¾ cup golden
     granulated sugar
   1 cinnamon stick
   1 fresh bay leaf
   2.5ml/½ tsp hot paprika
   2.5ml/½ tsp salt

1 Peel the papaya and cut it lengthways in half. Remove the seeds with a small teaspoon. Cut the flesh into small chunks and place them in a large saucepan.

2 Add the onion slices and raisins to the papaya chunks, then stir in the vinegar. Bring to a boil, lower the heat and simmer for 10 minutes.

3 Add all the remaining ingredients and bring to the boil, stirring all the time. Check that all the sugar has dissolved, then lower the heat and simmer for 50–60 minutes or until the relish is thick and syrupy.

4 Ladle into hot sterilized jars. Seal and label and store for 1 week before using. Keep chilled after opening.

Melon, Grape, Fig and Rhubarb Recipes

Whether alone or with other fruits, melons, rhubarb, figs and grapes make wonderful desserts, pies, cakes and preserves. Don't miss Red Grape and Cheese Tartlets, One-crust Rhubarb Pie or Greek Yogurt and Fig Cake.

MELON TRIO WITH GINGER BISCUITS

THE EYE-CATCHING COLOURS OF THESE THREE DIFFERENT MELONS REALLY MAKE THIS DESSERT, WHILE THE CRISP BISCUITS PROVIDE A PERFECT CONTRAST IN TERMS OF TEXTURE.

SERVES FOUR

INGREDIENTS
- ¼ watermelon
- ½ honeydew melon
- ½ charentais melon
- 60ml/4 tbsp stem ginger syrup

For the biscuits
- 25g/1oz/2 tbsp unsalted butter
- 25g/1oz/2 tbsp caster sugar
- 5ml/1 tsp clear honey
- 25g/1oz/¼ cup plain flour
- 25g/1oz/¼ cup luxury glacé mixed fruit, finely chopped
- 1 piece of stem ginger in syrup, drained and finely chopped
- 30ml/2 tbsp flaked almonds

1 Remove the seeds from the melons, cut them into wedges, then slice off the rind. Cut all the flesh into chunks and mix in a bowl. Stir in the ginger syrup, cover and chill until ready to serve.

2 Meanwhile, make the biscuits. Preheat the oven to 180°C/350°F/ Gas 4. Melt the butter, sugar and honey in a saucepan. Remove from the heat and stir in the remaining ingredients.

3 Line a baking sheet with non-stick baking paper. Space four spoonfuls of the mixture on the paper at regular intervals, leaving plenty of room for spreading. Flatten the mixture slightly into rounds and bake for 15 minutes or until the tops are golden.

4 Let the biscuits cool on the baking sheet for 1 minute, then lift each one in turn, using a fish slice, and drape over a rolling pin to cool and harden. Repeat with the remaining ginger mixture to make eight biscuits in all.

5 Serve the melon chunks with some of the syrup and the ginger biscuits.

COOK'S TIP
For an even prettier effect, scoop the melon flesh into balls with the large end of a melon baller.

PORT-STEWED RHUBARB WITH VANILLA DESSERTS

RHUBARB IS ONE OF THOSE FRUITS THAT SELDOM REALIZES ITS FULL POTENTIAL. IT HAS QUITE A SHORT SEASON, SO IF YOU CAN REMEMBER IT IS WORTH FREEZING SOME FOR USE LATER IN THE YEAR.

SERVES FOUR

INGREDIENTS
  115g/4oz/½ cup granulated sugar
  150ml/¼ pint/⅔ cup water
  pared rind and juice of 1 orange
  1 cinnamon stick
  300ml/½ pint/1¼ cups ruby port
  275g/10oz/2 cups rhubarb, cut into
    2.5cm/1in pieces
For the vanilla desserts
  ¾ vanilla pod
  175ml/6 fl oz/¾ cup double cream
  175ml/6fl oz/¾ cup creamy milk
  45ml/3 tbsp caster sugar
  30ml/2 tbsp water
  7.5ml/1½ tsp powdered gelatine

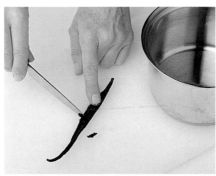

1 Start by making the vanilla desserts. Grease four individual pudding moulds or tins. Split the vanilla pod and scrape the seeds into a small saucepan. Add the pod, cream, milk and caster sugar. Simmer gently for 5 minutes, stirring.

2 Meanwhile, pour the water into a ramekin and sprinkle the gelatine over the surface. Set aside to sponge for 5 minutes. Place the ramekin in a pan of hot water and leave until the gelatine is dissolved, stirring occasionally.

3 Add the gelatine mixture to the hot milk mixture and stir until dissolved. Remove the vanilla pod and pour the mixture into the moulds or tins. Cool, then chill overnight or until set.

4 Put the sugar into a pan and add the water, orange rind and juice, and the cinnamon stick. Bring to the boil over a low heat, stirring occasionally until the sugar has dissolved. Increase the heat and boil for 1 minute.

5 Add the port, let the syrup return to the boil, then lower the heat and simmer for 15 minutes or until it has reduced and thickened. Remove the orange rind and cinnamon stick, add the rhubarb, cover and simmer gently for 2–3 minutes without stirring. Cool.

6 To serve, run a knife around the edge of each vanilla dessert to loosen it, then unmould on to a dessert plate. Serve each dessert with a spoonful or two of the rhubarb with its syrup.

COOK'S TIP
Rhubarb yields a lot of juice when cooked, so make sure the syrup has reduced well before adding the fruit.

FIG AND WALNUT TORTE

THIS RECIPE IS BASED ON THE TRADITIONAL MIDDLE EASTERN SPECIALITY, BAKLAVA. IT IS SWEET, STICKY AND DELICIOUS, AND THE FIGS ADD A REFRESHING TOUCH. SINCE IT IS QUITE RICH, PLAN ON CUTTING THE TORTE INTO FAIRLY SMALL DIAMONDS — LOVELY WITH A CUP OF STRONG BLACK COFFEE.

MAKES 20–25 PIECES

INGREDIENTS
  75g/3oz/⅓ cup butter, melted, plus
    extra for greasing
  175g/6oz/1½ cups walnuts,
    finely chopped
  115g/4oz/1 cup ground almonds
  75g/3oz/⅓ cup caster sugar
  10ml/2 tsp ground cinnamon
  9 large sheets of filo pastry, thawed
    if frozen, each cut into two
    30 × 20cm/12 × 8in rectangles
  4 fresh figs, sliced
  Greek yogurt, to serve
For the syrup
  350g/12oz/1½ cups caster sugar
  4 whole cloves
  1 cinnamon stick
  2 strips of lemon rind

1 Preheat the oven to 160°C/325°F/
Gas 3. Generously grease a 30 × 20cm/
12 × 8in shallow baking tin with melted
butter. Mix together the walnuts, ground
almonds, sugar and cinnamon in a bowl
and set aside.

2 Fit a sheet of filo pastry in the base
of the baking tin. Brush with some of
the melted butter and place another
sheet of filo on top. Repeat this until
you have layered up eight sheets.

COOK'S TIP
Paper-thin filo pastry is delicate and
dries out quickly. Work with one sheet
at a time, and keep the other sheets
covered or they will dry out.

3 Spoon half the nut mixture evenly
over the filo pastry, right to the edges,
and top with the fig slices.

4 Place two filo sheets on top of the
figs, brushing each with more melted
butter as before, then evenly spoon
over the remaining nut mixture.

5 Layer the remaining filo sheets on
top, buttering each one. Brush any
remaining melted butter over the top of
the torte, then score the surface with a
sharp knife to give a diamond pattern.
Bake for 1 hour until golden.

6 Meanwhile, make the syrup. Place all
the ingredients in a saucepan and mix
well. Heat, stirring, until the sugar has
dissolved. Bring to the boil, lower the
heat and simmer for 10 minutes until
syrupy, stirring occasionally.

7 Allow the syrup to cool for about
15 minutes, then strain it evenly over
the hot torte.

8 Allow to cool and soak for 2–3 hours,
then cut the torte into diamonds or
squares and serve with Greek yogurt.
Store the torte in an airtight tin for up to
three days.

VARIATION
If you like, replace the chopped walnuts
with coarsely chopped pistachio nuts, or
use finely chopped cashew nuts for an
ultra-rich flavour.

RED GRAPE AND CHEESE TARTLETS

FRUIT AND CHEESE IS A NATURAL COMBINATION IN THIS SIMPLE RECIPE. LOOK OUT FOR THE PALE, MAUVE-COLOURED OR RED GRAPES THAT TEND TO BE SLIGHTLY SMALLER THAN BLACK GRAPES. THESE ARE OFTEN SEEDLESS AND HAVE THE ADDED ADVANTAGE OF BEING SWEETER.

MAKES SIX

INGREDIENTS

    350g/12oz sweet shortcrust pastry,
      thawed if frozen
    225g/8oz/1 cup curd cheese
    150ml/¼ pint/⅔ cup double cream
    2.5ml/½ tsp pure vanilla essence
    30ml/2 tbsp icing sugar
    200g/7oz/2 cups red grapes, halved,
      seeded if necessary
    60ml/4 tbsp apricot conserve
    15ml/1 tbsp water

VARIATIONS

Use cranberry jelly or redcurrant jelly for the glaze. There will be no need to sieve either of these. Also vary the fruit topping, if you like. Try blackberries, blueberries, raspberries, sliced strawberries, kiwi fruit slices, banana slices or well-drained pineapple slices.

1 Preheat the oven to 200°C/400°F/ Gas 6. Roll out the pastry and line six deep 9cm/3½in fluted individual tartlet tins. Prick the bases and line with non-stick baking paper and baking beans. Bake for 10 minutes, remove the paper and beans, then return the cases to the oven for 5 minutes until golden and fully cooked. Remove the pastry cases from the tins and cool on a wire rack.

2 Meanwhile, beat the curd cheese, double cream, vanilla essence and icing sugar in a bowl. Divide the mixture among the pastry cases. Smooth the surface and arrange the halved grapes on top.

3 Sieve the apricot conserve into a pan. Add the water and heat, stirring, until smooth. Spoon over the grapes. Cool, then chill before serving.

ONE-CRUST RHUBARB PIE

THIS METHOD CAN BE USED FOR ALL SORTS OF FRUIT AND IS REALLY FOOLPROOF. IT DOESN'T MATTER HOW ROUGH THE PIE LOOKS WHEN IT GOES INTO THE OVEN; IT COMES OUT LOOKING FANTASTIC!

SERVES SIX

INGREDIENTS

350g/12oz shortcrust pastry, thawed
    if frozen
1 egg yolk, beaten
25g/1oz/3 tbsp semolina
25g/1oz/¼ cup hazelnuts,
    coarsely chopped
30ml/2 tbsp golden granulated sugar

For the filling

450g/1lb rhubarb, cut into
    2.5cm/1in pieces
75g/3oz/⅓ cup caster sugar
1–2 pieces stem ginger in syrup,
    drained and finely chopped

COOK'S TIP
Egg yolk glaze brushed on to pastry gives it a nice golden sheen. However, be careful not to drip the glaze on the baking sheet, or it will burn and be difficult to remove.

1 Preheat the oven to 200°C/400°F/ Gas 6. Roll out the pastry to a circle 35cm/14in across. Lay it over the rolling pin and transfer it to a large baking sheet. Brush a little egg yolk over the pastry. Scatter the semolina over the centre, leaving a wide rim all round.

2 Make the filling. Place the rhubarb pieces, caster sugar and chopped ginger in a large bowl and mix well.

3 Pile the rhubarb mixture into the middle of the pastry. Fold the rim roughly over the filling so that it almost covers it. Some of the fruit will remain visible in the centre.

4 Glaze the pastry rim with any remaining egg yolk and scatter the hazelnuts and golden sugar over. Bake for 30–35 minutes or until the pastry is golden brown. Serve warm.

FRESH FIG FILO TART

FIGS COOK WONDERFULLY WELL AND TASTE SUPERB IN THIS TART — THE RIPER THE FIGS, THE BETTER.

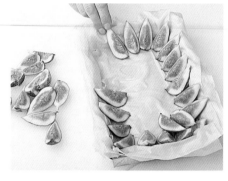

2 Using scissors, cut off any excess pastry, leaving a little overhanging the edge. Arrange the figs in the filo case.

3 Sift the flour into a bowl and stir in the caster sugar. Add the eggs and a little of the milk and whisk until smooth. Gradually whisk in the remaining milk and the almond essence. Pour the mixture over the figs; bake for 1 hour or until the batter has set and is golden.

SERVES SIX TO EIGHT

INGREDIENTS
    five 35 × 25cm/14 × 10in sheets filo
      pastry, thawed if frozen
    25g/1oz/2 tbsp butter, melted, plus
      extra for greasing
    6 fresh figs, cut into wedges
    75g/3oz/¾ cup plain flour
    75g/3oz/⅓ cup caster sugar
    4 eggs
    450ml/¾ pint/1¾ cups creamy milk
    2.5ml/½ tsp almond essence
    15ml/1 tbsp icing sugar, for dusting
    whipped cream or Greek yogurt,
      to serve

1 Preheat the oven to 190°C/375°F/ Gas 5. Grease a 25 × 16cm/10 × 6¼in baking tin with butter. Brush each filo sheet in turn with melted butter and use to line the prepared tin.

4 Remove the tart from the oven and allow it to cool in the tin on a wire rack for 10 minutes. Dust with the icing sugar and serve with whipped cream or Greek yogurt.

GREEK YOGURT AND FIG CAKE

BAKED FRESH FIGS, THICKLY SLICED, MAKE A DELECTABLE BASE FOR A FEATHERLIGHT SPONGE.
FIGS THAT ARE A BIT ON THE FIRM SIDE WORK BEST FOR THIS PARTICULAR RECIPE.

SERVES SIX TO EIGHT

INGREDIENTS
  6 firm fresh figs, thickly sliced
  45ml/3 tbsp clear honey, plus extra
    for glazing cooked figs
  200g/7oz/scant 1 cup butter,
    softened
  175g/6oz/¾ cup caster sugar
  grated rind of 1 lemon
  grated rind of 1 orange
  4 eggs, separated
  225g/8oz/2 cups plain flour
  5ml/1 tsp baking powder
  5ml/1 tsp bicarbonate of soda
  250ml/8fl oz/1 cup Greek yogurt

1 Preheat the oven to 180°C/350°F/ Gas 4. Grease a 23cm/9in cake tin and line the base with non-stick baking paper. Arrange the figs over the base of the tin and drizzle over the honey.

2 In a large mixing bowl, cream the butter and caster sugar with the lemon and orange rinds until the mixture is pale and fluffy, then gradually beat in the egg yolks.

3 Sift the dry ingredients together. Add a little to the creamed mixture, beat well, then beat in a spoonful of Greek yogurt. Repeat this process until all the dry ingredients and Greek yogurt have been incorporated.

4 Whisk the egg whites in a grease-free bowl until they form stiff peaks. Stir half the whites into the cake mixture to slacken it slightly, then fold in the rest. Pour the mixture over the figs in the tin, then bake for 1¼ hours or until golden and a skewer inserted in the centre of the cake comes out clean.

5 Turn the cake out on to a wire rack, peel off the lining paper and cool. Drizzle the figs with extra honey before serving.

MELON AND STAR ANISE JAM

MELON AND GINGER ARE CLASSIC COMPANIONS. THE ADDITION OF STAR ANISE IMPARTS A WONDERFUL ORIENTAL FLAVOUR TO THE JAM. IT'S SPLENDID ON TOASTED FRUIT AND SPICE MUFFINS.

MAKES 450G/1LB

INGREDIENTS

2 charentais or cantaloupe melons,
  peeled and seeded
450g/1lb/2 cups granulated sugar
2 star anise
4 pieces stem ginger in syrup,
  drained and finely chopped
finely grated rind and juice of
  2 lemons

COOK'S TIPS

Use this jam in savoury dishes instead of honey to add a spicy, non-cloying sweetness. Jams require a large amount of sugar for proper jelling – don't cut back.

1 Cut the melons into small cubes and layer with the granulated sugar in a large non-metallic bowl. Cover with clear film and leave overnight so the melons can release their juices.

2 Tip the melons and juice into a large saucepan and add the star anise, ginger, lemon rind and juice.

3 Bring to the boil, then lower the heat. Simmer for 25 minutes or until the melon has become transparent and the setting point has been reached. Test for this by spooning a small amount of the juice on to a chilled plate. If it wrinkles when you push a finger through the cooled liquid, it is ready to be potted.

4 Spoon the jam into hot sterilized jars. Seal, label and store in a cool, dry place. Once a jar has been opened, keep it in the fridge.

FIG AND DATE CHUTNEY

THIS RECIPE IS USUALLY MADE WITH DRIED FIGS AND DATES, BUT IT WORKS PERFECTLY WELL WITH FRESH FRUIT AND HAS A SUPERB FLAVOUR. TRY IT WITH CREAM CHEESE ON BROWN BREAD.

MAKES 450G/1LB

INGREDIENTS
1 orange
5 large fresh figs, coarsely chopped
350g/12oz/2½ cups fresh dates,
   peeled, stoned and chopped
2 onions, chopped
5cm/2in piece of fresh root ginger,
   peeled and finely grated
5ml/1 tsp dried crushed chillies
300g/11oz/1½ cups golden
   granulated sugar
300ml/½ pint/1¼ cups spiced
   preserving vinegar
2.5ml/½ tsp salt

1 Finely grate the rind of the orange, then cut off the remaining pith and segment the orange.

2 Place the orange segments in a large heavy-based saucepan with the chopped figs and dates. Add the rind, then stir in the onions, grated ginger, dried chillies, golden granulated sugar, spiced preserving vinegar and salt. Bring to the boil, stirring gently until all the sugar has dissolved.

3 Lower the heat and simmer gently for 1 hour or until the mixture has thickened and become pulpy, stirring often to prevent the mixture from sticking to the base of the pan.

4 Spoon the chutney into hot sterilized jars. Seal while still hot and label once the jars are cold. Store for 1 week before using. Once a jar has been opened, keep it in the fridge.

VARIATION
If you would rather use dried figs and dates to make the chutney, you will need to increase the amount of spiced preserving vinegar by 150ml/¼ pint/⅔ cup to 450ml/¾ pint/scant 2 cups. Stone the dates and coarsely chop the figs and dates.

INDEX

ACKNOWLEDGEMENTS

Photographs are by Don Last and William Lingwood except those on the following pages: p25 ml Harry Smith Horticultural Photographic Collection (HSHC); p47 t Clive Simms; p53 tl HSHC; b/tr The Garden Picture Library (GPL); p54 br GPL; p56 br Clive Simms (CS); p58 m HSHC, tr A-Z Botanical/Bjorn Svenson; p59 br GPL, tl Derek St. Romaine (DSR), bl HSHC; p60 b HSHC; p64 t DSR; p65 bl/br DSR; p75 b CS; p77 b GPL; p86 l Peter McHoy; p91 l HSHC, b CS; p92 t HSHC; p94 b GPL; p97 t HSHC; p99 t CS; p104 t CS; and p110 t GPL.